DAY HIKING

Snoqualmie Region

Previous page: Mount Stuart rises behind a partially frozen Lake Ingalls.

Next page: Two hikers climbing Bare Mountain

Hiker crossing a log bridge over the Greenwater River

Close-up of Columbia Lewisia in the Teanaway

Opposite: Views across Pete Lake toward the Cascade Crest
Above: Autumn views of Mount Rainier from the Naches Peak Trail

Fall colors surrounding granite rocks near the Kendall Katwalk

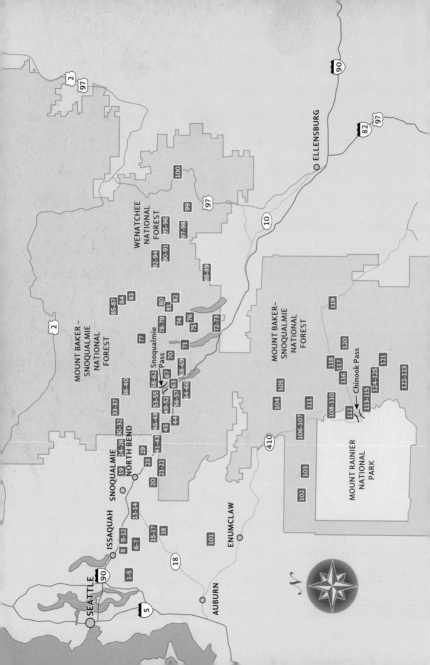

View of Rattlesnake Ledge from the East Rattlesnake Mountain Trail

DAY HIKING

Snoqualmie Region

cascade foothills/I-90 corridor/alpine lakes

Dan A. Nelson
photography by
Alan L. Bauer

THE MOUNTAINEERS BOOKS

THE MOUNTAINEERS BOOKS
*is the nonprofit publishing arm of The Mountaineers Club, an
organization founded in 1906 and dedicated to the exploration,
preservation, and enjoyment of outdoor and wilderness areas.*

1001 SW Klickitat Way, Suite 201, Seattle, WA 98134

© 2007 by Dan A. Nelson

Manufactured in the United States of America

Copy Editor: Julie Van Pelt
Cover and Book Design: The Mountaineers Books
Layout: Peggy Egerdahl
Cartographer: Moore Creative Designs

Cover photograph: *Rampart Lakes surrounded by fall color*
Frontispiece: *Thorp Mountain Lookout*

Maps shown in this book were produced using *National Geographic*'s TOPO!
software. For more information, go to *www.nationalgeographic.com/topo.*

Library of Congress Cataloging-in-Publication Data
Nelson, Dan A.
    Day hiking Snoqualmie region / Dan A. Nelson ; photographs by Alan
Bauer. — 1st ed.
        p. cm.
    Includes index.
    ISBN 978-1-59485-046-2 (paperbound)
    1. Hiking—Washington (State)—Snoqualmie Pass Region—Guidebooks. 2. Snoqualmie Pass
Region (Wash.)—Guidebooks. I. Title.
GV199.42.W22S567 2007
796.5109797—dc22

                        2007004172

 Printed on recycled paper

Table of Contents

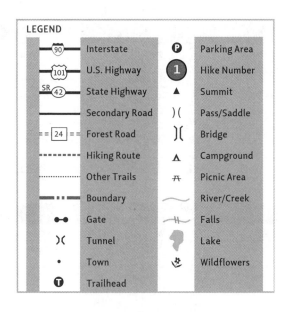

LEGEND

Symbol	Name	Symbol	Name
90	Interstate	P	Parking Area
101	U.S. Highway	1	Hike Number
SR 42	State Highway	▲	Summit
	Secondary Road	) (	Pass/Saddle
24	Forest Road	)(	Bridge
	Hiking Route	⌂	Campground
	Other Trails	🎋	Picnic Area
	Boundary		River/Creek
●—●	Gate		Falls
)(	Tunnel		Lake
•	Town	✿	Wildflowers
T	Trailhead		

A Quick Guide to the Hikes

Use this guide to quickly find a hike you'll like. These hike listings are organized according to popular features, followed by a summary of additional information. To pick a hike:

- Glance over the categories to find the one you want.
- Narrow your choices to those close to where you are or where you're going: IA means Issaquah Alps, NB means North Bend Area, SPW means Snoqualmie Pass Corridor West, SP means Snoqualmie Pass Area, SPE means Snoqualmie Pass Corridor East, TC means Teanaway Country, and CP means Chinook Pass Area.
- Find a hike with a distance and difficulty level that will work well for you.

Note that mileage for some hikes is one-way and for others is round-trip; refer to the full description for these and other details and driving directions.

No.	Hike Name	Area	Miles	Difficulty	Highlights
MOST FAMILY-FRIENDLY HIKES					
2.	Redtown Meadow	IA	1.5	easy	wildlife, native plants, restored meadow
23.	Twin Falls	NB	3.0	easy to moderate	moss-laden forest, waterfalls
34.	Middle Fork Snoqualmie: Upstream	NB	6.0	easy to moderate	bridge over river, bird-watching
53.	Denny Creek	SPW	4.0	easy	creek, multiple waterfalls
63.	Iron Horse Trail: The Tunnel	SP	6.0	moderate	tunnel to explore
101.	Flaming Geyser State Park	CP	3.0	easy	river, forest
122.	Twin Sisters Lakes	CP	5.0	easy to moderate	lakes, forest, wildlife
BEST HIKES TO LAKES FOR WADING OR SWIMMING					
49.	Talapus and Ollalie Lakes	SPW	4.0	easy to moderate	mountain lakes, wildlife
77.	Pete Lake	SPE	9.0	moderate	old-growth forest, wildlife, lakes
104.	Greenwater and Echo Lakes	CP	14.0	moderate	solitude, old-growth forest, lakes
112.	Sheep Lake and Sourdough Gap	CP	7.0	easy to moderate	lake, wildlife, huckleberry bushes
124.	Cougar Lakes	CP	8.0	moderate	lakes, wildlife, huckleberry bushes

No.	Hike Name	Area	Miles	Difficulty	Highlights
BEST HIKES ALONG CREEKS AND RIVERS					
5.	Wilderness Peak	IA	4.0	moderate	creek, boardwalks
33.	Middle Fork Snoqualmie: Downstream	NB	1.5	moderate	riverbanks, forest, wildlife
34.	Middle Fork Snoqualmie: Upstream	NB	6.0	easy to moderate	bridge over river, bird-watching
54.	Melakwa Lake	SPW	9.0	moderate to strenuous	creek, forest, mountain lake
78.	Cooper River	SPE	6.0	easy to moderate	mountain river, bird-watching
125.	Fish Lake	CP	14.0	moderate	wildlife, creeks, river crossing
BEST HIKES FOR VIEWING WATERFALLS					
3.	Coal Creek Falls	IA	2.5	easy to moderate	wildflowers
23.	Twin Falls	NB	3.0	easy to moderate	moss-laden forest
37.	Otter and Big Creek Falls	NB	10.0	moderate	solitude, bridges over creeks
53.	Denny Creek	SPW	4.0	easy	creek
55.	Franklin Falls	SPW	2.0	easy	historic wagon track
70.	Rachel Lake	SPE	8.0	moderate to strenuous	alpine lake
BEST HIKES FOR FINDING SOLITUDE					
27.	Mount Teneriffe	NB	14.0	strenuous	views, old logging road
48.	Little Bandera Mountain	SPW	7.0	moderate to strenuous	wildflowers, views
76.	French Cabin Mountain	SPE	6.0	strenuous	wildflowers, views
82.	Sasse Ridge	SPE	9.0	moderate	wildflowers, views from ridge
91.	Eldorado and Turnpike Passes	TC	8.0	moderate to strenuous	wildflowers, wildlife, views
105.	Arch Rock	CP	12.0	easy to moderate	rock bluffs
121.	Nelson Ridge and Mount Aix	CP	12.0	strenuous	panoramic views

No.	Hike Name	Area	Miles	Difficulty	Highlights
BEST HIKES FOR BIRD-WATCHING					
14.	Northwest Timber Trail	IA	5.0	easy to moderate	high bridge, waterfall
42.	Deception Crags	SPW	1.0	easy	rock climbers
66.	Mirror Lake	SP	2.0	easy to moderate	wildlife, lake
69.	Twin Lakes and Lake Lillian	SPE	9.0	moderate	alpine lakes, huckleberry bushes
78.	Cooper River	SPE	6.0	easy to moderate	mountain river
97.	Navaho Pass	TC	11.0	moderate	bird-watching, wildflowers, mountain views
BEST HIKES FOR PICKING BERRIES					
52.	Granite Mountain	SPW	8.0	strenuous	wildflowers, old fire lookout, summit views
60.	Snow Lake	SP	8.0	moderate to strenuous	picturesque lake, wildlife
68.	Margaret Lake	SPE	6.0	moderate	wildflowers, lake
69.	Twin Lakes and Lake Lillian	SPE	9.0	moderate	alpine lakes, bird-watching
82.	Sasse Ridge	SPE	9.0	moderate	solitude, wildflowers, views from ridge
112.	Sheep Lake and Sourdough Gap	CP	7.0	easy to moderate	swimming lake, wildlife
115.	American Lake	CP	14.0	moderate	panoramic views
HIKES THAT FEATURE LOCAL HISTORY					
2.	Redtown Meadow	IA	1.5	easy	wildlife, native plants, restored meadow
8.	Poo Poo Point	IA	7.4	moderate	Gap Creek Bridge and falls, launch site for hang gliders
22.	Iron Horse Trail: Washington Creek	NB	6.0	easy to moderate	high trestle over creek
46.	Ira Spring Trail	SPW	6.0	moderate to strenuous	creek, mountain lake
56.	Asahel Curtis Nature Trail	SPW	0.5	easy	interpretive loop
63.	Iron Horse Trail: The Tunnel	SP	6.0	moderate	tunnel to explore
101.	Flaming Geyser State Park	CP	3.0	easy	river, forest

No.	Hike Name	Area	Miles	Difficulty	Highlights
HIKES THROUGH WONDERFUL FORESTS					
15.	Middle Tiger	IA	9.0	moderate	forest, wildlife, native plants
39.	Dingford Creek–Hester Lake	NB	12.0	moderate to strenuous	lakes, old-growth forest, views
77.	Pete Lake	SPE	9.0	moderate	old-growth forest, wildlife, lake
104.	Greenwater and Echo Lakes	CP	14.0	moderate	solitude, old-growth forest, lakes
106.	Snoquera Falls	CP	6.0	easy to moderate	rain forest, small waterfall
HIKES WITH OUTSTANDING VIEWS					
20.	Rattlesnake Ledge	NB	4.0	moderate to strenuous	views
25.	Mount Si	NB	8.0	strenuous	wildflowers, views from summit meadow
52.	Granite Mountain	SPW	8.0	strenuous	wildflowers, huckleberry bushes, old fire lookout, summit views
59.	Kendall Katwalk	SP	11.0	moderate to strenuous	old-growth forest, wildflowers, views
80.	Davis Peak	SPE	11.0	strenuous	panoramic views from summit
86.	Cathedral Rock	SPE	9.0	moderate to strenuous	meadows, lakes, views of rock monolith
108.	Norse Peak	CP	10.6	moderate to strenuous	panoramic views, wildflowers, wildlife
121.	Nelson Ridge and Mount Aix	CP	12.0	strenuous	solitude, panoramic views

Acknowledgements

This book and book series would not have been possible without the support of my partner, Donna Meshke. Donna has stood by me, supported me, and has kept our home in order while I built my freelance writing career. Throughout the years of frequent trips away from home and odd hours as I worked under deadline pressures, Donna has kept me grounded, focused, and happy. She also has been invaluable as a partner in the field, joining me on many research trips and providing a fresh perspective for me. Thank you, Donna, for the life we share.

Introduction

The more advanced we become with labor-saving technology, the less time we have to ourselves. All those time-saving tools merely open the door for other time-eating traps at work and home. Americans are working more hours each year, with less vacation time taken, than they have at any time since World War II.

This helps explain why more and more hikers are foregoing multiday backpacking trips in favor of day-long outings. With fewer free hours—and more hobbies competing for that free time—hikers seem to favor trail excursions that can be done in a day.

This Day Hiking series steps in to help modern hikers get their wilderness fix, offering up the best routes in a region that can be enjoyed as day trips. Of course, the length of day will vary, depending on where you start—drive times to, say, the Teanaway Valley are considerably longer for hikers starting from Olympia than those coming from Issaquah.

Day Hiking: Snoqualmie focuses on hikes in the southern portion of the central Cascades—that is, the trails found off I-90, State Route 18, State Route 410, and US 97 from Blewett Pass south. These routes explore some of the Cascades' most varied terrain, delving into deep forested valleys, cresting high craggy peaks, and exploring dry pine basins and broad alpine meadows. You'll find some of the richest ecosystems and some of the most abundant and varied wildlife available in the country.

The trails cross the habitat of blacktail deer as well as their larger cousins, mule deer. There are Rocky Mountain elk (*wapiti*) and their chief predator, mountain lions (a.k.a. cougars or pumas). There are snowy white mountain goats and dun-colored bighorn sheep. Scan the skies and you might see eagles (bald and golden) as well as an array of other raptors, big and small. You might hear the screech of an owl, the *thump-thump-thump* of grouse, and the trilling calls of a multitude of songbirds.

This region is home to ancient cedar and hemlock forests, as well as stands of tall Douglas-fir. Massive ponderosa pines fill the eastern slopes, which are also dotted with beautiful larches that change from soft emerald green to radiant golden hues each year. From forest to meadow to alpine slopes, you'll also enjoy glorious bursts of color thanks to a plethora of wildflowers—from the beautiful (though unfortunately named) skunk cabbage to aptly named carpet pinks (a.k.a. spreading phlox). You'll find forest floors covered in the tall stalks of beargrass with their bulbous blooms, and hillsides covered in the ubiquitous lupine.

A mushroom grows from a mossy forest floor.

Best of all for those who love to hike, the trails of the central Cascades are just as varied as the environs they cross, and plentiful too. I hope this book will help you find your own special moments in this wonderful wild country.

USING THIS BOOK

These Day Hiking guidebooks strike a fine balance. They were developed to be as easy to use as possible while still providing enough detail to help you explore a region. As a result, these guidebooks include all the information you need to find and enjoy the hikes, but leave enough room for you to make your own discoveries as you venture into areas new to you.

What the Ratings Mean

Every trail described in this book features a detailed "trail facts" section. Not all of the details here are facts, however.

Each hike starts with two subjective ratings: each has a **rating** of 1 to 5 stars for its overall appeal, and each route's **difficulty** is rated on a scale of 1 to 5. This is subjective, based on the author's impressions of each route, but the ratings do follow a formula of sorts.

WHOSE LAND IS THIS?

All of the hikes in this book are on public land. That is, they belong to you and me and the rest of the citizenry. As fellow guidebook writer Craig Romano points out in *Day Hiking: Olympic Peninsula*, what's confusing is just who exactly is in charge of this public trust. Several different governing agencies manage the lands described in his guide and in this one as well.

The largest of the agencies, and the one managing most of the hikes in this book, is the U.S. Forest Service. A division of the Department of Agriculture, the Forest Service strives to "sustain the health, diversity, and productivity of the Nation's forests and grasslands to meet the needs of present and future generations." The agency purports to do this under the doctrine of "multiple-use"—the greatest good for the greatest number, frequently resulting in conflict. Supplying timber products, managing wildlife habitat, and developing motorized and nonmotorized recreation options have a tendency to conflict with each other. Some of these uses may not exactly sustain the health of the forest either.

The Mount Baker–Snoqualmie and Wenatchee National Forests manage over 3.9 million acres of land in the Cascades. Much has been heavily logged. Eleven areas within these forests, however, have been afforded stringent protections as federal wilderness areas. Several hikes in this guide are in the Alpine Lakes Wilderness, the Clearwater Wilderness, the Norse Peak Wilderness, and the William O. Douglas Wilderness.

Other public lands you'll encounter on the hikes in this book are Washington State parks, managed primarily for recreation and preservation; Washington State Department of Natural Resources lands, managed primarily for timber harvesting, with pockets of natural area preserves; and county parks, which are often like state parks but on a regional level.

It's important that you know who manages the land you'll be hiking on, for each agency has its own fees and rules. Confusing? Yes, but it's our land and we should understand how it's managed for us. And remember that we have a say in how our lands are managed, too, and can let the agencies know whether we like what they're doing or not.

Dennis Long taking waypoints on a summit

The overall rating is based on scenic beauty, natural wonder, and other unique qualities, such as solitude potential and wildlife-viewing opportunities.

The difficulty rating is based on trail length, the steepness of the trail, and how difficult it is to hike. Generally, trails that are rated more difficult (4 or 5) are longer and steeper then average. But it's not a simple equation. A short, steep trail over talus slopes may be rated 5, while a long, smooth trail with little elevation gain may be rated 2.

To help explain those difficulty ratings, you'll also find the **round-trip mileage** (unless otherwise noted as one-way), total **elevation gain**, and **high point** for each hike. The distances are not always exact mileages—trails weren't measured with calibrated instruments—but the mileages are those used by cartographers and land managers (who have measured many of the trails). The elevation gains report the cumulative difference between the high and low point on the route. It's worth noting that not all high points are at the end of the trail—a route may run over a high ridge before dropping to a lake basin, for instance.

Another subjective tool you'll find is the hikeable **season**. Many trails can be enjoyed from the time they lose their winter snowpack right up until they are buried in fresh snow the following fall. But snowpacks vary from year to year, so a trail that is open in May one year may be snow-covered until mid-July the next. The hiking season for each trail is an estimate, but before you venture out it's worth contacting the land manager to get current conditions.

To help with trip planning, each hike also lists which **maps** you'll want to have on your hike, as well as what agency to **contact** to get current trail conditions. Hikes in this guidebook use Green Trails maps, which are based on the standard 7.5-minute USGS topographical maps. Green Trails maps are available at most outdoor retailers in the state, as well as at many U.S. Forest Service visitors centers.

Given that we now live in a digital world, **GPS coordinates** for each trailhead are provided—use them both to get to the trail and to help you get back to your car if you get caught out in a storm or wander off-trail.

Finally, the **status** of several "Endangered," "Threatened," or "Saved" trails is noted for trails that are in danger of disappearing due to lack of maintenance, or have been saved thanks to volunteer efforts. The imperiled trails may be officially recognized as trails in trouble, but not always. Sometimes, we listed trails as "Threatened" or "Endangered" even though land managers may consider them fine—this is especially true when destructive uses are allowed, such as motorcycle use of trails on steep terrain or in sensitive meadow or wetland areas.

You will also note small icons throughout the book. Trails that we found to be dog-friendly, kid-friendly, good for wildlife viewing or of historical interest are marked by these icons. The icons are meant to be merely helpful suggestions, however, and should not be a limiting factor for your hiking. If you and the kids want to hike a trail that does not have a "kid" icon, go for it! Same holds true for dogs, though you might want to check with the land manager before venturing out with your dog since canines are restricted in some areas, especially on trails outside the National Forest Service lands.

 Kid-friendly

Dog-friendly

Wildlife viewing

Historical

Endangered trail

Saved trail

The route descriptions themselves provide a basic overview of what you might find on your hike, directions to get you to the trailhead, and in some cases additional highlights beyond the actual trails you'll be exploring.

Of course, you'll need some information long before you ever leave home. So, as you plan your trips consider the following several issues.

PERMITS AND REGULATIONS

You can't set foot out your door these days without first making sure you're not breaking the rules. In an effort to keep our wilderness areas wild and our trails safe and well-maintained, the land managers—especially the National Park Service and the U.S. Forest Service—have implemented a sometimes complex set of rules and regulations governing the use of public lands.

Virtually all trails in national forests in Washington (and Oregon) fall under the Region 6 forest pass program. Simply stated, in order to park legally at these designated national forest trailheads, you must display

a Northwest Forest Pass decal on your windshield. These sell for $5 per day or $30 for an annual pass good throughout Washington and Oregon (which constitute Region 6). The Northwest Forest Pass is also required at most trailheads within the North Cascades National Park Complex.

In addition to the parking pass, when you hike in wilderness areas you must pick up and fill out a wilderness permit at the trailhead registration box (sometimes located at the wilderness boundary if the trail doesn't immediately enter a designated wilderness). These are free and unlimited (though that may change).

WEATHER

Mountain weather in general is famously unpredictable, but the Cascade Range stretches that unpredictability to sometimes-absurd lengths. The high, jagged nature of the mountains, coupled with their proximity to the Pacific Ocean, makes them magnets for every bit of moisture in the atmosphere.

As moist air comes rushing in off the Pacific, it hits the western front of the Cascades. The air is pushed up the slopes of the mountains, often forming clouds and eventually rain, feeding the wet rain forests that dominate the western slopes. By the time the airstream crests the Cascades and starts down the east slopes, the clouds have lost their moisture loads, leaving the eastside forests dry and filled with open stands of drought-resistant pine.

Where east meets west the wet clouds hit the dry heat, often creating thunderstorms. Hikers on the trail must be aware of this potential, because such storms can brew up any month of the year. Thunderstorms can also develop quickly, with little warning, and a hiker stuck on a high pass becomes a good target for a lightning bolt (see "All Lit Up" for how to avoid this).

Rain's coming: a classic Mount Rainier lenticular cloud

ALL LIT UP

The following are suggestions for reducing the dangers of lightning should thunderstorms be forecast or develop while you are in the mountains:

- Use a NOAA weather radio (a radio tuned in to one of the national weather forecast frequencies) to keep abreast of the latest weather information.
- Avoid travel on mountain tops and ridge crests.
- Stay well away from bodies of water.
- If your hair stands on end, or you feel static shocks, move immediately—the static electricity you feel could very well be a precursor to a lightning strike.
- If there is a shelter or building nearby, get into it. Don't take shelter under trees, however, especially in open areas.
- If there is no shelter available, and lightning is flashing, remove your pack (the metal stays or frame are natural electrical conduits) and crouch down, balancing on the balls of your feet until the lighting clears the area.

Of course, thunderstorms aren't the only weather hazard hikers face. A sudden rain-squall can push temperatures down 15 or 20 degrees Fahrenheit in a matter of minutes. Even if you're dressed for hot summer hiking, you should be prepared for such temperature drops and the accompanying soaking rain if you want to avoid hypothermia.

If the temperature drop is great enough, you can miss the rain and get hit instead by snow. Snowstorms have blown through the Cascades every month of the year, with as much as a foot falling on some routes in late August.

Besides fresh-fallen snow, summer hikers also need to be aware of snowfields left over from the previous winter's snowpack. Depending on the severity of the past winter, and the weather conditions of the spring and early summer, some trails may melt out in June while others will remain snow-covered well into August or beyond—some years, sections never melt out. In addition to making for treacherous footing and difficulties in routefinding, these lingering snowfields can be prone to avalanches or slides.

ROAD AND TRAIL CONDITIONS

Trails in general change little year to year. Though they truly are man-made structures in rugged wilderness settings, trails are quite durable. But change can and does occur, and sometimes it occurs very quickly. One brutal storm can alter a river's course, washing out sections of trail in moments. Wind can drop trees across trails by the hundreds, making the paths unhikeable. And snow can obliterate trails well into the heart of summer.

Access roads face similar threats and are in fact more susceptible to washouts and closures than the trails themselves. With this in mind, each hike in this book lists the land manager's contact information so you can call or email prior to your trip and ensure that your chosen road and trail are open and safe to travel.

On the topic of trail conditions, it is vital that we thank the countless volunteers who donate tens of thousands of hours to trail maintenance each year. The Washington Trails Association (WTA) alone coordinates upward of sixty thousand hours of volunteer trail maintenance each year.

As massive as the volunteer efforts have become, there is always a need for more. Our wilderness trail system faces increasing threats, including (but by no means limited to) ever-shrinking trail funding, inappropriate trail uses, and conflicting land-management policies and practices.

With this in mind, this guide includes several trails that are threatened and in danger of becoming unhikeable. These Endangered Trails are found throughout the region and are marked with the following icon in this book:

On the other side of the coin, we've also been blessed with some great trail successes

The late WTA trail guru Greg Ball loads his truck after a work party.

in recent years, thanks in large part to that massive volunteer movement spearheaded by WTA. As you enjoy these Rescued Trails, stop to consider the contributions made by your fellow hikers that helped protect our trail resources. These Rescued Trails are marked with this icon:

WILDERNESS ETHICS

As wonderful as volunteer trail maintenance programs are, they aren't the only way to help save our trails. Indeed, these on-the-ground efforts provide quality trails today, but to ensure the long-term survival of our trails—and the wildlands they cross—we all must embrace and practice sound wilderness ethics.

Strong, positive wilderness ethics include making sure you leave the wilderness as pure or purer than it was when you found it. As the adage says, "take only pictures, leave only footprints." But sound wilderness ethics go deeper than that, beyond simply picking up after ourselves when we go for a hike. Wilderness ethics must carry over into our daily lives. We need to ensure that our elected officials and public land managers recognize and respond to our wilderness needs and desires. If we hike the trails on the weekend, but let the wilderness go neglected—or worse, allow it to be abused—on the weekdays, we'll soon find our weekend haunts diminished or destroyed.

TRAIL GIANTS

I want to add here a personal note. As I began my career as a guidebook author, I was blessed with the opportunity to learn from the men and women who helped launch the guidebook genre for The Mountaineers Books. Throughout the 1990s I enjoyed many conversations with Ira Spring—we would talk for hours about our favorite trails and how we needed to diligently fight for those trails.

I exchanged frequent correspondence with Harvey Manning, debating the best means of saving wildlands. I was advised and mentored by Louise Marshall. I worked alongside Greg Ball—founder of the WTA's volunteer trail maintenance program—for more than a decade.

In short, I served my apprenticeship with masters of the trail trade. From them, and from my own experiences exploring the wonderful wildlands of Washington, I discovered the pressing need for individual activism. When hikers get complacent, trails suffer. We must, in the words of the legendary Ira Spring, "get people onto trails. They need to bond with the wilderness." This green bonding, as Ira called it, is essential in building public support for trails and trail funding.

As you get out and hike the trails described here, consider that many of these trails would have long ago ceased to exist without the phenomenal efforts of people like Ira Spring, Harvey Manning, Louise Marshall, and Greg Ball, not to mention the scores of unnamed hikers who joined them in their push for wildland protection, trail funding, and strong environmental stewardship programs.

When you get home, bear in mind these people's actions and then sit down and write a letter to your congressperson asking for better trail funding. Call your local Forest Service office to say that you've enjoyed the trails in their jurisdiction and that you want these routes to remain wild and accessible for use by you and your children.

And if you're not already a member, consider joining an organization devoted to wilderness, backcountry trails, or other wild-country issues. Organizations like The Mountaineers Club, Washington Trails Association, Volunteers for Outdoor Washington, the Cascade chapter of the Sierra Club, the Conservation Northwest, the Cascade Land Conservancy, and countless others leverage individual

Mittens waits for the signal to get going again on Tiger Mountain.

contributions and efforts to help ensure the future of our trails and the wonderful wilderness legacy we've inherited.

TRAIL ETIQUETTE

Anyone who enjoys backcountry trails should recognize their responsibility to those trails and to other trail users. We each must work to preserve the tranquility of the wildlands by not only being sensitive to the environment, but to other trail users as well.

The trails in this book are open to an array of uses. Some are open to hikers only, but others also allow horseback riders, mountain bikers, hikers with dogs, and—on occasion—motorcycles.

When you encounter other trail users—whether they are hikers, climbers, runners, bicyclists, or horseback riders—the only hard-and-fast rule is to follow common sense and exercise simple courtesy. It's hard to overstate just how vital these two things—common sense and courtesy—are to maintaining an enjoyable, safe, and friendly situation when different types of trail users meet. See "The

Golden Rules of Trail Etiquette" for what you can do during trail encounters to make everyone's trip more enjoyable.

Also part of trail etiquette is to pack out everything you packed in, even biodegradable things like apple cores. The phrase, "leave only footprints, take only pictures," is a worthy slogan to live by when visiting the wilderness.

Another important Leave No Trace principle focuses on the business of taking care of personal business. The first rule of backcountry bathroom etiquette says that if an outhouse exists, use it. This seems obvious, but all too often folks find that backcountry toilets are dark, dank affairs and they choose to use the woods rather than the rickety wooden structure provided. It may be easier on your nose to head off into the woods, but this disperses human waste around popular areas. Privies, on the other hand, concentrate the waste and thus minimize contamination of area waters. The outhouses get even higher environmental marks if they feature removable holding tanks that can be air-lifted out. These johns and their accompanying stacks of tanks aren't exactly aesthetically pleasing, but having an ugly outhouse tucked into the corner of the woods is better than finding toilet paper strewn about.

When privies aren't provided, the key factor to consider is location. You'll want to choose a site at least 200 to 300 feet from water, campsites, and trails. A location well out of sight of trails and viewpoints will give you privacy and reduce the odds of other hikers stumbling onto the site after you leave. Other factors to consider are ecological: surrounding vegetation and some direct sunlight will aid decomposition.

Once you pick your place, start digging. The idea is to make like a cat and bury your waste. You need to dig down through the organic duff into the mineral soil below—a hole 6 to 8 inches deep is usually adequate. When

THE GOLDEN RULES OF TRAIL ETIQUETTE

- **Right-of-way.** When meeting other hikers, the uphill group has the right-of-way. There are two general reasons for this. First, on steep ascents hikers may be watching the trail and not notice the approach of descending hikers until they are face-to-face. More importantly, it is easier for descending hikers to break their stride and step off the trail than it is for those who have gotten into a good, climbing rhythm. But by all means if you are the uphill trekker and you wish to grant passage to oncoming hikers, go right ahead with this act of trail kindness.

- **Moving off-trail.** When meeting other user groups (like bicyclists or horseback riders), the hiker should move off the trail. This is because hikers are more mobile and flexible than other users, making it easier for them to step off the trail.

- **Encountering horses.** When meeting horseback riders, the hiker should step off the downhill side of the trail unless the terrain makes this difficult or dangerous. In that case, move to the uphill side of the trail, but crouch down a bit so you don't tower over the horses' heads. Also, make yourself visible so as not to spook the big beastie, and talk in a normal voice to the riders. This calms the horses. If hiking with a dog, keep your buddy under control.

- **Stay on trails**, and practice minimum impact. Don't cut switchbacks, take shortcuts, or make new trails. If your destination is off-trail, stick to snow and rock when possible so as not to damage fragile alpine meadows. Spread out when traveling off-trail; don't hike in line if in a group, as this greatly increases the chance of compacting thin soils and crushing delicate plant environments.

- **Obey the rules** specific to the trail you are visiting. Many trails are closed to certain types of use, including hiking with dogs or riding horses.

- **Hiking with dogs.** Hikers who take their dogs on the trails should have their dog on a leash or under very strict voice command at all times.

- **Avoid disturbing wildlife,** especially in winter and in calving areas. Observe from a distance, resisting the urge to move closer to wildlife (use your telephoto lens). This not only keeps you safer, but it prevents the animal from having to exert itself unnecessarily to flee from you.

- **Take only photographs.** Leave all natural things, features, and historic artifacts as you found them for others to enjoy.

- **Never roll rocks off trails or cliffs.** You risk endangering lives below you.

- These are just a few of the things you can do to maintain a safe and harmonious trail environment. And while not every situation is addressed by these rules, you can avoid problems by always remembering that common sense and courtesy are in order.

Gary Jackson pauses to drink water along Quartz Creek.

you've taken care of business, refill the hole and camouflage it with rocks and sticks—this helps prevent other humans, or animals, from digging in the same location before decomposition has done its job.

WATER

You'll want to treat your drinking water in the backcountry. Wherever humans have gone, germs have gone with them—and humans have gone just about everywhere. That means that even the most pristine mountain stream may harbor microscopic nasties like *Giardia* cysts, *Cryptosporidium*, or *E. coli*.

Treating water can be as simple as boiling it, chemically purifying it (adding tiny iodine tablets), or pumping it through one of the new-generation water filters or purifiers (Note: Pump units labeled as filters generally remove everything but viruses, which are too small to be filtered out. Pumps labeled as purifiers use a chemical element—usually iodine—to render viruses inactive after all the other bugs are filtered out). Never drink untreated water, or your intestines will never forgive you.

CLEANUP

When washing your hands, rinse off as much dust and dirt as you can in just plain water first. If you still feel the need for a soapy wash, collect a pot of water from a lake or stream and move at least 100 feet away. Apply a tiny bit of biodegradable soap to your hands, dribble on a little water, and lather up. Use a bandanna or towel to wipe away most of the soap, and then rinse with the water in the pot.

WILDLIFE
Bears

There are an estimated thirty to thirty-five thousand black bears in Washington, and the big bruins can be found in every corner of the state. The central and southern Cascades

BEAR IN MIND

Here are some suggestions for helping to avoid running into an aggressive bear:

- **Hike in a group** and hike only during daylight hours.
- **Talk or sing as you hike.** If a bear hears you coming, it will usually avoid you. When surprised, however, a bear may feel threatened. So make noises that will identify you as a human—talk, sing, rattle pebbles in a tin can—especially when hiking near a river or stream (which can mask more subtle sounds that might normally alert a bear to your presence).
- **Be aware** of the environment around you, and know how to identify bear sign. Overturned rocks and torn-up deadwood logs often are the result of a bear searching for grubs. Berry bushes stripped of berries—with leaves, branches, and berries littering the ground under the bushes—show where a bear has fed. Bears will often leave claw marks on trees and, since they use trees as scratching posts, fur in the rough bark of a tree is a sign that says "A bear was here!" Tracks and scat are the most common signs of bear's recent presence.
- **Stay away from abundant food sources and dead animals.** Black bears are opportunistic and will scavenge food. A bear that finds a dead deer will hang around until the meat is gone, and it will defend that food against any perceived threat.
- **Keep dogs leashed and under control.** Many bear encounters have resulted from unleashed dogs chasing a bear: The bear gets angry and turns on the dog. The dog gets scared and runs for help (back to its owner). And the bear follows right back into the dog owner's lap.
- **Leave scented items at home**—the perfume, hair spray, cologne and scented soaps. Using scented sprays and body lotions makes you smell like a big, tasty treat.
- **Fish cleaning.** Never clean fish within 100 feet of camp.

are especially attractive to the solitude-seeking bears. Watching the bears graze through a rich huckleberry field or seeing them flip dead logs in search of grubs can be an exciting and rewarding experience—provided, of course, that you aren't in the same berry patch.

Bears tend to prefer solitude to human company and will generally flee long before you have a chance to get too close. There are times, however, when bears either don't hear hikers approaching, or they are more interested in defending their food source—or their young—then they are in avoiding a confrontation. These instances are rare, and there are things you can do to minimize the odds of an encounter with an aggressive bear (see "Bear in Mind").

Cougars

Very few hikers ever see a cougar in the wild. Not only are these big cats some of the most solitary, shy animals in the woods, but there are just twenty-five hundred to three thousand of them roaming the entire state of Washington. Still, cougars and hikers do sometimes encounter each other. In these cases hikers should, in my opinion, count their blessings—they will likely never see a more majestic animal than a wild cougar.

To make sure the encounter is a positive one, hikers must understand the cats. Cougars are shy but very curious. They will follow hikers simply to see what kind of beasts we are, but they very rarely (as in, almost never) attack adult humans. See "Cool Cats" for how to make the most of your luck.

COOL CATS

If you encounter a cougar, remember that these animals rely on prey that can't, or won't, fight back. So, as soon as you see the cat:

- **Do not run!** Running may trigger a cougar's attack instinct.
- **Stand up and face it.** Virtually every recorded cougar attack on humans has been a predator-prey attack. If you appear as another aggressive predator rather than as prey, the cougar will back down.
- **Try to appear large.** Wave your arms or a jacket over your head.
- **Pick up children and small dogs.**
- **Maintain eye contact** with the animal. The cougar will interpret this as a show of dominance on your part.
- **Back away slowly** if you can safely do so.

A pair of bobcats resting under a rocky ledge

GEAR

No hiker should venture far up a trail without being properly equipped, starting with the feet. A good pair of boots can make the difference between a wonderful hike and a horrible death march. Keep your feet happy and you'll be happy.

But you can't talk boots without talking socks. Only one rule here: wear whatever is most comfortable unless it's cotton. Corollary to that rule: never wear cotton.

Cotton is a wonderful fabric when your life isn't on the line—it's soft, light, and airy. But get it wet and it stays wet. That means blisters on your feet. Wet cotton also lacks any insulation value. In fact, get it wet and it sucks away your body heat, leaving you susceptible to hypothermia. So leave your cotton socks, cotton underwear, and even the cotton T-shirts at home. The only cotton I carry on the trail is my trusty pink bandanna (pink because nobody else I know carries pink, so I always know which is mine).

While the "to pack" list varies from hiker to hiker, there are a few things each and every one of us should have in our packs. For instance, every hiker who ventures more than a few hundred yards away from the road should be prepared to spend the night under the stars (or under the clouds, as may be more likely). Mountain storms can whip up in a hurry, catching sunny-day hikers by surprise. What was an easy-to-follow trail during a calm, clear day can disappear into a confusing world of fog and rain—or even snow—in a windy tempest. Therefore, every member of the party should pack the Ten Essentials and a few other items that aren't necessarily essential, but would be good to have on hand in an emergency.

The Ten Essentials

1. **Navigation (map and compass):** Carry a topographic map of the area you plan

to be in and knowledge of how to read it. Likewise a compass—again, make sure you know how to use it.

2. **Sun protection (sunglasses and sunscreen):** In addition to sunglasses and sunscreen (SPF 15 or better), take along physical sun barriers such as a wide-brimmed hat, long-sleeve shirt, and long pants.

3. **Insulation (extra clothing):** This means more clothing than you would wear during the worst weather of the planned outing. If you get injured or lost, you won't be moving around generating heat, so you'll need to be able to bundle up.

4. **Illumination (flashlight/headlamp):** If caught after dark, you'll need a headlamp or flashlight to be able to follow the trail. If forced to spend the night, you'll need it to set up emergency camp, gather wood, and so on. Carry extra batteries and bulb too.

5. **First-aid supplies:** Nothing elaborate needed—especially if you're unfamiliar with how to use less familiar items. Make sure you have plastic bandages, gauze bandages, some aspirin, and so on. At minimum a Red Cross first-aid training course is recommended. Better still, sign up for a Mountaineering Oriented First-Aid course (MOFA) if you'll be spending a lot of time in the woods.

6. **Fire (firestarter and matches):** An emergency campfire provides warmth but it also has a calming effect on most people. Without one the night can be cold, dark, and intimidating. With one the night is held at arm's length. A candle or tube of firestarting ribbon is essential for starting a fire with wet wood. And of course matches are an important part of this essential. You can't start a fire without them. Pack them in a waterproof container and/or buy the waterproof/windproof variety. Book matches

DAY HIKER'S CHECKLIST
ALWAYS CARRY THE TEN ESSENTIALS
- See list on left

THE BASICS
- Daypack (just big enough to carry all your gear)

CLOTHING
- Polyester or nylon shorts/pants
- Short-sleeve shirt
- Long-sleeve shirt
- Warm pants (fleece or micro-fleece)
- Fleece jacket or wool sweater
- Wicking long underwear
- Noncotton underwear
- Bandanna

OUTERWEAR
- Raingear
- Wide-brimmed hat (for sun/rain)
- Fleece/stocking hat (for warmth)
- Gloves (fleece/wool and shell)

FOOTWEAR
- Hiking boots
- Hiking socks (not cotton!). Carry one extra pair. When your feet are soaked with sweat, change into the clean pair, and rinse out the dirty pair and hang them on the back of your pack to dry. Repeat as often as necessary during the hike.
- Liner socks
- Extra laces
- Gaiters
- Moleskin (for prevention of blisters) and Second Skin (for treatment of blisters). Carry both in your first-aid kit.

Take care before leaving the trailhead, and pay attention to information posted on kiosks.

are useless in wind or wet weather and disposable lighters are unreliable.

7. **Repair kit and tools (including a knife):** A knife is helpful, a multitool is better. You never know when you might need a small pair of pliers or scissors, both of which are commonly found on compact multitools. A basic repair kit includes such things as a 20-foot length of nylon cord, a small roll of duct tape, some 1-inch webbing and extra webbing buckles (to fix broken pack straps), and a small tube of superglue.

8. **Nutrition (extra food):** Pack enough so that you'll have leftovers after an uneventful trip—those leftovers will keep you fed and fueled during an emergency.

9. **Hydration (extra water):** Figure what you'll drink between water sources, and then add an extra liter. If you plan on relying on wilderness water sources, be sure to include some method of purification, whether a chemical additive, such as iodine, or a filtration device.

10. **Emergency shelter:** This can be as simple as a few extra-large garbage bags, or something more efficient such as a reflective space blanket or tube tent.

TRAILHEAD CONCERNS

Sadly, the topic of trailhead and trail crime must be addressed. As urban areas continuously encroach upon our green spaces, societal ills follow along.

But by and large our hiking trails are safe places—far safer than most city streets. Common sense and vigilance, however, are still in order. This is true for all hikers, but particularly so for solo hikers. Be aware of your surroundings at all times. Leave your itinerary with someone back home. If something doesn't feel right, it probably isn't. Take action by leaving the place or situation immediately. But remember, most hikers are friendly, decent people. Some may be a little introverted, but that's no cause for worry.

By far your biggest concern should be with trailhead theft. Car break-ins are a far too common occurrence at some of our trailheads. Do not—absolutely under no circumstances—leave anything of value in your vehicle while out hiking. Take your wallet, cell phone, and listening devices with you, or better yet, don't bring them along in the first place. Don't leave anything in your car that may appear valuable. A duffle bag on the back seat may contain dirty T-shirts, but a thief may think there's a laptop in it. If you do leave a duffle of clothes in the car, unzip it so prowlers can see that it does indeed just have clothes inside. Save yourself the hassle of returning to a busted window by not giving criminals a reason to clout your car.

If you arrive at a trailhead and someone looks suspicious, don't discount your intuition. Take notes on the person and his or her vehicle. Record the license plate and report the behavior to the authorities. Don't confront the person. Leave and go to another trail.

While most car break-ins are crimes of opportunity, organized bands intent on stealing IDs have also been known to target parked cars at trailheads. While some trailheads are regularly targeted and others rarely if at all, there's no sure way of preventing this from happening to you other than being dropped off at the trailhead or taking the bus (rarely an option, either way). But you can make your car less of a target by not leaving anything of value in it.

ENJOY THE TRAILS

Above all else, I hope you can safely enjoy the trails in this book. These trails exist for our enjoyment and for the enjoyment of future generations. We can use them and protect them at the same time if we are careful with our actions and forthright with our demands on Congress to continue and further the protection of our country's wildlands.

Throughout the twentieth century wilderness lovers helped secure protection for the lands we enjoy today. As we enter the twenty-first century we must see to it that those protections continue and that the last bits of wildlands are also preserved for the enjoyment of future generations.

Please, if you enjoy these trails, get involved. Something as simple as writing a letter to Congress can make a big difference.

A treed raccoon waits for the photographer to move along.

A NOTE ABOUT SAFETY

Safety is an important concern in all outdoor activities. No guidebook can alert you to every hazard or anticipate the limitations of every reader. Therefore, the descriptions of roads, trails, routes, and natural features in this book are not representations that a particular place or excursion will be safe for your party. When you follow any of the routes described in this book, you assume responsibility for your own safety. Under normal conditions, such excursions require the usual attention to traffic, road and trail conditions, weather, terrain, the capabilities of your party, and other factors. Keeping informed on current conditions and exercising common sense are the keys to a safe, enjoyable outing.

—The Mountaineers Books

Opposite: Fog-filled Snoqualmie Valley and the Cascades from the Tiger Mountain Trail

issaquah alps

Western Washington boasts many wonderful and unique features, but one thing truly sets the Seattle-area megalopolis apart from all other urban areas: the Issaquah Alps. These peaks comprise the section of the Cascade foothills straddling the I-90 corridor, from the North Bend area to Bellevue. In the mid-1970s, Mountaineers Books author Harvey Manning gave these low but spectacular peaks the moniker "Alps" as a way to help promote, and thus preserve, the beautiful wildlands before they were marred by developers. Recreation became the focus for the public lands within the Alps, and the land management agencies—from King County Parks to the Washington State Department of Natural Resources—helped make this a trail user's mecca in a state already rich in hiking opportunities.

The Issaquah Alps offer residents of the Puget Sound basin wonderful year-round hiking. The trails in this region range from short, scenic strolls along rivers and streams, to long hikes into rich forest ecosystems, to even a few view-rich mountain summits. Best of all, these wildland trails are mere minutes from downtown Seattle, so even the busiest corporate type can get off work at 5:00 PM and, with Superman-like speed, convert into a hiker type and be on a pristine trail by 6:00 PM for an evening hike.

① Wildside Trail–De Leo Wall

RATING/ DIFFICULTY	ROUND-TRIP	ELEV GAIN/ HIGH POINT	SEASON
***/2	4 miles	350 feet/ 950 feet	Year-round

Map: Green Trails Cougar Mountain No. 203S; **Contact:** King County Parks, (206) 296-8687, *www.metrokc.gov*; **GPS:** N 47 32.090, W 122 07.728

🏠 *Humans have been trekking through this Cougar Mountain forest for ages. Native Americans wandered the slopes for as long as seven thousand years, and after the new Americans moved west, trappers, prospectors, loggers, and traders pushed goods through the wagon traces along the slopes above Coal Creek basin. Today, hikers and horse riders can enjoy the cool forests and gentle trails year-round, even November through May when the high-country Cascades are locked in snow.*

GETTING THERE

From I-90 take exit 13 onto Lakemont Boulevard. Drive south on Lakemont Boulevard, which becomes Newcastle–Coal Creek Road. After crossing "The Pass" and starting down, cross Coal Creek and find the trailhead on the east side of the road at a sharp bend in Newcastle–Coal Creek Road.

ON THE TRAIL

Red Town. Coal Creek Town. Rainbow Town. There's a lot of American history here, going back nearly 150 years. Of course, the Native American history goes back much farther. Local tribes hunted these woods, gathered foodstuffs in the meadows, and harvested cedar for various uses.

As you hike the Wildside Trail (W1) you'll cross the clear waters of Coal Creek in a deep gorge, striding past an old homesite (the Wash House). Stay left at the junction with the Rainbow Town Trail to continue a scenic woodland walk to a high old mine site, where you'll find a massive concrete piling. Once, a massive cable nearly a half mile long was used to haul

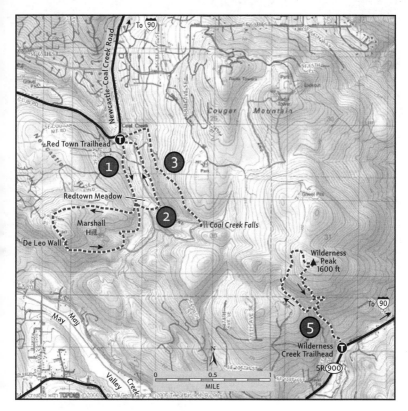

ore-laden containers up the steep slope below—this section of trail, dubbed the Steam Hoist Trail, is named for the massive coal-fired engines that powered that ore-hauling cable system.

The trail continues past this bit of Americana to Curious Valley—a U-shaped gorge carved by glaciers at the tail end of the last ice age—before it loops around the upper flank of Marshall Hill. An old millpond still sits, cool and dark, in the woods on Marshall Hill. Its waters once rushed down an old closed flume system to power lumber mills down in Coal Creek valley.

Past the pond, the trail leads across the spine of De Leo Wall. Here you'll find views from the open madrona forest atop the wall. Leave the spine of De Leo Wall by descending gradually toward Newcastle Hills to rejoin the Wildside Trail in the Coal Creek valley near Redtown Meadow.

EXTENDING YOUR TRIP

Several linkages exist to make this, and other area hikes, longer. A secondary trail links Curious Valley on the southwestern end of this route to the trails leading to Redtown Meadow (Hike 2) and Coal Creek Falls (Hike 3).

Mount Rainier and a lenticular cloud as seen from the De Leo Wall

2 Redtown Meadow

RATING/ DIFFICULTY	ROUND-TRIP	ELEV GAIN/ HIGH POINT	SEASON
***/1	1.5 miles	150 feet/ 800 feet	Year-round

Loop

```
800'
750'
700'
650'
    0            0.75           1.5
```

Map: Green Trails Cougar Mountain No. 203S;
Contact: King County Parks, (206) 296-8687,
www.metrokc.gov; **GPS:** N 47 32.090, W 122
07.728; **Status:** Rescued

Sometimes we humans do get it right and this area proves it. The old mining community of Red Town built a ball field in a previously spectacular meadowland, and when King County Parks reclaimed Cougar Mountain, a few advocates—most notably the venerable guidebook author and wildlands protector, Harvey Manning, and his daughter and fellow advocate, Penny Manning—fought to restore the meadow to its natural state. Hundreds of volunteers helped plant native grasses, trees, and shrubs, clearing out invasive species such as Scotch broom and blackberry vines. They toted tons of topsoil and cleared human relics. As the native plants took root and flourished, native birds and beasts moved in and prospered. Today, this area offers a stunning experience of a native foothills forest meadow—complete with mosquitoes, so come fall through spring to avoid these summer pests.

GETTING THERE

From I-90 take exit 13 onto Lakemont Boulevard. Drive south on Lakemont Boulevard, which becomes the Newcastle–Coal Creek Road. After crossing "The Pass" and starting down, cross Coal Creek and find the trailhead on the east side of the road at a sharp bend in Newcastle–Coal Creek Road.

ON THE TRAIL

Leave the trailhead and follow the Wildside Trail (W1). Stay right at the first three junctions, then go left at about 0.25 mile from the trailhead and in mere yards go right to stay on the Wildside Trail (this short jog to the left was on the Rainbow Town Trail).

The Wildside Trail reaches a junction with the Red Town Trail on the left at just 0.7 mile. The Redtown Meadow awaits you. Stop and enjoy the fragrant meadows—many of the wildflowers bloom April through May—but don't tromp through the fragile field please. Benches invite those who want to spend some quality time contemplating this native restoration.

Once you've had your fill, continue on the Red Town Trail as it sweeps left around the upper Coal Creek basin before turning north and rolling back down toward the trailhead.

3 Coal Creek Falls

RATING/ DIFFICULTY	ROUND-TRIP	ELEV GAIN/ HIGH POINT	SEASON
***/2	2.5 miles	350 feet/ 1000 feet	Year-round

One-way

Map: Green Trails Cougar Mountain No. 203S;
Contact: King County Parks, (206) 296-8687, www.metrokc.gov; **GPS:** N 47 32.090, W 122 07.728

Water, water everywhere and quite a drop it takes! Cougar Mountain's Coal Creek Falls is the primary attraction here, but it's the water underfoot that really makes the area special. Such abundance helps keep the forest

Trail passing Coal Creek near the Redtown Meadow

*green and fragrant, with wildflowers in sea-
son—and abundant summer mosquitoes.
Come in November through May, when the
nights are too cold for these pesky biters
and the falls are full of runoff. In the spring
you'll find skunk cabbage, and through the
early summer you'll enjoy plump, juicy
salmonberries. And at the end, you'll enjoy
the cool cascade of Coal Creek Falls.*

GETTING THERE

From I-90 take exit 13 onto Lakemont Boulevard. Drive south on Lakemont Boulevard,
which becomes Newcastle–Coal Creek Road.
After crossing "The Pass" and starting down,
cross Coal Creek and find the trailhead on
the east side of the road at a sharp bend in
Newcastle–Coal Creek Road.

ON THE TRAIL

From the trailhead, head up toward Red Town.
The route you want veers left onto Cave Hole
Trail. Once upon a time, mules pulled wagon-
loads of coal down this trace, and later, as the
coal veins played out, folks used it as an access
route to another easily accessible fuel source:
firewood. Today's trail uses that same old track.

As you climb away from the old Red Town
site, you'll notice areas where the ground
seems to have slumped in on itself—these
are the cave holes that give the trail its name.
The holes formed when miners pushed their
underground extractions too close to the surface, leaving a void that eventually caved in,
creating a "cave hole" in the ground above.

Less than 1 mile after leaving the trailhead,
you'll find the Coal Creek Falls Trail leading
off to the right. The path meanders around
the upper slopes of Curious Valley before
slanting down into a small gulch carved by the
tumbling waters of Coal Creek. Here, about
1.25 miles out, you'll find the falls.

Opposite: Coal Creek Falls

Coal Creek Falls can be spectacular during
the rainy season of January–March, thundering
down the rocky chute. Venture out during a particularly cold spell and you'll find marvelous ice
sculptures formed by the splashing and spray
from the falls. By midsummer, the falls usually
shrinks to nothing more than a small splatter-
ing of dribbling streams between the rocks.

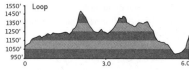

4 Anti-Aircraft Peak

RATING/ DIFFICULTY	ROUND-TRIP	ELEV GAIN/ HIGH POINT	SEASON
****/3	6 miles	625 feet/ 1525 feet	Year-round

Map: Green Trails Cougar Mountain No. 203S;
Contact: King County Parks, (206) 296-8687,
www.metrokc.gov; **GPS:** N 47 32.465, W 122
05.762

*If you want views from Cougar Moun-
tain, this is the trail to take—best in
November through May, to avoid the summer clouds of mosquitoes. The route climbs
to one of the highest points in the western
Issaquah Alps, and along the way you'll find
plenty of open viewpoints to take in the
scenery of the central Puget Sound basin.
The military early on recognized the value of
these high peaks and built a missile launch
and missile-command radar station atop
Anti-Aircraft Peak.*

GETTING THERE

From I-90 take exit 13 onto Lakemont
Boulevard. Drive south on Lakemont Boulevard,

which becomes Newcastle–Coal Creek Road. After crossing "The Pass," turn left (east) onto Cougar Mountain Way. Continue about 0.5 mile before turning right (south) onto 166th Way. Drive about 0.75 mile to a gate and park, being sure not to block the gate.

ON THE TRAIL

The route starts by rounding the gate and heading up the road toward the Newcastle Brick Works clay pit. At about 0.75 mile you'll leave the road by veering left onto the Klondike Swamp Trail. This swampy basin was once a shallow impoundment behind a long dam across these headwaters of Coal Creek. The lake behind the dam filled with sediment (largely the result of runoff from area logging), creating the current boggy swamp.

Birds of all varieties thrive in this accidental ecosystem—even wood ducks!

A mile into your hike through this rich environment, go left onto Lost Beagle Trail. (Was that lost beagle lured away by the abundant wildlife? Perhaps, so keep your own dog on-leash please). The trail climbs slightly through the wild woods to a reminder of this area's military might—a high fence around Radar Park. Continue along the trail as it skirts the park perimeter and, shortly after crossing the access road leading into the park compound, stop and enjoy the best views of the day at a small knob locals have dubbed Million Dollar View. The panoramic splendor includes Mount Baker in the North Cascades (on especially clear days) to the Seattle skyline and the Olympic Mountains beyond.

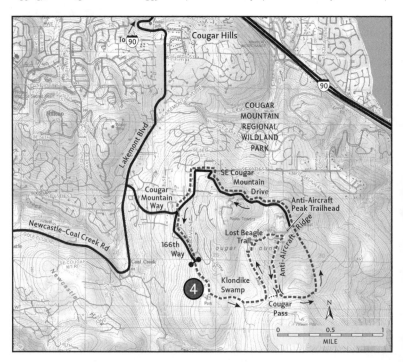

Mount Pilchuck and Three Fingers from Anti-Aircraft Peak

After soaking in the scenery at the top, descend along the Shangri La Trail a short 0.1 mile before going right and then right again at the very next junction. This puts you on Anti-Aircraft Ridge Trail. Shortly, you'll encounter yet another fork in the trail. (Warning: There are myriad trails here, and if signposts get knocked down it's easy to take a wrong turn—a great reason to carry a map.) To the right is Lost Beagle Trail, leading straight back to your starting point. Go left instead to descend along Anti-Aircraft Ridge.

You'll soon find yourself at Cougar Pass (elev. 1250 ft)—about 1.25 miles from Million Dollar View. This pass separates the drainages of Coal Creek and West Tibbetts Creek. Go right to cut your hike short (this leads straight down to the Klondike Swamp Trail), or stay left for the longer loop. This path skirts another swamp before merging into Tibbetts Marsh Trail. Stay right and climb a long 0.25 mile to the blue-sky views above the open cuts of the clay pits (elev. 1375 ft). Hop on SE Cougar Mountain Drive here and follow it west and then south to 166th Way and your waiting vehicle.

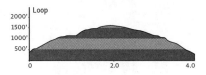

⑤ Wilderness Peak

RATING/ DIFFICULTY	ROUND-TRIP	ELEV GAIN/ HIGH POINT	SEASON
***/3	4 miles	1200 feet/ 1600 feet	Year-round

Map: Green Trails Cougar Mountain No. 203S; **Contact:** King County Parks, (206) 296-8687, *www.metrokc.gov*; **GPS:** N 47 32.465, W 122 05 **See map on page 37**

🐾 *If your definition of wilderness includes remote wildlands untouched by the hands of man, this is a misnamed peak. But if you can accept that wilderness includes lands returned to a state of wildness, you'll love this simple little Cougar Mountain hike in a natural wonderland that's just minutes from an urban jungle. Though the trail* is usually hikeable year-round (snowfall is scarce at this elevation), the route is best enjoyed in the fall through spring because mosquitoes buzz here in great numbers during the summer.

GETTING THERE

From I-90 take exit 15 onto Newcastle Way (State Route 900). Drive south about 2.5 miles to the Wilderness Creek trailhead.

ON THE TRAIL

The Wilderness Creek Trail crosses a sturdy, picturesque bridge over the pretty creek before climbing immediately up a series of switchbacks to lead you up and out of the creek canyon. The creek itself can be seen frequently from the trail as it tumbles down the steep draw, rushing over rocks and dropping over small falls. At around 0.5 mile you'll reach a trail fork.

To the right is the path you'll return on. For now, go left and you'll soon recross the creek and continue up the creek valley. Here, the forest boasts stands of maple, cottonwood, alder, and fir. This mixed forest allows great light penetration to the forest floor, which makes the moisture-rich creek valley an emerald basin of mosses and ferns that seem to cover every surface. From huge boulders to old, rotting logs, greenery grows everywhere. This rich world of green can be a wonderful place to escape the heat of summer. But for our purposes it's simply a grand landscape to enjoy while hiking on to greater adventures.

Continue up the trail as it veers up the lower slopes of nearby Ring Road Peak (not-so-creatively named for the old road that circled 'round the peak to its top). At the next trail junction stay right to recross the creek again, and then move onto a long section of boardwalk trail that keeps you above the murk on

Wilderness Creek footbridge on the way up Wilderness Peak

Big Bottom Bog. The forest here is largely very old second growth and even some native deciduous stands.

After crossing the boggy bottomlands at the upper end of the creek valley, the trail starts up the flank of Wilderness Peak. You'll find yourself among majestic old Douglas-firs in a forest largely untouched by man—only a few old stumps reveal the hand of hardworking independent loggers (gypos) who harvested single trees. Look closely and you'll see the notches cut for the sawyers' springboards—long planks stuck into the axe-hewn notches so the loggers could stand and saw through the tree trunk above the wide spread at root level.

After hiking just 1.3 miles you'll cross Sky Bear Pass at 1320 feet, and in another 0.25 mile find yourself at Far Country Lookout. At the junction here, go right to ascend to the summit of forest-crowned Wilderness Peak. You'll find scant views other than of the forest around you. Continue on down the far side of the peak to Big View Cliff on the southern slope before reaching that original trail split at the top of the first set of switchbacks you encountered on your trek out.

Washington Trails Association construction on Crystal Creek

Squak Mountain's East Side Loop

6

RATING/ DIFFICULTY	ROUND-TRIP	ELEV GAIN/ HIGH POINT	SEASON
****/3	7 miles	1700 feet/ 2025 feet	Year-round

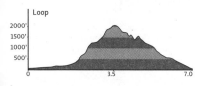

Map: Green Trails Cougar Mountain No. 203S;
Contact: King County Parks, (206) 296-8687,

www.metrokc.gov; **GPS:** N 47 28.908, W 122 03.248

It's appropriate that this hike begins in the heart of Issaquah. In the language of the native tribes, Ishquowh means "sound of water birds." The raspy name of this mountain destination, meanwhile, comes from the raucous calls of the herons that migrate through this area in the spring and fall— their mighty squak, squak, squak! echoes off the forested slopes of Squak Mountain.

GETTING THERE

From I-90 take the Front Street exit into Issaquah, and drive south on Front Street to turn

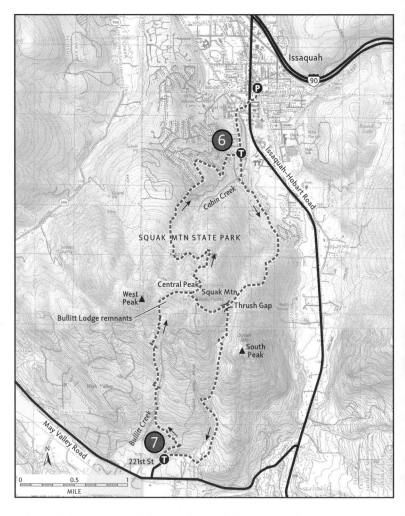

right onto Bush Street. Free parking is provided in the Issaquah Trail Center parking lot.

ON THE TRAIL

From the parking area, head east on Bush Street to its junction with Front Street. Cross at the light and turn south onto Newport Way.

Follow Newport Way as it crosses Issaquah Creek and then continue south on Wildwood Boulevard as it climbs out of town, soon turning to gravel road as it follows the creek up a gentle slope. When you reach the old Issaquah Creek Dam, you'll find a paved trail winding past some apartments and condominiums. A

Pacific Tree Frog

fast pace gets you past these buildings in just a few minutes and you'll soon reach the Squak Mountain Access trailhead on the left side of the street, about 1 mile from your starting point. There is *very* limited parking here, for those that can't or won't make the hike through town.

That first mile serves to remind you of what you are about to leave behind. As you start up the trail, you'll enter a world that is in transition back into a natural wonderland. The trail is an old road once used by coal miners and loggers. For the first 0.75 mile on this road-turned-trail path, stay left at the first two trail junctions before turning right to continue climbing.

At roughly 2 miles from your car, you'll find yet another fork in the trail (elev. 1450 ft). Turn right and follow the Central Peak Trail as it climbs gently for another mile to the summit of Central Peak—the peak bristles with radio and cell-phone towers. You'll find a few broken views from around the legs of the towers.

Leave the summit by walking 0.25 mile down the dirt service road before turning left onto a steep woodland path. Turn left at the next trail junction (about 0.25 mile after leaving the service road), and continue descending along an ancient logging road turned trail. This trail ends at a T junction near an old mill site.

Turn right onto the East Side Trail and meander through a bright woodland, crossing the multiple headwater streams of Cabin Creek, before reaching the trail end and the short walk back through town to your car.

7 Phils Trail–Thrush Gap Loop

RATING/ DIFFICULTY	ROUND-TRIP	ELEV GAIN/ HIGH POINT	SEASON
★★★★/3	5 miles	1650 feet/ 2025 feet	Mar–Nov

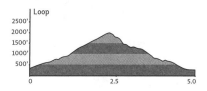

Map: Green Trails Cougar Mountain No. 203S; **Contact:** King County Parks, (206) 296-8687, *www.metrokc.gov*; **GPS:** N 47 28.908, W 122 03.248

Horse crossing bridge over Phils Creek

Squak Mountain is like the quiet cousin at a family reunion. Tiger Mountain is the boisterous brother, Cougar is the pretty sister, and Mount Si is the rowdy uncle. But Squak is lesser known and thus less commonly visited, which means the woodlands of Squak Mountain offer some of the most solitary exploration in the Issaquah Alps. And this route is the least used of the primary access points on scenic Squak.

GETTING THERE

From I-90 take exit 17 (Front Street), and turn right (south) onto Front Street and continue south through town. Front Street becomes Issaquah-Hobart Road as you leave town. In a couple of miles turn right (west) onto May Valley Road, and find the trailhead parking

area on the right (north) side of the road at 221st Street.

ON THE TRAIL

The trail leaves the parking area, heading west on the May Valley Trail and climbing quickly through mature second-growth forests of fir and hemlock. Cedars flourish in the boggy areas, where the trail rolls through on boardwalk sections.

At 1.1 miles the trail forks. Turn left and then back to the right, being sure to stay on the primary trail as you continue climbing—there are several boot-beaten trails angling away (illegal shortcuts carved by lazy hikers).

At 1.5 miles—shortly after crossing Bullitt Creek—the path tops 1300 feet and angles to the right along the creek gorge. The trail you want runs straight up the gorge, climbing at a rate of 1200 feet per mile. Fortunately, this pitch is only 0.25 mile long, getting you to 1600 feet about 1.8 miles into the hike.

The May Valley Trail you've been hiking intersects the Perimeter Trail at this point. Continue along the May Valley Trail into an old logged section of forest—small trees sprout from between old stumps—and in another 0.25 mile (2 miles into the hike) turn right onto the Bullitt Fireplace Trail.

At 2.2 miles you'll find the relics of the old Bullitt Lodge. All that remains of the once-grand structure is the old rock fireplace and a bit of foundation. You might stop here for a rest, or a light meal, making use of the nearby benches and picnic table. Continue along your path and in another 0.3 mile you'll top out on the radio-tower-laden summit of Central Peak.

To close the loop, leave the summit via the Old Griz Trail. No signposts mark the path, so you'll have to work to find it—but not too hard. Just walk up to the viewpoint at the summit and then follow the roadway guardrails northeast. The trail drops away through the gap between the end of the guardrail and the start of the cyclone fence around the radio towers. Descend on this path, heading north, and you'll soon feel isolated in the dense forests of northern Squak. About 0.5 mile after leaving the summit, turn right onto Phils Trail. The route now winds along the steep upper slope of Central Peak.

At 3.7 miles the trail crosses Thrush Gap and descends the Phils Creek gorge. At 4.4 miles continue straight through a trail junction, and in another 0.25 mile reach the short connector trail leading back to the trailhead.

8 Poo Poo Point

RATING/ DIFFICULTY	ROUND-TRIP	ELEV GAIN/ HIGH POINT	SEASON
****/3	7.4 miles	1650 feet/ 1850 feet	Mar–Nov

Map: Green Trails Tiger Mountain No. 204S; **Contact:** Department of Natural Resources, South Puget Sound Region, (360) 825-1631, *www.dnrwa.gov*; **GPS:** N 47 31.425, W 122 1.571

It's time to go back to high school. Or maybe flight school. This Tiger Mountain path starts at Issaquah High School and ends at Poo Poo Point, where many paraglider pilots learn to fly their featherweight crafts. In between, you'll find wonderful old forests to explore and a grand path to follow.

GETTING THERE
From I-90 take exit 17 (Front Street) and turn right (south). After 0.6 mile turn left (east) onto East Sunset Way, and in two blocks turn right onto 2nd Avenue SE. In about 0.5 mile park near the high school. The trail begins just south of the school on the switchback of the old railroad grade.

A happy dog shares the views from Poo Poo Point

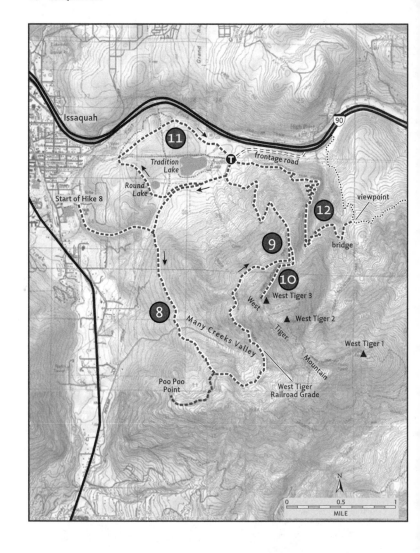

HIKE WITH KIDS

School just let out for summer and the kids are already bored and restless. What do you do? Take a hike!

This Day Hiking series features many scenic-but-gentle trails laced throughout our state lands and national forests and parks, offering wilderness adventures perfect for families with young kids. With the abundance of these easy-to-moderate hiking trails, there is no reason for anyone to miss out on the enjoyment of hiking. This pastime has grown to be truly a sport for people of all ages, all abilities.

The woods are full of things kids of all ages find fascinating. Besides bugs, birds, and animals there are all sorts of relics of human history to discover and explore, from rusting railroad spikes and mining equipment, to old fire lookouts and foresters' cabins, to Native American petroglyphs and rock art. There are fascinating geologic formations and countless forms of water bodies—streams, creeks, seeps, marshes, tarns, ponds, lakes, and bays.

Before heading out to discover your own great trail experiences, though, there are some things to consider. First and perhaps most important are the ages of the kids and their physical condition (not to mention your own). If you are new to hiking, or have been away from it for a while (like, since the kids were born), or if your kids are under fourteen years old, stick to trails of less than 1 mile in length. Both you and the kids will find this to be long enough, and many of the trails in that range offer plenty to see and experience.

Once the trip is planned, parents can do a few things to make sure their kids have fun—for instance, never hike with just one child. Kids need companions to compete with, play with, and converse with. One child and a pair of adults makes a hike seem too much like work for the poor kid. But let your child bring along a friend or two and all will have the time of their lives.

When starting out on the trail, adults need to set goals and destinations that are attainable for everyone. Kids and adults alike are more likely to enjoy the hike if they know there is a specific destination rather than just an idea of "going until we feel like turning back."

Then, when hiking, make sure to take frequent breaks and offer the kids "energy food" consisting of a favorite cookie or tasty treat. These snacks serve two purposes. The kids will be motivated to make it to the next break site, knowing they will get a good-tasting treat, and the sugar will help keep the kids fueled up and energized on the trail. For maximum benefit, make the energy foods a special treat that the kids especially like but maybe don't get as often as they'd like. Pack plenty of water, too, to wash down the snacks and to replace what is lost as sweat.

Finally, let the kids explore and investigate the trail environment as much as they like. Patience is more than a virtue here—it's a necessity. Take the time to inspect the tadpoles in trailside bogs, to study the bugs on the bushes, and to try spotting the birds singing in the trees. Just let the kids be kids. If you can then share in their excitement and enthusiasm, everyone will have a great time on the trail.

ON THE TRAIL

Hike up the old railway turned trail about 0.25 mile before veering right onto the service road known as the Old State Road. Walk around the gate on this road and continue about 1 mile. Just after crossing an old clear-cut, climb under some high-tension powerlines and continue up the rocky slope. Stay right at the next trail junction (to the left is the Section Line Trail) to hop onto the Poo Poo Point Trail. Limited views southwest reveal Squak Mountain.

Like so many Issaquah Alps trails, the Poo Poo Point Trail was born from an old road. The path is still wide enough for two hikers to trek side-by-side much of the time. More often, however, thick wildflowers and bushes (some laden with delicious salmonberries) line the route and crowd it down to a single-track trail.

At about 2 miles you'll cross a broad plateau (elev. 1150 ft) before starting up into Many Creeks Valley. Some of the creeks giving the valley its name are seasonal, running only in spring, while others—notably Gap Creek—runs year round. The well-built Gap Creek Bridge is at 2.5 miles, from which you can view the creek's stairstep falls and the remains of an old road bridge.

Past the creek, the trail continues to weave upward through the forest. You'll find some wonderful ancient trees, and plenty of reminders of the region's logging history (hint: look for old stumps with springboard notches). At 3.2 miles, stay right at the intersection with the West Tiger Railroad Grade (Hike 9).

In just another 0.5 mile, you'll come out into a small parking area, complete with high-tech composting toilet. Follow the trail around to the right side of the parking area to burst out into the bright sunshine on the grass bench that is Poo Poo Point. Hang gliders and paragliders launch off this grassy swale most afternoons spring through early autumn. Non-pilots can rest on the grassy hillside above the launch area, enjoying views of Issaquah Valley, Lake Sammamish, and the Bellevue skyline beyond. On clear days, Mount Baker can even be seen in the distance.

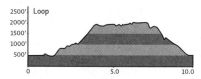

9 West Tiger Railroad Grade

RATING/ DIFFICULTY	ROUND-TRIP	ELEV GAIN/ HIGH POINT	SEASON
****/4	10 miles	1600 feet/ 2000 feet	Year-round

Map: Green Trails Tiger Mountain No. 204S; **Contact:** Department of Natural Resources, South Puget Sound Region, (360) 825-1631, www.dnr.wa.gov; **GPS:** N 47 31.779, W 121 59.742

Follow Tiger Mountain's finest old rail line while exploring some of the wildest and remotest stands of forest remaining on the mountain. You'll even find some outstanding views during this long, gentle hike. If you want to keep from swatting mosquitoes with every step, visit in fall through spring.

GETTING THERE

From I-90 take exit 20 and then turn right onto the frontage road paralleling the interstate. In just under 0.5 mile the road ends at a gate. The gate opens daily, though it is closed and locked at 7:00 PM. Park outside the gate if you'll be returning late in the day. Otherwise, continue another 0.4 mile to the Tradition Plateau trailhead.

ON THE TRAIL

Tiger Mountain's rich stands of timber and its close proximity to the booming city of Seattle proved too enticing for lumber barons to ignore. Trucking in the early 1900s wasn't efficient—to haul big loads you needed steam, and that meant railroads. As a result, short-line railroads were laid all over the mountain. Most wound through long series of switchbacks—the log trains would run forward up the first leg and out onto a long spur at the corner of the switchback turn. A lineman would switch the track so the train could back off the spur and continue backward up the next leg onto another corner spur. And so on until the log trains were at the top of the mountain. They'd then reverse the process to descend. Today, hikers enjoy those same switchbacks, though the rails are long gone and the remaining forest is mixed second and third growth, with a few remnant stands of old growth.

From the trailhead, head south on the Bus Trail as it swings around the east side of Tradition Lake. The trail pierces the second-growth forests of the lower flank of West Tiger. You'll cross under the high-tension powerlines and turn left onto the Section Line Trail, following the lines for more than 0.5 mile.

At 2.5 miles out, turn left onto the Poo Poo Point Trail, climbing steeply up the rocky slopes before climbing through the middle of Many Creeks Valley. At 5 miles out (elev. 1200 ft), cross Gap Creek on a stout bridge. Enjoy the views of the creek as it tumbles over a series of steps.

Beyond Gap Creek, the trail ascends steeply through a rare stand of old-growth Douglas-fir before crossing the West Tiger Railroad Grade at 5.6 miles. Turn left onto this trail to continue the loop (the right fork leads to Poo Poo Point, Hike 8). Stay on West Tiger Railroad Grade as it sweeps around the head of Many Creeks Valley, crossing as many as eight seasonal streams (and a couple year-round creeks). Stick to the main trail at all intersections and trail forks—there are many side trails leading away on both sides of the West Tiger Railroad Grade.

Lush sword ferns line the West Tiger Railroad Grade

At about 7 miles you'll cross the route's high point (2000 feet) on the ridge below West Tiger's summit. From here the trail descends gently for the next mile, before turning steep for the last 2 miles as it drops through a series of switchbacks, crosses Tradition Creek, and runs straight down to the trailhead.

10 West Tiger 3

RATING/ DIFFICULTY	ROUND-TRIP	ELEV GAIN/ HIGH POINT	SEASON
****/4	5 miles	2100 feet/ 2525 feet	Mar–Nov

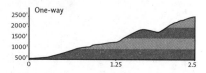

Map: Green Trails Tiger Mountain No. 204S; **Contact:** Department of Natural Resources, South Puget Sound Region, (360) 825-1631, *www.dnr.wa.gov*; **GPS:** N 47 31.779, W 121 59.742

Don't expect solitude here—this is perhaps the most heavily used trail on Tiger Mountain, and for good reason. Fortunately, there is plenty of room to share. This close-to-the-city wildland trail provides stunning views, great forestlands, and ample opportunities to see birds and critters. West Tiger—one of the sprawling mountain's four primary peaks (West, Middle, South, and East)—is itself a tri-crowned peak. Numbered 1 through 3, the third of the West Tiger peaks offers the best views, despite being the lowest of the triplets.

GETTING THERE

From I-90 take exit 20 and then turn right onto the frontage road paralleling the interstate. In just under 0.5 mile the road ends at a gate. The gate opens daily, though it is closed and locked at 7:00 PM. Park outside the gate if you'll be returning late in the day. Otherwise, continue another 0.4 mile to the Tradition Plateau trailhead.

ON THE TRAIL

Start up the Bus Trail, and after just 0.25 mile veer left onto the West Tiger 3 Trail. Stay to the right just after that trail fork (the second left leads to the seemingly endless Tiger Mountain Trail, or TMT). Sticking to West Tiger 3 Trail can be problematic if trail signs are missing or hard to find, since multiple trails slant away left and right over the next 2 miles. Stick to the primary path as it ascends a long series of steep switchbacks.

At 2 miles out, the trail crosses the West Tiger Railroad Grade (elev. 1960 ft). Continue upward, heading into a tight series of switchbacks. The trail gets steeper, it seems, the closer you get to the top. But finally, you burst out onto the summit of West Tiger 3 (elev. 2525 ft), just 2.5 miles from the trailhead.

The open views you'll find here sweep in Squak Mountain, the sprawling town of Issaquah, the blue waters of Lake Sammamish, the skyscrapers of Bellevue, and even the snowy crown of Mount Baker far to the north. On hot summer days you might see hang gliders and paragliders launching off Poo Poo Point (just to your south), riding the thermal lift that spins out of Many Creeks Valley and off the summit.

EXTENDING YOUR TRIP

You can return the way you came, or descend to the north along the Section Line Trail. If you choose this route, continue downhill for nearly 1 mile before turning right on a small connector trail (elev. 1100 ft). This 0.75-mile-long path contours around the Tradition Creek valley to intercept the West Tiger 3 Trail about 1 mile above the trailhead.

Gary Jackson on the West Tiger 3 summit

11 Tradition Lake Loop

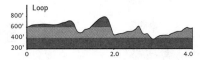

RATING/ DIFFICULTY	ROUND-TRIP	ELEV GAIN/ HIGH POINT	SEASON
****/2	4 miles	400 feet/ 800 feet	Year-round

Map: Green Trails Tiger Mountain No. 204S;
Contact: Department of Natural Resources,
South Puget Sound Region, (360) 825-1631,
www.dnr.wa.gov; **GPS:** N 47 31.779, W 121
59.742

*When the pressures of the office
get too much, this Tiger Moun-
tain trail is just close enough to hike after
business hours, and just wild enough to
make you forget those urban cares for a few
hours. The plethora of trails around the Tradition Lake plateau make for an array of
loop options, this one being the longest of
the short loops possible. You'll find yourself
wandering deep green woods. You'll smell
the rich foliage bursting from the damp
earth of woodland swamps. You'll hear the
song of countless birds. And you'll see a
spectrum of native flora and fauna, all within a few moments' walk of the busy interstate corridor.*

GETTING THERE

From I-90 take exit 20 and then turn right
onto the frontage road paralleling the interstate. In just under 0.5 mile the road ends at a
gate. The gate opens daily, though it is closed
and locked at 7:00 PM. Park outside the gate if
you'll be returning late in the day. Otherwise,
continue another 0.4 mile to the Tradition Plateau trailhead.

ON THE TRAIL

This route makes use of several trails. Start
on the Bus Trail as it climbs south before
sweeping west along the long slope of West
Tiger Mountain. The path crosses several
small creeks (some running year-round, some
seasonal freshets) before reaching the Bonne-
ville powerlines at 0.8 mile. Cross under them
and slant west onto the Wetlands Trail.

In another 0.1 mile, you'll find a small spur
path that drops a short hop down to the small
basin of Round Lake. Look for songbirds
around this pond any time of year, and in the
winter you might see migratory waterfowl
resting here.

Continue along the trail as it runs northwest, descending slightly before reaching a

A hiker pauses at the Tradition Lake viewpoint.

junction at 1.8 miles. Go right (to the second trail on the right—the first is Big Tree Trail) to follow Brink Trail as it swings around at about the 400-foot-elevation level for another short mile to yet another junction.

Stay left to continue along the Swamp Trail as it stays near the same elevation for another mile. This path pierces some thick foliage, utilizing raised boardwalks for a good portion of the route. Volunteers from the Issaquah Alps Trail Club chopped this route out of the swamp vegetation below Tradition Lake—so it can be hot and buggy during the midday heat of summer. But come evening, it can be a cool escape from the hot urban jungle.

The trail ends at the powerline access road just west of the trailhead. Hike the last few hundred yards back to the trailhead on this road.

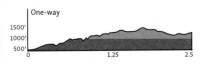

12 Tiger Mountain Trail: North

RATING/ DIFFICULTY	ROUND-TRIP	ELEV GAIN/ HIGH POINT	SEASON
***/3	5 miles	1100 feet/ 1500 feet	Mar–Nov

One-way

1500'
1000'
500'
0   1.25   2.5

Map: Green Trails Tiger Mountain No. 204S; **Contact:** Department of Natural Resources, South Puget Sound Region, (360) 825-1631, www.dnr.wa.gov; **GPS:** N 47 31.779, W 121 59.742

The crown jewel of the Tiger Mountain trail network will be thirty years old in 2009: the Tiger Mountain Trail (TMT) officially opened on October 13, 1979. This long trail meanders across the three main Tiger peaks, running some 16 miles from the southeast side of the big mountain all the way across to the northwest corner of the Tiger Mountain State Forest. This hike—the northern end of the TMT—is one of the more scenic stretches you'll find, with grand views and plenty of natural habitat to explore.

GETTING THERE
From I-90 take exit 20 and then turn right onto the frontage road paralleling the interstate. In just under 0.5 mile the road ends at a gate. The gate opens daily, though it is closed and locked at 7:00 PM. Park outside the gate if you'll be returning late in the day. Otherwise, continue another 0.4 mile to the Tradition Plateau trailhead.

ON THE TRAIL
With the maze of trails leading away from the trailhead, make sure you are heading south on the path signed "TMT." The trail leads out from the parking lot on the Bus Trail. In just a few paces, turn left onto the West Tiger 3 Trail, then make a quick left again onto the TMT.

The TMT leads east along the Tradition Plateau, running under the broken canopy of a mixed-aged forest. In less than 1 mile the route turns south and climbs a steep series of switchbacks, ascending the northern spine of West Tiger Mountain. This steep climb can be a scorcher in midsummer, since the forest around the trail is mostly young alder and maple. This area was logged repeatedly through the first half of the twentieth century.

At around 1 mile (elev. 1350 ft) the trail sweeps southeast around the nose of the ridge and then climbs more gradually as it traverses into the headwaters of the West Fork High Point Creek. During this traverse of the ridge nose you'll encounter increasingly older and mature forest as past logging operations fall behind you. You'll find massive Douglas-firs and hemlocks—even a few cedars. A high, wide bridge spans the deep cut of the creek.

A final 0.75 mile leads around another ridge

A hiker crossing a footbridge along the TMT

nose into the main branch of High Point Creek. Just past the creek crossing you'll intersect the High Point Trail at a viewpoint. Turn back here and enjoy a relaxing hike back down the forested path.

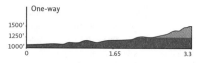

13 East Tiger: Silent Swamp

RATING/ DIFFICULTY	ROUND-TRIP	ELEV GAIN/ HIGH POINT	SEASON
***/2	6.6 miles	450 feet/ 1550 feet	Year-round

Map: Green Trails Tiger Mountain No. 204S; **Contact:** Department of Natural Resources, South Puget Sound Region, (360) 825-1631, *www.dnr.wa.gov;* **GPS:** N 47 28.376, W 121 54.614

You'll want to visit this Tiger Mountain swamp during the wet season to really enjoy all it has to offer—July and August can be uncomfortably hot and prime time for mosquitoes. Plus, if you head out during the winter waterfowl migration, you might find a rare treat: wood ducks in the marshy areas. But any time of year can be an adventure here, with a bounty of wild plants and animals to enjoy.

GETTING THERE

From I-90 take exit 25 and drive southwest 3.1 miles on State Route 18. Turn right (north) onto a small gated road and park well clear of the main highway without blocking the gate (if you miss this pullout, go to the Tiger Mountain summit to turn around—the pullout is 1.2 miles northeast of the summit).

ON THE TRAIL

Don't be put off by the fact that the first 2.3 miles of this "trail" follows a narrow gravel road. You may be walking on road, but you won't be competing with car traffic—the road is only used by forest managers and a very few lease holders (such as companies with radio towers on the summits).

From the parking area at the road gate, hike north along the East Side Road and in 2.3 miles you'll find the start of the true Silent Swamp Trail on your left (elev. 1420 ft). The trail climbs away from the road and then veers right onto an old railroad grade (Tiger Mountain is littered with old railroad right-of-ways).

The trail sweeps around a small ridge, climbing to 1550 feet, before rolling out into

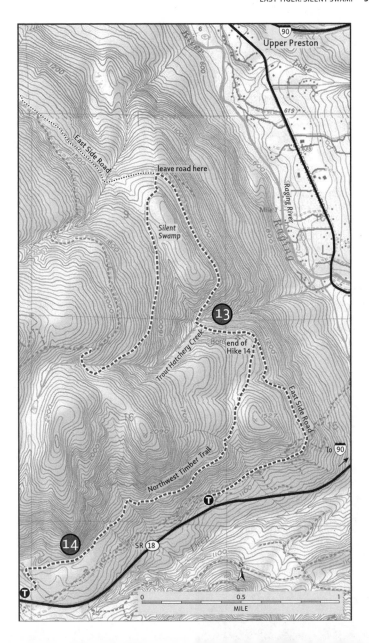

Silent Swamp. This mecca of wetland habitat seems to be an isolated wilderness, making you forget that you hiked in on a road, and that two busy highways are just a few miles away. The ridge you hiked around blocks the white noise of the ever-flowing traffic on the interstate, and a heavily forested slope shelters you from the noisy diesel trucks climbing State Route 18.

Silent Swamp, though seemingly pristine and truly wild, is misnamed. Indeed, no true wild swamp is silent. The bogs here are alive with the sounds of nature. Frogs, birds, insects, trickling water. Burbling mud. Deer splashing through the marshes. Silent Swamp is a veritable symphony.

The trail crosses the swampy basin and reaches a fork just 1 mile after leaving the East Side Road. Turn around here, since the best of scenery is now behind you. Go back and enjoy it once more before returning to your car.

Monster stumps of Silent Swamp

14 Northwest Timber Trail

RATING/ DIFFICULTY	ROUND-TRIP	ELEV GAIN/ HIGH POINT	SEASON
***/2	5 miles	200 feet/ 1500 feet	Year-round

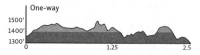

Map: Green Trails Tiger Mountain No. 204S; **Contact:** Department of Natural Resources, South Puget Sound Region, (360) 825-1631, *www.dnr.wa.gov*; **GPS:** N 47 28.015, W 121 55.997

 With little elevation change and a modest distance, this is a great Tiger Mountain trail for after work, especially on hot summer days. The cool forest tempers the worst summer heat wave, while the lush forests provide all the relaxation you could want. As you trek along this multiuse trail (open to horses and mountain bikes as well as hikers), keep silent and you're likely to hear the raucous calls of ravens, the screams of hawks, the chirps of juncos, and the rat-a-tat-tats of woodpeckers.

GETTING THERE
From I-90 take exit 25 and drive south on State Route 18 to the Tiger Mountain summit. At the summit, turn right (west) into the large parking lot.

ON THE TRAIL
Head for the gated road farthest to the right as you start walking out of the parking area. You'll walk a scant 0.25 mile on this road before turning right onto the well-signed path. The forest is a mix of old maples and alders—many draped beautifully with long beards of moss and lichen—as well as hemlocks and firs.

The trail contours northeast along the base of Beaver Hill for 2 miles, crossing a few creek basins along the way. One of these features a high bridge over the deep creek gorge. Below the bridge, waters cascade over a rocky ledge, creating a pretty waterfall to entertain hikers. The trail continues on, slowly descending toward Trout Hatchery Creek. The trail ends at a junction with the East Side Road.

EXTENDING YOUR TRIP

Turn around and retrace your steps, or link to Hike 13 (Silent Swamp).

(15) Middle Tiger

RATING/ DIFFICULTY	ROUND-TRIP	ELEV GAIN/ HIGH POINT	SEASON
***/3	9 miles	1127 feet/ 2607 feet	Year-round

One-way

```
3000'
2500'
2000'
1500'
1000'
      0            2.25           4.5
```

Map: Green Trails Tiger Mountain No. 204S; **Contact:** Department of Natural Resources, South Puget Sound Region, (360) 825-1631, www.dnr.wa.gov; **GPS:** N 47 28.015, W 121 55.997

When you want to simply stretch your legs and enjoy the woods, this is the trail to explore. The summit of Middle Tiger is wooded, so you won't find grand views. In fact, the entire route is wooded. But that's okay. This area is rich with wildlife, from the winged variety (woodpeckers, flickers, red-tailed hawks, Stellar's jays) to the four-legged kind (deer, bobcats, black bears, cougars, martens, coyotes, raccoons, beavers). There are also the usual suspects when it comes to forest flora—with a variety of trees, bushes, wildflowers, ferns, and

Douglas squirrel on the branch of a cedar tree

mosses—and the usual suspects in summer when it comes to mosquitoes, so visit in fall through spring for swat-free hiking.

GETTING THERE

From I-90 take exit 25 and drive south on State Route 18 to the Tiger Mountain summit. At the summit, turn right (west) into the large parking lot. Drive through the first lot, and turn left onto a gravel road. Continue about 0.25 mile to a second, larger parking lot on the right. The road is gated just past this lot.

ON THE TRAIL

The first leg of this hike starts on the West Side Road. The wide road is still used for limited logging operations, and a few individuals have keys to the gate so they can get their hang gliders to the launch site on Poo Poo Point (Hike 8). But for the most part, only hikers, horses, and the occasional mountain bike use the road. The road meanders a bit, but generally rolls west, maintaining a mild up-and-down action as it contours around the slopes below East and Middle Tiger.

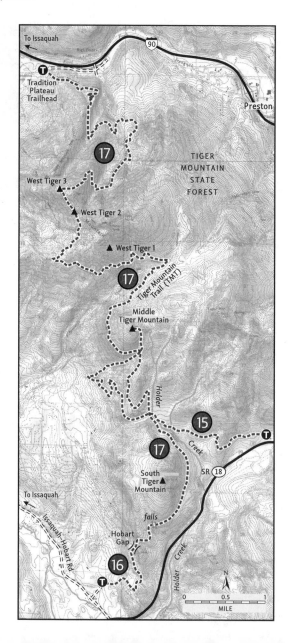

Two hikers pass a huge blowdown heading toward Middle Tiger.

At 1.8 miles the road crosses Holder Creek (elev. 1600 ft), where you'll also encounter a junction with the Tiger Mountain Trail (TMT). Continue west along the road for another 1.6 miles—at the end of this leg, you'll pass through a pair of switchback turns as you descend into a narrow creek valley. Look for the trail on the right (uphill) side of the road.

Head up the path, passing a jumble of a collapsed railroad trestle. The trail climbs steeply out of the creek canyon. Stay right at the first junction (about 0.1 mile in from the road) and you'll find a fairly level 0.25-mile run through thick bramble of salmonberries and devil's club. At about 1 mile from the road you'll cross the TMT at Milan's Crossing (elev. 2180 ft). From here it's a straight, steep climb over the final 0.3 mile to the Middle Tiger summit at 2607 feet (yes, that's more than 400 feet in 0.3 mile! Steep!!).

EXTENDING YOUR TRIP

Retrace your steps, or you can detour on the descent by turning left (east) on the TMT at that first junction near the summit. This will drop you down to the roadway in 1.6 miles, but when you hit the road you'll be just 1.8 miles from your car.

16 Tiger Mountain Trail: South

RATING/ DIFFICULTY	ROUND-TRIP	ELEV GAIN/ HIGH POINT	SEASON
***/2	4 miles	600 feet/ 1100 feet	Year-round

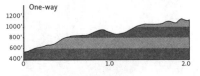

Map: Green Trails Tiger Mountain No. 204S; **Contact:** Department of Natural Resources, South Puget Sound Region, (360) 825-1631, *www.dnr.wa.gov*; **GPS:** N 47 26.553, W 121 58.656

The Tiger Mountain Trail (TMT) is to Tiger Mountain what the Pacific Crest Trail is to the Cascades—a long, winding trail that crosses many summits and offers a long thru hike or short section hikes. This is the shortest, but possibly most scenic, of the main TMT sections. It's an outstanding introduction to Tiger Mountain and its wonderful wildland trails.

GETTING THERE

From Issaquah head east on Front Street (which becomes Issaquah-Hobart Road after it leaves town). About 6 miles past the city limits, turn left (north) onto SE Tiger Mountain Road. Continue for 1 mile before parking on the left shoulder at a wide pullout. The trail is on the right.

ON THE TRAIL

As you set off up the wide trail, look for the old historical marker that reads "Route of Woods-Iverson Railroad Grade." The trail climbs gently but steadily for the next 1.5 miles through very old mixed-species forest. There are hemlocks, alders, and firs, as well as maples and even a few madronas.

At 1.5 miles, the climb turns into a traverse as the trail slants along the slope, heading for Hobart Gap (elev. 1100 ft), just shy of 2 miles out. A short hop past the gap, you'll find a picture-perfect little waterfall on the trailside creek. Stop here for photos and a snack before turning back.

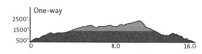

17 Tiger Mountain Trail

RATING/ DIFFICULTY	ONE-WAY TRIP (SHUTTLE)	ELEV GAIN/ HIGH POINT	SEASON
*****/5	16 miles	2200 feet/ 2607 feet	Mar–Nov

Map: Green Trails Tiger Mountain No. 204S; **Contact:** Department of Natural Resources, South Puget Sound Region, (360) 825-1631, *www.dnr.wa.gov*; **GPS:** N 47 26.553, W 121 58.656

Hiking the crown jewel of Tiger Mountain State Forest is a rite of passage for serious Issaquah Alps explorers. The trip isn't to be

The Tiger Mountain Trail passing through Hobart Gap

taken lightly, however. It requires a long day and good conditioning. It also requires some planning, as you'll need to arrange for a car at the trail's end. The 16-mile route weaves around or over most of the primary peaks on Tiger, and since it crosses scores of other trails and not all the intersections are well-marked, good routefinding skills are essential.

GETTING THERE
From Issaquah head east on Front Street (which becomes Issaquah-Hobart Road after it leaves town). About 6 miles past the city limits, turn left (north) onto SE Tiger Mountain Road. Continue for 1 mile before parking on the left shoulder at a wide pullout. The trail is on the right.

ON THE TRAIL
The Tiger Mountain Trail (TMT) was first conceived of in 1972, with construction getting underway in 1977. The first official hike on the new trail was in 1979. The route can be hiked north to south, but most Tiger Mountain aficionados agree it is best traveled south to north, as described here.

The trail begins climbing steadily right from the start, heading north onto the wooded slopes of South Tiger Mountain. At 1.5 miles, after passing under a band of cliffs, the trail pops out on an old railroad grade turned road at Hobart Gap, the first trail junction you'll encounter. Stay right on the railroad grade—occasionally, you'll see railroad ties still embedded in the trail tread.

At 2.2 miles, the TMT rolls under the high-tension powerlines. The long clearing under the powerlines reveals views of the East Tiger summit. Head straight across this clearing, keeping a sharp eye out for trail signs, to find the trail heading off into the woods on the far side.

The path continues to make use of the old railroad grade to a junction with Road 1400 at 2.9 miles. Follow this road about 0.5 mile

Mile 5 marker along the Tiger Mountain Trail

to Holder Creek and the West Side Road. Turn left onto the West Side Road and in just 0.2 mile you'll encounter the old TMT trailhead (used when the West Side Road was still open to public traffic).

Turn right onto the TMT as it rolls north on the old Holder Creek Railroad Grade. At 5 miles out, you'll cross Karls Gap. An optional 0.5-mile side trail leads to the (treed) summit of Middle Tiger (elev. 2607 ft). Continue on the main trail and you'll enjoy broken views of Mount Rainier and the country between you and that big peak.

Around the halfway point, the trail runs through the woods alongside Fifteenmile

Creek. An interesting bit of human history can be found here—a massive steel cable lies across the trail. This 2-inch braided bit of steel was suspended overhead and used to drag huge logs out of the forest to a landing where they could be loaded on rail cars.

The TMT crosses Fifteenmile Gap at 9.3 miles, and 1 mile later the trail bursts out onto the sun-drenched viewpoint of Ricks Rock (elev. 2250 ft). Outstanding views are found here and continue on as you hike north to West Tiger 2. At 10.5 miles, you'll stride through Mannings Reach—named for guidebook author and legendary wildland protector Harvey Manning—which marks the high point of the TMT (elev. 2600 ft).

From Mannings Reach, you'll descend past junctions with the West Tiger Railroad Grade, West Tiger 3 Trail, and the West Tiger 2 Trail. Grand views can be found at West Tiger 2.

The rest of the TMT is a rolling descent to the Tradition Plateau Trailhead.

18 Taylor Mountain

RATING/ DIFFICULTY	ROUND-TRIP	ELEV GAIN/ HIGH POINT	SEASON
**/2	4 miles	550 feet/ 1100 feet	Year-round

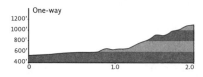

Map: Green Trails Tiger Mountain No. 204S; **Contact:** King County Parks, (206) 296-8687, *www.metrokc.gov*; **GPS:** N 47 26.012, W 121 58.360; **Status:** Rescued

Holder Creek

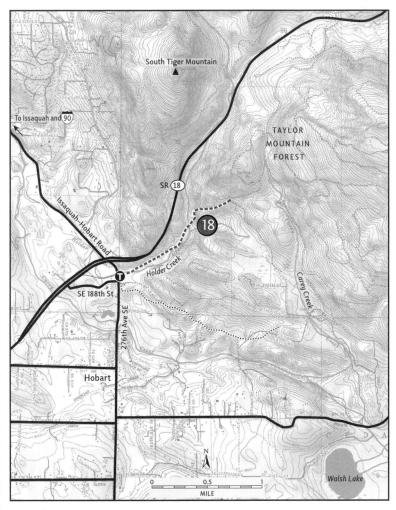

Taylor Mountain represents an experiment in forest management. Over the decades, loggers took what they could from the 1700-acre forest, leaving behind a mess of scrub brush and second- (and third-) growth trees. But that young forest has filled in nicely and nature is once more proving that, given the chance, it can recover on its own.

GETTING THERE

From I-90 take exit 17 (Front Street), and turn right (south) onto Front Street and continue south through Issaquah. Front Street becomes

Issaquah-Hobart Road as you leave town. Continue south along this road to its junction with State Route 18. Cross under SR 18 and drive another 0.25 mile, passing Holder Creek at SE 188th Street. Park near Holder Creek.

ON THE TRAIL

Few true trails exist as yet in the Taylor Mountain Forest, but there are some rough-hewn routes, and there are many miles of old logging road to explore. The best bet is to grab a map (Taylor Mountain is well represented on the corner of the Green Trails Tiger Mountain map) and go exploring.

A faint trail leads away from the Issaquah-Hobart Road alongside Holder Creek. You can follow this path for up to 2 miles as it parallels the creek along its first mile. Enjoy the lush green maple and alder groves, heavily laden with moss and fern that flank the creek. The last mile of this path climbs the long ridge that separates Holder Creek from Carey Creek. You'll find an old logging road at 1100 feet near the 2-mile mark. Turn around here.

EXTENDING YOUR TRIP

Another option is to hike the old logging road that leaves the trailhead area and angles east around the flank of Taylor Mountain. This road-turned-trail meanders through young stands of forest and brush-filled clear-cuts as it climbs for more than 1 mile before descending gently into the Carey Creek valley. You'll hit the creek at around 2 miles. Enjoy the riparian wonderland of Carey Creek (a vital salmon spawning habitat for the Cedar River watershed) before returning the way you came.

Opposite: View of Garfield Mountain from the Middle Fork Snoqualmie Trail

north bend area

Hiker on summit of Bare Mountain looking out at Glacier Peak

North Bend sits near the confluence of the three forks of the Snoqualmie River, and hikers have long enjoyed the wildland experiences found on the array of trails that weave through these river drainages. Many of the trails around North Bend draw more hikers on any given summer weekend than you would see in a year on similar trails a bit farther away. A good part of the reason for this is proximity to population centers. The North Bend area can be reached quickly and easily by hikers coming from the west (via I-90), from the south (via State Route 18), and from the north (via State Routes 202 and 203). The real key, though, to the area's popularity is the quality of the trails: from low river-valley hikes such as the Middle Fork Snoqualmie Trail to high climbs on rugged trails that make worthy destinations for peak baggers (Mount Si, for instance). The North Bend area offers some of the best hiking in the central Cascades, and much of it can be enjoyed year-round.

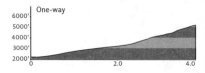

19 Bare Mountain

RATING/ DIFFICULTY	ROUND-TRIP	ELEV GAIN/ HIGH POINT	SEASON
***/5	8 miles	3250 feet/ 5353 feet	June–Nov

Maps: Green Trails Mount Si No. 174 and Skykomish No. 175; **Contact:** Mount Baker-Snoqualmie National Forest, Snoqualmie Ranger District, North Bend office, (425) 888-1421, *www.fs.fed.us/r6/mbs*; **Notes:** Northwest Forest Pass required; **GPS:** N 47 38.373, W 121 31.699

Any time you can hike to the site of an old fire-watch station, you know you'll have grand views—after all, those fire spotters needed a 360-degree panorama to be effective. Bare Mountain stands as one of those old fire-tower sites and, nestled in the westernmost part of the Cascades, this trail offers a unique opportunity to enjoy a wild-country hike with views of the Puget Sound lowlands.

GETTING THERE

From Seattle drive east on I-90 to exit 31 (North Bend). Drive through North Bend on Main Street, then turn north onto Ballaratt Street and follow it out of town. This road becomes North Fork Road SE. About 4 miles after leaving the North Bend city limits, the road forks. Stay left and continue another 17 miles to the Forest Service boundary, where the road becomes Forest Road 57. Just after crossing Lennox Creek, stay right at the next junction to continue on FR 57. At mile 23 find the trailhead on the left.

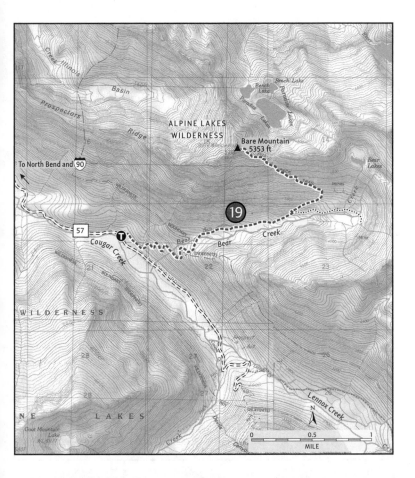

ON THE TRAIL

The trail uses an old miners road for the first 2 miles as it climbs along the flank of Bare Mountain and into the Bear Creek valley. You'll cross the creek about 0.5 mile out, then cross it again just under a mile into your hike. At about 1 mile, you'll enter the Alpine Lakes Wilderness amid a moist meadow as the trail straightens out to parallel Bear Creek for the next mile.

At mile 2 you'll find a trail junction, where the trail leaves the old miners road. Turn left and hike up the southern flank of Bare Mountain, winding upward through a long series of sweeping switchbacks.

After 2 miles of climbing, you'll find yourself atop the 5353-foot summit of Bare Mountain, with its grand views in all directions. To the south, Mount Rainier towers above the lesser Cascade peaks. To the west is the sprawling green world of the Snoqualmie Valley and the Puget Sound basin. North is mighty Mount Baker, and westward lies the bulk of the Alpine Lakes Wilderness.

20 Rattlesnake Ledge

RATING/ DIFFICULTY	ROUND-TRIP	ELEV GAIN/ HIGH POINT	SEASON
*****/4	4 miles	1160 feet/ 2078 feet	Mar–Nov

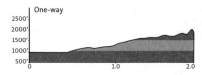

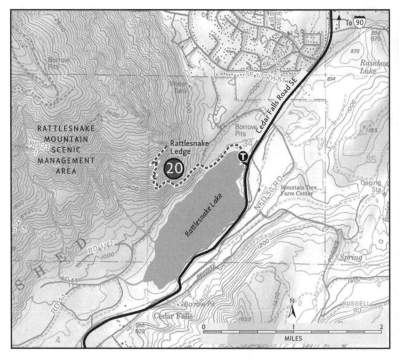

Matt Jackson enjoying the view of Mount Si from Rattlesnake Ledge

Map: Green Trails Rattlesnake Mountain/ Upper Snoqualmie Valley No. 205S **Contact:** Mount Baker–Snoqualmie National Forest, Snoqualmie Ranger District, North Bend office, (425) 888-1421, *www.fs.fed.us/r6/ mbs*; **Notes:** Northwest Forest Pass required; **GPS:** N 47 26.007, W 121 46.052

You won't find better views anywhere else this close to Seattle. Rattlesnake Ledge is a monolithic block of rock on the eastern end of Rattlesnake Ridge, towering high over the cool waters of Rattlesnake Lake and the Snoqualmie River valley. Looking up from the trailhead, the site is daunting—the rock face looks sheer and impregnable. Fortunately, the cliff face isn't too broad, and hearty Washington Trails Association volun-teers have carved a path through the steep forests flanking the rock face. Indeed, the original trail, which was daunting in its own right, has been largely replaced with a new, more secure pathway.

GETTING THERE

From Seattle drive 32 miles east on I-90 to exit 32 (436th Avenue SE). Turn right (south) on 436th Avenue SE (Cedar Falls Road SE) and drive about 4 miles to the well-developed Rat-tlesnake Lake parking area on the right.

ON THE TRAIL

From the parking lot, round the gate and walk the old road 0.25 mile to a grassy swath on the west side of Rattlesnake Lake. A well-signed path leads off to the right. The rebuilt trail climbs steeply from the get-go, gaining more than 1000 feet in just over 1.5 miles. Of course, the old trail made that gain in just 1 mile, so please keep the complaints to a minimum as you slog up the switchbacks. Those new hairpin turns add a little distance to the hike, but they also level the trail a tad, making it a bit easier on the thighs.

After a seemingly endless upward march, you'll suddenly burst out of the forest onto the snout of the rock ledge. The views are unbe-lievable. Peer southeast into the rarely seen Cedar River watershed, with Chester Morse Lake dominating the close-in scenery. This big lake supplies Seattle with a significant portion of its drinking water. The rest of the watershed is filled with untrammeled forest—the watershed is closed to most human access to ensure that the water remains uncontaminated. Look farther east and you'll see the peaks leading to Snoqualmie Pass and, of course, massive Mount Si is just across the valley.

Cedar Butte turn-off from Iron Horse Trail

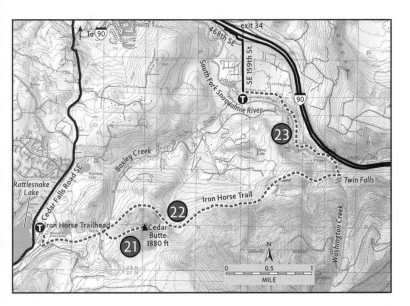

21 Cedar Butte

RATING/ DIFFICULTY	ROUND-TRIP	ELEV GAIN/ HIGH POINT	SEASON
***/3	3 miles	900 feet/ 1880 feet	Year-round

Map: Green Trails Rattlesnake Mountain/Upper Snoqualmie Valley No. 205S; **Contact:** Washington State Parks, (360) 902-8844, www.parks.wa.gov; **GPS:** N 47 26.007, W 121 46.052

 *Cedar Butte may be the least visited mountain in the Snoqualmie Pass corridor. The smallish butte stands between the popular Rattlesnake Lake and the remote Chester Morse Lake in the Cedar River watershed area. This butte's lack of popularity, though, has more to do with its lack of publicity than its dearth of scenery. Indeed, Cedar Butte offers plenty of scenic spectacle.*

GETTING THERE
From Seattle drive east on I-90 to exit 32 (436th Avenue SE). Turn right (south) on 436th Avenue SE (Cedar Falls Road SE) and drive about 4.5 miles, passing the Rattlesnake Lake parking area, until you find the Iron Horse Trailhead parking area on the left.

ON THE TRAIL
From the trailhead, start east along the wide ribbon of the Iron Horse Trail. When you reach Boxley Creek, you have another 0.25 mile or so before finding the start of the well-established path (about 1 mile from the parking area) up Cedar Butte. Turn right (south) onto the sometimes-signed Cedar Butte Trail.

Signage is only "sometimes" because this is technically an unofficial trail—the signs are installed and maintained by unauthorized volunteers rather than official agency staff. Still, even if the signs are down, the trail gets enough use and maintenance that it is easy to find if you look for it.

After leaving the Iron Horse, you'll cross an old logged-over area, then climb steeply up the face of Cedar Butte. Once at the summit, enjoy the expansive views to the north—Mount Si, Teneriffe, and Mailbox stand tall on the horizon.

22 Iron Horse Trail: Washington Creek

RATING/ DIFFICULTY	ROUND-TRIP	ELEV GAIN/ HIGH POINT	SEASON
***/2	6 miles	300 feet/ 1100 feet	Year-round

Maps: Green Trails Rattlesnake Mountain/ Upper Snoqualmie Valley No. 205S and Snoqualmie Pass No. 207; **Contact:** Washington State Parks, (360) 902-8844, *www.parks.wa .gov*; **GPS:** N 47 26.007, W 121 46.052

The Iron Horse Trail runs down the middle of the linear John Wayne State Park. The trail utilizes the old rail line known as the Milwaukee Road, which carried locomotives of the Chicago-Milwaukee-St. Paul-Pacific Railroad. The trail runs from Rattlesnake Lake to Idaho and is the only east-west cross-state trail.

GETTING THERE

From Seattle drive east on I-90 to exit 32 (436th Avenue SE). Turn right (south) on 436th Avenue SE (Cedar Falls Road SE) and drive about 4.5 miles, passing the Rattlesnake Lake parking area, until you find the Iron Horse Trailhead parking area on the left.

ON THE TRAIL

From Rattlesnake Lake start up the old rail-trail as it crosses Boxley Creek and heads east along the northern flank of Cedar Butte (Hike 21). The trail is relatively flat and wide enough for a family of four to walk side by side. Take your time and enjoy the walk along this historic route.

At 3 miles out, you'll find yourself on a towering trestle spanning the deep cut of Washington Creek. This massive wooden structure offers those with acrophobia a chance to experience their fear, while the rest of you can experience the stunning views out over the lower South Fork Snoqualmie Valley and its intersection with the broad Middle Fork Valley. Mount Si and Mailbox Peaks stand tall to the north, marking the west and east flanks of the Middle Fork Valley.

EXTENDING YOUR TRIP

If you seek more miles, continue east. Just past Washington Creek a small trail to the left drops onto the Twin Falls Trail, leading to the pretty cascades described in Hike 23.

23 Twin Falls

RATING/ DIFFICULTY	ROUND-TRIP	ELEV GAIN/ HIGH POINT	SEASON
****/2	3 miles	500 feet/ 1000 feet	Year-round

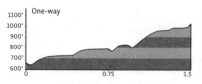

Trestle along the Iron Horse Trail

Map: Green Trails Rattlesnake Mountain/Upper Snoqualmie Valley No. 205S **Contact:** Washington State Parks, (360) 902-8844, *www.parks.wa.gov*; **GPS:** N 47 27.205, W 121 42.344

Twin Falls run year-round for one very good reason: the area around North Bend receives more than 90 inches of rain each year. Seattle—just 35 miles west—gets half that much. The South Fork Snoqualmie River takes that massive amount of rainfall and puts it to use entertaining hikers. The river squeezes into a narrow rocky gorge before tumbling over a very impressive stairstep falls. Then, when the water has been churned into a frothy torrent, it plunges over a 150-foot rock wall, creating the stunning cascade of the Lower Twin Falls.

GETTING THERE

From Seattle drive east on I-90 to exit 34. Turn south on 468th Avenue SE and proceed about 0.5 mile. Immediately before the South Fork Snoqualmie River bridge, turn left (east) on SE 159th Street and drive 0.5 mile to the trailhead parking lot at the road's end.

ON THE TRAIL

The first 0.7 mile of the trail pass through moss-laden forest along the shores of the South Fork Snoqualmie River. This flat mile provides kids plenty of opportunity to explore massive old nurse logs (fallen trees that act as nurseries for newly sprouted trees) and other interesting forest formations. Given the bounty of rain, and the lush forest growth, this area feels almost like an Olympic Peninsula rain forest—just without the massive cedars and hemlocks.

After this long, flat run the trail climbs gently up a series of long switchbacks. About 1 mile out, you'll find a short spur trail on the right—this leads to a fantastic overlook of the lower falls, the mighty 150-foot cascade. Back on the main trail, you'll continue to climb another 0.5 mile or so to a bridge that takes you over the river gorge, directly between two of the stairstep falls.

24 Little Si

RATING/ DIFFICULTY	ROUND-TRIP	ELEV GAIN/ HIGH POINT	SEASON
****/4	5 miles	1200 feet/ 1576 feet	Year-round

Maps: Green Trails Mount Si No. 174 and Bandera No. 206; **Contact:** Department of Natural Resources, South Puget Sound Region, (360) 825-1631, *www.dnr.wa.gov*; **GPS:** N 47 29.267, W 121 45.378

Rock climbers use the first half of this trail to get to the rock faces on the east end of Little Si. Hikers use the full trail to sweep around the west end and climb the tall knob on the easier (though still a bit rocky) route. Like its big sibling, Mount Si, Little Si offers phenomenal views of the Upper Snoqualmie Valley after a nice hike through forests and over rocks. The trail is steep initially, then mellow, then steep again as it scrambles straight up the northern spine to the 1576-foot summit.

GETTING THERE

From Seattle drive east on I-90 to exit 32 (436th Avenue SE). Turn left (north) over the freeway and drive 0.5 mile to North Bend Way. Turn left (west), and in 0.25 mile turn right (north) on Mount Si Road. Shortly after

Lower Twin Falls on the South Fork Snoqualmie River

crossing the bridge, the road banks right. Just after this curve, look for a paved parking area on the left side of the road (if you get to the intersection with 444th Avenue SE, you've gone too far).

ON THE TRAIL

This area was logged extensively, but in the intervening decades the forest has regenerated nicely, and a diverse collection of evergreens and deciduous trees shade the trail.

As you near the hulk of rocky bluff known as Little Si, the trail levels off into a swampy area. Small streams link bogs filled with trillium and skunk cabbage. The trail is generally

high and dry, though you will encounter an area of mud or three.

At around 1.5 miles, views open up onto the high, craggy rock of the southeastern face of Little Si. You might see rock climbers crawling up the rock routes here. Continue along the trail as it loops north and then west to the gentler north face of Little Si.

The trail turns and runs straight up this northern spine, climbing steeply up the rocky ridge—you'll be forced to use your hands at times as you scramble up the biggest rocks—until finally capping out on the 1576-foot summit on the southern edge of the rocky prominence. Enjoy stellar views of the North Bend valley before heading back the way you came.

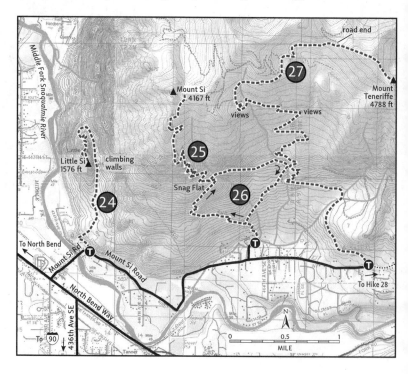

Rocky cliffs on the eastern face of Little Si

Maps: Green Trails Mount Si No. 174 and Bandera No. 206; **Contact:** Department of Natural Resources, South Puget Sound Region, (360) 825-1631, *www.dnr.wa.gov*; **GPS:** N 47 29.376, W 121 43.409

Mount Si should be experienced at least once by every hiker. In fact, a significant number of Puget Sound residents do just one hike per year, and these annual hikers almost invariably turn to Mount Si every time. In the early spring, mountain-loving backpackers and climbers use the trail as a tune-up for the coming season. Others come because the trail is one of few that becomes snow-free early in the year. Land managers estimate that Si draws between thirty thousand and fifty thousand visitors a year, making it the most heavily used trail in the state. As a result, on any sunny summer weekend the trail will be crowded—almost to the point of having to take a number and get in line. Really, it's not that bad, and the steep trail soon separates the serious hiker from the casual mall walker. And Si's payoff is incredible: views of the Upper Snoqualmie Valley, the Puget Sound basin, and far beyond.

GETTING THERE

From Seattle drive east on I-90 to exit 32 (436th Avenue SE). Turn left (north) over the freeway and drive 0.5 mile to North Bend Way. Turn left (west), and in 0.25 mile turn right (north) on Mount Si Road. The large trailhead parking lot is on the left, 2.5 miles down the road.

ON THE TRAIL

From the broad parking lot, the trail climbs moderately for 1 mile to the first views of the long hike. Here, at around 1600 feet, you'll find wonderful views from atop a rocky bluff on the side of the mountain. Hikers short on

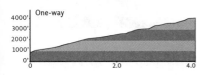

25 Mount Si

RATING/ DIFFICULTY	ROUND-TRIP	ELEV GAIN/ HIGH POINT	SEASON
*****/5	8 miles	3150 feet/ 3900 feet	May–Nov

Hikers lunching on top of Mount Si

time and stamina could turn around here for a modest 2-mile outing.

As you near the 1.8-mile mark, you'll sweep alongside a small brook, with grassy banks on which to rest. This is Snag Flat—the site of an old burn, as evidenced by the blackened scars on the trunks of many of the old Douglas-firs in the area.

The trail then pushes on, never wavering from its steep ascent, until you finally crest the last slope and step out into the wildflower-filled meadow at the summit, or rather, the summit basin. The true summit of Si is atop the big rock "haystack" that towers over the edge of the meadow. The haystack does sport a scramble path to its summit, but the route is tricky, with incredible exposure (one slip and you'll plummet hundreds—thousands?—of feet). It's best **NOT** to attempt the Haystack, especially considering the added danger of

other people kicking loose rock down, creating deadly missiles from above. Besides, the views atop the rock are no better than those you'll enjoy from the meadows at its base.

26 Talus Loop

RATING/ DIFFICULTY	ROUND-TRIP	ELEV GAIN/ HIGH POINT	SEASON
***/3	3.7 miles	1750 feet/ 2120 feet	Year-round

Maps: Green Trails Mount Si No. 174 and Bandera No. 206; **Contact:** Department of Natural Resources, South Puget Sound Region, (360) 825-1631, www.dnr.wa.gov; **GPS:** N 47 29.267, W 121 45.378

If you want to experience the ever-popular Mount Si without the thigh-burning workout of going to the top, follow the Talus Loop Trail instead and find old-growth and old second-growth forests on the flanks of this popular mountain.

GETTING THERE
From Seattle drive east on I-90 to exit 32 (436th Avenue SE). Turn left (north) over the freeway and drive 0.5 mile to North Bend Way. Turn left (west), and in 0.25 mile turn right (north) on Mount Si Road. The large trailhead parking lot is on the left, 2.5 miles down the road.

ON THE TRAIL
Leaving the trailhead, you'll climb moderately, weaving through the forests as the trail angles up the southern flank of Mount Si. At about 0.8 mile out, the trail forks. The main trail goes left, and so should you (the right is your return route). Over the next mile you'll climb steeply, first on a long traverse, then through some gentle turns. The route here pierces cool, dark forests, bringing you wonderful relief from summer heat, and decent protection from the driving winter rains.

A small rest bench awaits you at 1.4 miles, then at 1.8 miles the trail splits again at Snag Flat Interpretive Area. The main Mount Si summit trail continues north, climbing steeply past this 2120-foot junction. Head right instead to explore the wonderfully diverse ecosystem on Snag Flat.

The path heads east, crossing a small creek basin, then contours around a long forested slope. A few more creeks are crossed before the trail turns back to the west just before dropping into the Roaring

Creek valley. After walking a total of 3 miles, you'll be back at the first trail junction, where you'll turn right and descend back to the trailhead.

Rick Russell passes the Snag Flat area.

27 Mount Teneriffe

RATING/ DIFFICULTY	ROUND-TRIP	ELEV GAIN/ HIGH POINT	SEASON
****/5	14 miles	3800 feet/ 4788 feet	Mar–Nov

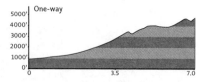

Maps: Green Trails Mount Si No. 174 and Bandera No. 206; **Contact:** Department of Natural Resources, South Puget Sound Region, (360) 825-1631, www.dnr.wa.gov; **GPS:** N 47 29.170, W 121 42.072

Typically, a moderate grade is one of the key benefits of hiking an old, closed road. Unfortunately, loggers and miners sometimes ignored the good health of their vehicles in the interest of enjoying expedited travel times—in these cases, roads pitched steeply upward. Mount Teneriffe sports one such truck-killing road. But a gradient that cripples trucks is a mere leg-stretcher for hikers. This road walk is not nearly as steep as the trail up adjacent Mount Si (Hike 25). And unlike Si, Teneriffe is only lightly used, so you stand a good chance of enjoying a solitary adventure on this Si sibling.

GETTING THERE

From Seattle drive east on I-90 to exit 32 (436th Avenue SE). Turn left (north) over the

Photographer Alan L. Bauer on the summit of Mount Teneriffe

freeway and drive 0.5 mile to North Bend Way. Turn left (west), and in 0.25 mile turn right (north) on Mount Si Road. Continue past the Mount Si parking area (at 2.5 miles) to a wide turnaround area about a mile beyond. Park here, well clear of the road.

ON THE TRAIL
Start up the gated road on the left. Since you're hiking on an old logging road, you shouldn't be surprised that portions of the trek pass through old clear-cuts. But the logging took place in decades past, so even those areas scraped bare have sprouted fine young forests.

The two-track trail climbs through these young forest groves and stump-filled "meadows" for 2 miles, gaining a mere 500 feet in that distance. Then the angle increases and the road starts to switchback up another 2 miles. During this climb you'll pass through one massive forty-year-old clear-cut that has **NOT** regenerated well (the scar of the clear-cut can still be seen from the freeway). You'll also witness the erosion that such land-clearing practices precipitate—small run-off streambeds have been eroded into deep rock-rimmed gullies by the meltwaters that rush down treeless slopes.

At 4 miles (elev. 3200 ft) you can enjoy wondrous views, thanks in part to the above bemoaned clear-cut: to the south lies the Cedar River watershed, Rattlesnake Ledge, and the long spine of Rattlesnake Ridge, not to mention Mailbox Peak and the summits of the Middle Fork Snoqualmie Valley. This makes a fine place to turn around if you want a shorter hike.

Shortly after crossing a creek, around 3600 feet, a side trail angles off toward Mount Si. Ignore it and stick to the road walk. About 2 miles after the viewpoint, you'll crest the ridge at 4200 feet. Standing here in a broad saddle below the true summit, you have a choice. Stop here to enjoy views that are even grander

Yellow violets growing up through sword fern fronds

than those found below. Or leave the road and hike another 0.5 mile along a boot-beaten path up the ridge crest to the summit knoll at 4788 feet.

28 CCC Road: Lower Trailhead

RATING/ DIFFICULTY	ROUND-TRIP	ELEV GAIN/ HIGH POINT	SEASON
**/2	8 miles	550 feet/ 1650 feet	Year-round

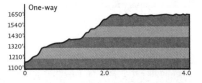

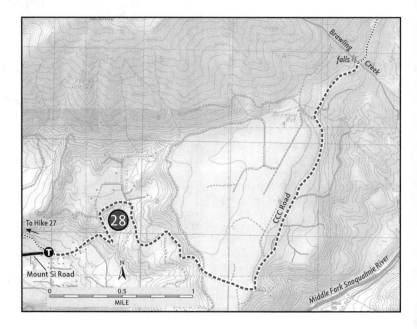

Maps: Green Trails Mount Si No. 174 and Bandera No. 206; **Contact:** Mount Baker–Snoqualmie National Forest, Snoqualmie Ranger District, North Bend office, (425) 888-1421, www.fs.fed.us/r6/mbs; **Notes:** Northwest Forest Pass required; **GPS:** N 47 29.170, W 121 42.072

After logger and miners punched hastily built roads into the Middle Fork Snoqualmie River valley in the first couple decades of the twentieth century, the area was abandoned until the 1930s, when the Depression-busting programs of FDR came into play. The best known of these was the Civilian Conservation Corps (CCC), which put unemployed men to work in the woods building trails, national park lodges, and roads. In the 1960s this CCC road was used to give clear-cutting loggers fast access to the Middle Fork's forests. Now that the big timber is mostly gone, the road is reverting to trail, and the forests are regenerating into something hikers can enjoy.

GETTING THERE

From Seattle drive east on I-90 to exit 32 (436th Avenue SE). Turn left (north) over the freeway and drive 0.5 mile to North Bend Way. Turn left (west), and in 0.25 mile turn right (north) on Mount Si Road. Continue past the Mount Si parking area (at 2.5 miles) to a wide turnaround area about a mile beyond. Park here, well clear of the road.

ON THE TRAIL

The hike starts with a walk up the final mile of the Mount Si Road—closed to vehicle traffic after the turnaround. The road is steep, though easy to walk. At 1300 feet you leave this rough gravel road and, rounding a locked gate, jump onto the CCC Road (trail).

The CCC workers bulldozed their road onto the gravelly moraine left by the ancient glacier that carved the valley. By staying on this high rocky ridge, the route provides outstanding views for much of the journey. Look south to Rattlesnake Ridge and Ledge, and east to Mailbox Peak. The peaks of the Upper Snoqualmie Valley also peek into view.

At 3.5 miles from the parking area (2.5 miles from the CCC gate), you'll find a trail junction on the left. This old two-track trail leads to Green Mountain. Stay right and in another 0.5 mile or so, bang into Brawling Creek and its tumbling waterfalls. This is an ideal lunch spot and turnaround point.

EXTENDING YOUR TRIP

If you like, you can press on for added miles along the CCC Road (see Hikes 30 and 32).

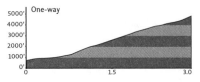

29 Mailbox Peak

RATING/ DIFFICULTY	ROUND-TRIP	ELEV GAIN/ HIGH POINT	SEASON
****/5	6 miles	4100 feet/ 4926 feet	May–Nov

Map: Green Trails Bandera No. 206; **Contact:** Mount Baker–Snoqualmie National Forest, Snoqualmie Ranger District, North Bend office, (425) 888-1421, *www.fs.fed.us/r6/mbs*; **Notes:** Northwest Forest Pass required; **GPS:** N47 28.045; W121 40.491

Mailbox Peak as seen from across the Middle Fork Snoqualmie River valley

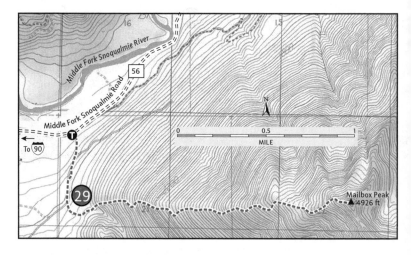

Wimpy hikers, turn the page. This trail offers nothing for you but pain and heartbreak. If you think you've got the goods to scramble up more than 1000 feet per mile, read on. Mailbox Peak brings a serious burn to the thighs of even the best-conditioned athletes, but the rewards make it all worthwhile. From the top of this jutting lump of rock, you'll enjoy spectacular views of the lower Snoqualmie River valleys. The entire Issaquah Alps range sprawls at your feet, with the rocky-topped Mount Si directly across the Middle Fork Valley and the sheer wall of Rattlesnake Ledge just across the South Fork Valley. After soaking in the views, pull the summit register out and leave your signature—you'll find the tattered pages of a notebook in an old metal mailbox wedged above the summit rocks.

GETTING THERE

From Seattle, drive east on I-90 to exit 34 (Edgewick Road). Turn left (north) onto 468th Street and follow it to the junction with the Middle Fork Snoqualmie Road (Forest Road 56). Turn right and continue up the Middle Fork Snoqualmie Road to the end of the pavement (about 3 miles from the I-90 exit). Turn right onto a gated road and park, being sure not to block the gate.

ON THE TRAIL

Start hiking by rounding the gate and walking up the road (avoiding all side roads). At around 0.5 mile from your car, watch for a sign on the left marking the Mailbox Peak Trail. This trail is rough-hewn, since it was built by boots and only recently received any real trail work—and that done mostly by ad hoc volunteers.

The trail leaves the road and turns near vertical, climbing ever-more steeply over the next 2.5 miles—the first 0.5 mile of road walking gains only a few hundred feet of elevation, leaving about 3800 feet for the last 2.5 miles. That means you'll be climbing about 1500 feet per mile, and most hikers consider anything over 1000 feet per mile to be steep!

The first mile of climbing makes use of a few switchbacks—though a few more would moderate the pitch more reasonably. From there on, turns and twists become fewer and farther between. The trail climbs with ruthless focus—to get to the top in as direct a line as possible. As you move above 4000 feet, the forest falls away, the views open, and all pretense of switchbacks disappears. You'll now be scrambling up steep, open hillsides. An old forest fire scoured the slope here, removing the tree cover but making space for a wonderful mix of heather, beargrass, and dense huckleberry thickets.

Finally, after one last scramble through the rocky crown around the summit, you're there, standing beside the battered mailbox on the top of Mailbox Peak. After you catch your breath, pat yourself on the back—because if you're on the summit, you've conquered perhaps the most difficult hike in this book!

Blowout Creek along the CCC Road

30 CCC Road: Blowout Creek Trailhead

RATING/ DIFFICULTY	ROUND-TRIP	ELEV GAIN/ HIGH POINT	SEASON
***/2	7 miles	620 feet/ 1520 feet	May–Oct

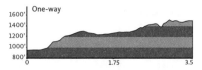

Map: Green Trails Mount Si No. 174; **Contact:** Mount Baker–Snoqualmie National Forest, Snoqualmie Ranger District, North Bend office, (425) 888-1421, *www.fs.fed.us/r6/mbs*; **Notes:** Northwest Forest Pass required; **GPS:** N 47 30.953, W 121 36.805

In the 1930s the Civilian Conservation Corps (CCC) took unemployed men out of America's cities and put them to work in the nation's forests. This jobs program helped get our country out of the Great Depression, as well as building some of the most impressive man-made features in our national parks and forests. The CCC Road isn't one of the program's most impressive accomplishments, but it is one of its lasting legacies. Originally built for logging in the Middle Fork Snoqualmie River valley, the road has become a primary recreational resource in this wonderland of the Middle Fork.

GETTING THERE

From Seattle, drive east on I-90 to exit 34 (Edgewick Road). Turn left (north) onto 468th Street and follow it to the junction with the Middle Fork Snoqualmie Road (Forest Road 56). Turn right and continue up the Middle Fork Snoqualmie Road 7.4 miles (or 2 miles after crossing a bridge over the Middle Fork) to a gated road on the left. Park here, well off the main road and without blocking the gated road. Start your hike by rounding the gate and starting up that side road.

ON THE TRAIL

Hiking up the gated road, you'll climb alongside Blowout Creek for nearly 1 mile before intersecting the CCC Road. About half of your total elevation gain will have been accomplished.

Once on the CCC Road (elev. 1300 ft), turn left and follow the twin-track trail west. You'll find stunning panoramas between the trees periodically as you walk the gradually climbing trail.

At just under 3.5 miles from your car, you'll hear the sounds of falling water. Soon, you'll see it—Brawling Creek in its rough-and-tumble plummet down the rocky run of waterfalls.

EXTENDING YOUR TRIP

Brawling Creek is your turnaround point, though you can press on for added miles if you'd like (see Hike 28 for the western end of the CCC Road).

31 Bessemer Mountain

RATING/ DIFFICULTY	ROUND-TRIP	ELEV GAIN/ HIGH POINT	SEASON
****/4	13 miles	4100 feet/ 5028 feet	July–Oct

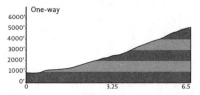

Map: Green Trails Mount Si No. 174; **Contact:** Mount Baker–Snoqualmie National Forest,

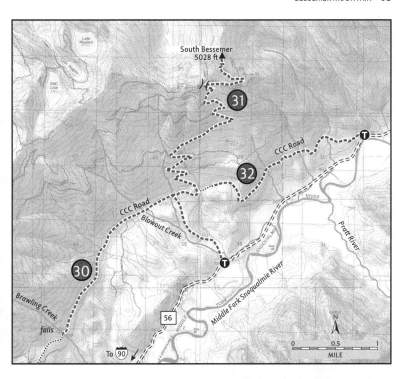

Snoqualmie Ranger District, North Bend office, (425) 888-1421, *www.fs.fed.us/r6/mbs*; **Notes:** Northwest Forest Pass required; **GPS:** N 47 30.953, W 121 36.805

The Middle Fork Snoqualmie River valley gives us hope. Once a wasteland of illegal trash dumping, rampant gunplay, and illicit drug manufacturing (and use), this area is now a premiere recreation destination. The Bessemer Mountain route is one of the valley's great success stories. On this old roadway built by folks eager to extract as much of the area's natural resources as

Abandoned logging equipment on Bessemer Mountain

possible, you'll discover that the greatest resource remains—the power of nature to heal itself. You'll explore fantastic mixed-age, diverse second-growth forests. You'll gawk at awesome views. And if you're lucky, you'll see and/or hear some of the native wildlife whose populations have rebounded.

GETTING THERE

From Seattle, drive east on I-90 to exit 34 (Edgewick Road). Turn left (north) onto 468th Street and follow it to the junction with the Middle Fork Snoqualmie Road (Forest Road 56). Turn right and continue up the Middle Fork Snoqualmie Road for 7.4 miles (or 2 miles after crossing a bridge over the Middle Fork) to a gated road on the left. Park here, well off the main road and without blocking the gated road. Start your hike by rounding the gate and starting up that side road.

ON THE TRAIL

Hike up the road, which parallels Blowout Creek (Hike 30) to its junction with the CCC Road. Turn right onto the CCC Road and in less than 0.5 mile you'll encounter a fork in the path at about 1300 feet elevation. Turn left, rounding the gate in the road, and climb the steep two-track trail as it ascends the flank of Bessemer Mountain.

At about 3.5 miles, the road enters a wide clear-cut that clearly hasn't recovered from its shearing in the late 1970s. The road crosses this scar quickly, but stop and enjoy the one benefit such devastation offers—wide-open views. Look across the Middle Fork Valley to the deep slash of the Pratt River as it carves its way steeply down the opposite side of the valley. Look east and enjoy the tall crowns of the Snoqualmie area peaks: Mount Garfield, Chimney Rock, Lemah, and others.

Continuing on, the road climbs ever more steeply, entering a series of switchbacks. At each fork, stick with the trail, which climbs

ceaselessly upward. Finally, just over 5.5 miles out, you'll crest the ridge on a 4000-foot saddle. Grand views are found here, but don't stop now. Push on to the end of the road on a small bench—dubbed South Bessemer Summit—at 5028 feet.

32 CCC Road: Upper Trailhead

RATING/ DIFFICULTY	ROUND-TRIP	ELEV GAIN/ HIGH POINT	SEASON
***/2	4 miles	400 feet/ 1450 feet	Year-round

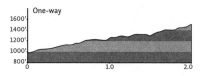

Map: Green Trails Mount Si No. 174; **Contact:** Mount Baker–Snoqualmie National Forest, Snoqualmie Ranger District, North Bend office, (425) 888-1421, *www.fs.fed.us/r6/mbs*; **Notes:** Northwest Forest Pass required; **GPS:** N 47 32.235, W 121 34.650

This old road built by workers in the Depression-era Civilian Conservation Corps (CCC) has been used to link lumber mills, provide miners easier access to their claims, and to give loggers faster access to the big trees of the lower Middle Fork Snoqualmie River. Today, closed to motors, the road provides a wonderful opportunity for hikers to explore the human and natural history of this region.

GETTING THERE

From Seattle, drive east on I-90 to exit 34 (Edgewick Road). Turn left (north) onto 468th Street and follow it to the junction with the Middle Fork Snoqualmie Road (Forest Road 56). Turn right and continue up the Middle

Dennis Long on the CCC Road by the moss cliffs

Bridge over the Middle Fork Snoqualmie River

Fork Snoqualmie Road for 9.8 miles (or 4.4 miles after crossing a bridge over the Middle Fork) to an overgrown road on the left, signed "CCC Road."

ON THE TRAIL

Nature has largely reclaimed this roadway, leaving us to enjoy a wide single-track trail as it climbs gently away from the Middle Fork Snoqualmie up onto the ridge above. The forest around the trail has recovered remarkably well from the savage clear-cutting that took place in the 1960s. This second-growth forest now sports massive trees, both evergreen and deciduous (maple and alder), giving the forest a diversity needed for true forest health.

After about 0.5 mile of hiking, stay left as the road forks. You'll soon ford a stream (avoid this in spring when snowmelt raises the water level to a torrent) and continue steadily, though gradually, upward.

At 1.5 miles, the screen of trees opens enough to allow you uninterrupted views across the broad Middle Fork to the deep cut of the Pratt River, leading up the opposite valley, away from the Middle Fork. Over the next 0.5 mile, you'll have partial views of the pretty river and the valley around you.

At 2 miles out, sweep under Tall Cliffs, a moss-laden rock face towering over the trail. Enjoy the cool shade under this emerald face before returning to the trailhead.

EXTENDING YOUR TRIP

Hikers looking for more mileage can link this hike with the route up Bessemer Mountain, described in Hike 31.

33 Middle Fork Snoqualmie: Downstream

RATING/ DIFFICULTY	ROUND-TRIP	ELEV GAIN/ HIGH POINT	SEASON
***/3	1.5 miles	100 feet/ 900 feet	Year-round

Maps: Green Trails Mount Si No. 174 and Skykomish No. 175; **Contact:** Mount Baker–Snoqualmie National Forest, Snoqualmie Ranger District, North Bend office, (425) 888-1421, *www.fs.fed.us/r6/mbs*; **Notes:** Northwest Forest Pass required; **GPS:** N 47 32.877, W 121 32.304

While most hikers cross the bridge and go left, heading upstream along the main Middle Fork Trail, savvy hikers looking for a solitary short hike will turn right and scramble downstream. There once was a popular trail on this side of the river, and hard-core backcountry anglers will still find their way up a faint boot-beaten path alongside Rainy Creek all the way to trout heaven at Rainy Lake. For most hikers, though, a simple hike alongside the Middle Fork will be sufficient escape.

GETTING THERE

From Seattle, drive east on I-90 to exit 34 (Edgewick Road). Turn left (north) onto 468th Street and follow it to the junction with the Middle Fork Snoqualmie Road (Forest Road 56). Turn right and continue up the Middle Fork Snoqualmie Road for 11.8 miles to the Middle Fork trailhead parking area on

the right. Cross the river on the impressively large metal and wood footbridge.

ON THE TRAIL

After crossing the bridge, turn right and follow a rough trail around the bridge abutment. The path drops to the river's edge and then cuts up the bank and meanders through the lush green forest nestled on the flat between the lower end of Stegosaurus Butte and the river. The trail is rough and, at times, hard to follow, since it is largely a boot-beaten track. Deer are frequently seen in this lush, moss- and fern-rich area— move quietly and keep your eyes moving and you might see an assortment of wildlife.

At roughly 0.75 mile, the path runs out on the gravelly bank of the river. A deep, glassy pool pushes against the foot of a cliff just beyond the trail's end. Stop and rest on the gravel bar, and enjoy the cold (!) waters. But

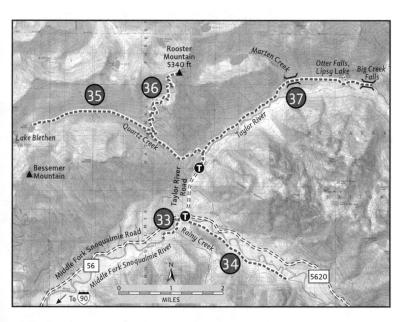

be aware: The pool is deep and, depending on riverflow levels and underwater structures, could be dangerous because the current creates an undertow.

Turn around here, since the route beyond is nearly impossible to find.

EXTENDING YOUR TRIP
If you don't mind bushwhacking and strenuous scrambling, you can turn off the main path about 0.5 mile after leaving the bridge and climb the fishermens path up Rainy Creek valley. No true trail exists, but there is at times a faint path leading to Rainy Lake and its population of small but feisty fish.

34 Middle Fork Snoqualmie: Upstream

RATING/ DIFFICULTY	ROUND-TRIP	ELEV GAIN/ HIGH POINT	SEASON
****/2	6 miles	200 feet/ 1100 feet	Year-round

Maps: Green Trails Mount Si No. 174 and Skykomish No. 175; **Contact:** Mount Baker–Snoqualmie National Forest, Snoqualmie Ranger District, North Bend office, (425) 888-1421, www.fs.fed.us/r6/mbs; **Notes:** Northwest Forest Pass required; **GPS:** N 47 32.877, W 121 32.304

The Middle Fork Snoqualmie River valley has come a long way. Once the playground of loggers and miners, the valley was stripped of many of its resources and then left torn and tattered. Soon came the unsavory characters, making the Middle Fork their own personal dumping ground. Drug users and meth producers fouled the forest with their toxic concoctions. Then came the Middle Fork Coalition, a hard-working group of volunteers who helped the Forest Service clean up the valley while developing plans for its future greatness. Roads were closed, trails were built, garbage dumps were cleaned up. Peace and quiet was restored. Today, the Middle Fork Snoqualmie is a recreationist's dream, and the Middle Fork Trail is one of the best recreational resources in the valley.

GETTING THERE
From Seattle, drive east on I-90 to exit 34 (Edgewick Road). Turn left (north) onto 468th Street and follow it to the junction with the Middle Fork Snoqualmie Road (Forest Road 56). Turn right and continue up the Middle Fork Snoqualmie Road for 11.8 miles to the Middle Fork trailhead parking area on the right. Cross the river on the impressively large metal and wood footbridge.

ON THE TRAIL
The Middle Fork Snoqualmie River is a fast-moving, cold river that few hikers would care to cross on their own. But when the Forest Service and a team of volunteers installed a bridge over the Middle Fork near the mouth of the Taylor River, hikers gained new trails to explore.

Walk across the bridge—stopping midspan to enjoy the views up- and downstream, as well as to marvel at the beautiful bridge (circa 1993)—and turn left to hike upstream alongside the tumbling river. The trail rolls in and out of the trees, sometimes dropping down close to the water's edge while at other times it pushes far into the forest. The Middle Fork is a trout-rich river, so it's not uncommon to see fish-eating birds along its banks. Blue herons and bald eagles are frequent visitors, so don't be surprised if a massive bird takes wing right before your eyes.

Around 0.75 mile into the hike, you'll pass under a tall granite wall, dubbed Stegosaurus Butte. These cliffs top out at 2000 feet (about 1100 feet above your head). Another mile on and you'll find the narrow path opening up

Child hiking up the Middle Fork Snoqualmie Trail

a bit as it takes advantage of an old railroad right-of-way—steam locomotives once used this route to pull railcars loaded with logs out of the forest.

The next 1.2 miles angle through the woods, finally dropping down to the riverside. Cool your feet in the icy waters—or maybe even wet a line if you're an angler (good fishing here at times!)—before heading back down to the trailhead.

35 Quartz Creek and Lake Blethen

RATING/ DIFFICULTY	ROUND-TRIP	ELEV GAIN/ HIGH POINT	SEASON
***/3	10 miles	2000 feet/ 3200 feet	Year-round

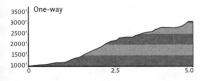

Map: Green Trails Mount Si No. 174; **Contact:** Mount Baker–Snoqualmie National Forest, Snoqualmie Ranger District, North Bend office, (425) 888-1421, *www.fs.fed.us/r6/mbs*; **Notes:** Northwest Forest Pass required; **GPS:** N 47 10.993, W 121 51.044

Loggers ravaged the Quartz Creek valley not too long ago—at least, not so long ago that clear-cuts have recovered. There are still great swaths of open hillside above the trail, but that's not all bad. For one thing, land managers are focusing on keeping this area as a recreational area. More importantly, the clear-cuts frequently boast thick huckleberry fields. Of course, if the berries aren't ripe you'll still enjoy the open and expansive views, since that's the other small benefit of take-it-all logging.

GETTING THERE

From Seattle, drive east on I-90 to exit 34 (Edgewick Road). Turn left (north) onto 468th Street and follow it to the junction with the

Middle Fork Snoqualmie Road (Forest Road 56). Turn right and continue up the Middle Fork Snoqualmie Road for 12.5 miles to the Taylor River Road (just past the Middle Fork trailhead parking area). Turn left onto the Taylor River Road and drive to a wide parking area at its end, in about 0.5 mile.

ON THE TRAIL

Start up the Taylor River Road/trail and in about 0.4 mile, when the road forks, stay left (Hike 37 to Big Creek Falls goes right). This old logging road-turned-trail sweeps uphill and curls back around to head west up the Quartz Creek valley. The route is steep, climbing continuously up the ever-narrowing canyon of Quartz Creek. More than 1.7 miles out, the road runs through a few switchbacks, climbing higher up the valley wall before rolling on up the valley for another 0.25 mile.

At this point, the trail forks (Hike 36 to Rooster Mountain goes right). Stay left to continue your ascent of Quartz Creek. Just past this split, the valley walls move apart, opening up more views of the valley. To the southwest, you'll see the heavily scarred slopes of Bessemer Mountain. Loggers have scraped most of the trees off this 5166-foot peak over the years, but young stands are starting to reclaim the clear-cuts.

Just past the 4-mile mark, the trail gets a bit more difficult as it angles past an old washout. In another 0.5 mile, the angle of your ascent lessens as the road forks once more. Stay left (the right fork dead-ends almost immediately). The last 0.5 mile is on rough-hewn trail. The path doesn't seem to have actually been built but simply kicked in by countless boots.

Lake Blethen is a pretty forest pond nestled among old cedars and Douglas-firs, backed by the high rocky walls of the Cascade Range.

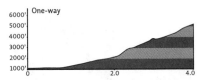

36 Rooster Mountain

RATING/ DIFFICULTY	ROUND-TRIP	ELEV GAIN/ HIGH POINT	SEASON
***/5	8 miles	4100 feet/ 5340 feet	May–Oct

Map: Green Trails Mount Si No. 174; **Contact:** Mount Baker–Snoqualmie National Forest, Snoqualmie Ranger District, North Bend office, (425) 888-1421, www.fs.fed.us/r6/mbs; **Notes:** Northwest Forest Pass required; **GPS:** N 47 10.993, W 121 51.044

If you're up for it, the steep hike up Rooster Mountain will have you crowing—in agony after the thigh-burning 4000-foot gain, and with pleasure over the outstanding views. The Rooster Mountain Trail takes advantage of old logging roads for much of the route, but then follows an old boot-built path up a side canyon above Quartz Creek. Not for the faint of heart, but this route does boast outstanding rewards for those willing to put in the (considerable) effort.

GETTING THERE

From Seattle, drive east on I-90 to exit 34 (Edgewick Road). Turn left (north) onto 468th Street and follow it to the junction with the Middle Fork Snoqualmie Road (Forest Road 56). Turn right and continue up the Middle Fork Snoqualmie Road for 12.5 miles to the Taylor River Road (just past the Middle Fork trailhead parking area). Turn left onto the

Opposite: Hiking through snow to the old broken bridge along Quartz Creek Road

Russian Butte as seen from Rooster Mountain

Taylor River Road and drive to a wide parking area at its end, in about 0.5 mile.

ON THE TRAIL

Follow the Taylor River Road/trail for about 0.4 mile to a Y junction, and stay left to climb through a broad, sweeping turn into the Quartz Creek valley. Following the old logging road up this narrow valley leads you in 2 miles to a road split at 2400 feet. The main Quartz Creek Trail follows the old roadbed to the left, to Lake Blethen (Hike 35). Rooster Mountain is off to the right.

As you veer right, you'll climb steeply for another few hundred yards before the roadbed disappears and you find yourself on a narrow, steep single-track path. The trail climbs ruthlessly, foregoing such extrava-

gances as switchbacks, for another 2 miles, gaining nearly 2900 feet in that distance. But you'll enjoy remarkable views for much of the climb, and once at the summit you'll be able to stare in wonder at peaks including Russian Butte and Bessemer Mountain.

37 Otter and Big Creek Falls

RATING/ DIFFICULTY	ROUND-TRIP	ELEV GAIN/ HIGH POINT	SEASON
***/3	10 miles	650 feet/ 1750 feet	Mar–Nov

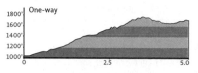

Maps: Green Trails Mount Si No. 174 and Skykomish No. 175; **Contact:** Mount Baker–Snoqualmie National Forest, Snoqualmie Ranger District, North Bend office, (425) 888-1421, *www.fs.fed.us/r6/mbs*; **Notes:** Northwest Forest Pass required; **GPS:** N 47 32.877, W 121 32.304

It seems impossible: Finding quiet solitude on a backcountry trail leading through ancient cathedral forests and past magnificent waterfalls less than a hour from Seattle. Yet the Taylor River Trail offers just that. While nearby Mount Si bristles with sweating hikers, and the Middle Fork

Otter Falls slides down hundreds of feet into Lipsy Lake

Snoqualmie Trail hosts hordes of outdoor enthusiasts, the Taylor River Trail—an old road that's been reclaimed by the forest—goes largely unnoticed and unused.

GETTING THERE

From Seattle, drive east on I-90 to exit 34 (Edgewick Road). Turn left (north) onto 468th Street and follow it to the junction with the Middle Fork Snoqualmie Road (Forest Road 56). Turn right and continue up the Middle Fork Snoqualmie Road for 12.5 miles to the Taylor River Road (just past the Middle Fork trailhead parking area). Turn left onto the Taylor River Road and drive to a wide parking area at its end, in about 0.5 mile.

ON THE TRAIL

Start up the Taylor River Road/trail and in about 0.4 mile, when the road forks, stay right—the left-hand trail leads to Lake Blethen (Hike 35) and Rooster Mountain (Hike 36). Weave up the valley, and cross an old bridge structure at Marten Creek, about 3 miles up the track. Modern planking has been added to the bridge deck to ensure safe crossing. But once across, peer under the bridge to gain an appreciation of the type of timber harvested from this area. Huge cedar logs serve as the spanners that support the bridge.

From here, the trail rolls gently onto the Big Creek bridge at about 5 miles. This structure appears to be out of place here. The wide concrete bridge belongs on a highway—somewhere other than a backcountry trail—but it's a remnant of the old road and a developer's dream, a dream that fortunately died. The wide road that was planned into the headwaters of the Taylor River valley never progressed much beyond a logging road, and even that has largely disappeared, leaving this primitive trail.

The Big Creek bridge may be the first thing to grab your attention when you reach the creek, but it fades into the background as soon as you step onto its deck. Big Creek Falls tumbles off the hillside on the north side of the bridge—over a series of granite steps and down smooth granite faces to create a sparkling tapestry of watery jewels. A deep plunge pool lies at the foot of the falls, just below the bridge itself.

Big Creek Falls makes an ideal lunch stop—the sun streams down onto the bridge deck and the concrete curbing along its edges serves as a fine bench.

EXTENDING YOUR TRIP

Be sure to pause on your way back to the trailhead and take a side trip to Otter Falls. Watch for a small sign and a cairn (pile of rocks) about 0.25 mile from Big Creek. A side trail leads north through the woods for a few hundred yards, ending at a wide but shallow pool of water at the base of a huge vertical granite slab. A ribbon of water slides down the smooth gray rock face to splash into the pool. This is Lipsy Lake and Otter Falls.

In a normal snow year, the falls sparkles and crashes as the melting snowpack feeds the creek, but even in a low-water year the falls is pretty, especially reflected in the calm waters of the lake, and especially when viewed in the quiet solitude that reigns along this valley trail from autumn through spring.

38 Rock Creek Falls

RATING/ DIFFICULTY	ROUND-TRIP	ELEV GAIN/ HIGH POINT	SEASON
***/3	11 miles	2100 feet/ 3400 feet	July–Oct

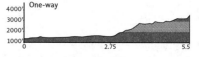

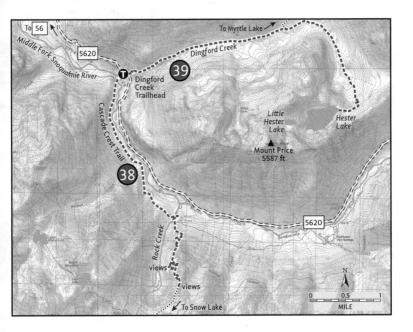

Map: Green Trails Snoqualmie Pass No. 207; **Contact:** Mount Baker–Snoqualmie National Forest, Snoqualmie Ranger District, North Bend office, (425) 888-1421, *www.fs.fed .us/r6/mbs*; **Notes:** Northwest Forest Pass required; **GPS:** N 47 31.041, W 121 27.253; **Status:** Endangered

❎ Once upon a time, the Cascade Crest Trail rolled through the Rock Creek valley, carrying hikers down from the ridge above Snoqualmie Pass. That old scenic high route later became the Pacific Crest Trail (PCT)—the brightest gem in the triple crown of the National Trail System (the PCT, Continental Divide Trail, and Appalachian Trail). While the PCT followed much of the old Cascade Crest route, this Rock Creek section was replaced when trail builders carved a new high route into the face of Kendall

Peak (see Hike 59, Kendall Katwalk). The Rock Creek Trail was forgotten for many years, but hiking legends Harvey Manning and Ira Spring refused to let a good trail die and they added the path to one of their last guidebooks. Here it is, in an abbreviated version, to ensure that this wonderful trail doesn't disappear.

GETTING THERE

From Seattle, drive east on I-90 to exit 34 (Edgewick Road). Turn left (north) onto 468th Street and follow it to the junction with the Middle Fork Snoqualmie Road (Forest Road 56). Turn right and continue up the Middle Fork Snoqualmie Road for 12.5 miles to the junction with Taylor River Road. Pass that junction to continue east on Forest Road 5620 about 5 miles to the Dingford Creek trailhead.

Log bridge at Rock Creek's beginnings in an outlet of Snow Lake

ON THE TRAIL

The hike starts with a cold-water footbath—you'll need to ford the Middle Fork Snoqualmie River. Do this only when water levels are low (August is an ideal time). Once over the river, you'll head off through the woods. Jump onto the well-graded Middle Fork Snoqualmie Trail and head upstream 2 miles. Just after crossing Rock Creek, turn left onto the Cascade Crest Trail and start a climb up a tight series of switchbacks alongside Rock Creek.

The trail can be rough and a bit brushy at times. Persevere, and soon (near the 2.5-mile mark) the trail levels out briefly as it skirts along an old railroad right-of-way. Then the climbing begins in earnest again. Over the next mile or so, the views behind you begin to open up as you climb out of the dense forest of the valley and into a more open, view-friendly forest. Since the best views are back over the valley behind you, you'll have good reason to pause and rest—uh, I mean, enjoy the views—frequently. The grandest views start at 3.5 miles, where you can stare out over the valley at the massive face of Mount Garfield.

This is a good turnaround point, though if you really want to experience the best this route has to offer, push on. The trail continues to weave upward through the creekside forests.

Finally, at about 5.5 miles, you'll find a stunning view up through the headwater basin of Rock Creek. Before you is the steep rocky slope of the valley headwall, and the bright white ribbon of a waterfall pouring down its face.

HOW TO HELP THIS TRAIL

The best way to help protect this trail is to hike it, and then let the local ranger district know that you have visited and think the trail is a valuable part of the backcountry trail network in this area. But don't just call: put it in writing. Send a letter, describing your experience and where you see need for improvements (e.g., reconstruction of trail tread, brush cutting, log removal, etc.). Send the letter to the ranger and to the good folks at the Washington Trails Association, the leading volunteer trail-maintenance organization in the state.

EXTENDING YOUR TRIP

If you're really serious about your scrambling (and bushwhacking), push on up the trail. It gets rougher and harder to follow, but in another 2 miles you'll find yourself on the shores of Snow Lake, which is typically accessed from the Alpental trailhead at Snoqualmie Pass (see Hike 60).

39 Dingford Creek–Hester Lake

RATING/ DIFFICULTY	ROUND-TRIP	ELEV GAIN/ HIGH POINT	SEASON
****/4	12 miles	2600 feet/ 3900 feet	July–Oct

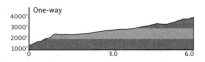

Map: Green Trails Skykomish No. 175; **Contact:** Mount Baker–Snoqualmie National Forest, Snoqualmie Ranger District, North Bend office, (425) 888-1421, *www.fs.fed.us/r6/mbs*; **Notes:** Northwest Forest Pass required; **GPS:** N 47 31.041, W 121 27.253

Pack a fishing pole and a camera. There are many meal-sized trout in this basin's lakes, and there are endless views to enjoy both on the trail and at the trail's end. The route pierces the old-growth forest in the valley as it enters the Alpine Lakes Wilderness and leads to glorious examples of the wilderness's namesake lakes. Hester Lake sprawls below Mount Price, and short scrambles are possible to Little Hester Lake and the scenic ridges around the basin.

GETTING THERE

From Seattle, drive east on I-90 to exit 34 (Edgewick Road). Turn left (north) onto 468th Street and follow it to the junction with the Middle Fork Snoqualmie Road (Forest Road

Fresh cougar tracks on a log in the snow

56). Turn right and continue up the Middle Fork Snoqualmie Road for 12.5 miles to the junction with Taylor River Road. Pass that junction to continue east on Forest Road 5620 about 5 miles to the Dingford Creek trailhead.

ON THE TRAIL

The Dingford Creek Trail climbs from the banks of the Middle Fork Snoqualmie River, heading north up the creek valley. The forest path immediately starts a sweat-popping climb, with a long series of switchbacks over the first mile. At the top of the last switchback, the trail ducks into the Alpine Lakes Wilderness and the grade levels out a bit. The surrounding forest, young second-growth near the trailhead, slowly returns to native old-growth status as the trail penetrates deeper into the wilderness.

At 3.5 miles the trail—and the creek—split. To the left the trail continues due north another 2.5 miles to Myrtle Lake, while the right fork heads due south to Hester Lake in just 2 miles. Both lakes are enjoyable and both hold pan-sized trout. Hester, however, offers somewhat better views, with the jagged peak of Mount Price looming above it.

The final couple of miles to Hester are rough and poorly maintained, making the final walk into the lake basin all the more rewarding. Stop and rest along the shores of the blue water lake, enjoying views of Mount Price and Big Snow Mountain.

EXTENDING YOUR TRIP

If you feel the need for more miles, detour off your return trip to make the 5-mile round-trip to Myrtle Lake. It is nestled in a deep rocky cirque at the end of a 2.5-mile trail that is just as rough and steep as the one leading to Hester.

40 Upper Middle Fork Snoqualmie Meadow

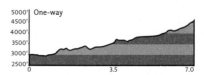

RATING/ DIFFICULTY	ROUND-TRIP	ELEV GAIN/ HIGH POINT	SEASON
★★★★/3	14 miles	1600 feet/ 4600 feet	Aug–Oct

Maps: Green Trails Skykomish No. 175 and Stevens Pass No. 176; **Contact:** Mount Baker–Snoqualmie National Forest, Snoqualmie Ranger District, North Bend office, (425) 888-1421, www.fs.fed.us/r6/mbs; **Notes:** Northwest Forest Pass required, high-clearance vehicle required for last few miles to trailhead; **GPS:** N 47 31.041, W 121 27.253; **Status:** Endangered

All you have to do to enjoy this trail is survive perhaps the worst road in the Cascades. But the long, slow drive (crawl) is worth it. You'll ramble through

A strange find: four-petaled western trillium

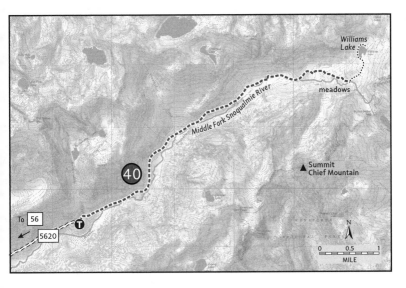

groves of ancient forests, cross massive avalanche chutes choked with slide alder and salmonberries, and enjoy endless views of the stunning peaks of the upper Snoqualmie River watershed. Reap maximum benefit by visiting in late summer through early fall: (1) because by September most of the mosquitoes are dead and gone; (2) because cooler nights add brilliant color to the vine maples and slide alders; and (3) because ripe huckleberries await at the upper end of the valley.

GETTING THERE

From Seattle, drive east on I-90 to exit 34 (Edgewick Road). Turn left (north) onto 468th Street and follow it to the junction with the Middle Fork Snoqualmie Road (Forest Road 56). Turn right and continue up the Middle Fork Snoqualmie Road for 12.5 miles to the junction with Taylor River Road. Pass that junction to continue east on Forest Road 5620 about 5 miles to the Dingford Creek trailhead. Continue east another 6.5 miles to the road end and trailhead. The last few miles are extremely rough and require a high-clearance vehicle. If you're in a lower-clearance passenger car, you'll have to hike a few extra miles (how many depends on road conditions).

ON THE TRAIL

If the last several miles of the road prove too rough for your vehicle, just walk those miles, and turn around early on the upper end of the trail. From the road end, the trail follows the north side of the river valley, angling steadily upward into the heart of the Alpine Lakes Wilderness. Though the trail climbs from beginning to end, the gain is gentle—no ruthless switchbacks to worry about here.

The long, straight trail crosses several small side creeks (some are seasonal—dry in late summer—others are raging trickles year-round). As you hike you'll find your eyes constantly drawn upward. The slopes on both sides are a patchwork of bright white granite, green forest, and (in autumn) brilliantly colored bands of vine maples.

The trail meanders in and out of forest,

sliding through meadows, skirting the base of alder-clogged avalanche chutes, and hopping over small creeks and gullies. This varied terrain and gentle climbing goes on for nearly 7 miles until the trail reaches a stunning little valley-bottom meadow dotted with small ponds and laced with wandering streams. Low-bush huckleberries fill the grassy meadows. If the berries aren't ripe, you can feast on the view of Summit Chief Mountain. This massive rock looms to your right (east), casting a remarkable reflection in the meadow ponds.

This is a great place for lunch before heading back downvalley for that long drive home.

HOW TO HELP THIS TRAIL

The best way to help protect this trail is to hike it, and then let the local ranger district know that you have visited and think the trail is a valuable part of the backcountry trail network in this area. But don't just call: put it in writing. Send a letter, describing your experience and where you see need for improvements (e.g., reconstruction of trail tread, brush cutting, log removal, etc.). Send the letter to the ranger and to the good folks at the Washington Trails Association, the leading volunteer trail-maintenance organization in the state.

EXTENDING YOUR TRIP

Turn left in the meadow, cross the small wooden bridge, and hike another mile to the shores of Williams Lake. There are great campsites on the north side of the lake, near the base of the talus slope. Beyond Williams Lake lie the Chain Lakes and days' worth of alpine scrambling.

Opposite: Pratt Lake

snoqualmie pass corridor: west

Savvy hikers know that the western side of the Snoqualmie Pass corridor means steep climbs and grand views. Not all trails in the region boast thigh-burning climbs, but the walls of the South Fork Snoqualmie Valley are brutally steep, and very tall. Few other parts of the Cascade Range offer such a collection of near-vertical trails and stellar views. Hike up the Ira Spring Trail with its 2500 feet of elevation gain in 3 miles and you'll think it can't get much steeper than that—until you go over to Granite Mountain and push up 3800 feet in 4 miles! Yes, you'll get a workout on these trails, but you'll also get phenomenal payoffs. The lakes nestled in deep bowls among these peaks are stunning, and the views from the high, craggy mountaintops are simply out of this world.

41 Mount Washington

RATING/ DIFFICULTY	ROUND-TRIP	ELEV GAIN/ HIGH POINT	SEASON
***/3	4 miles	1600 feet/ 2800 feet	Aug–Nov

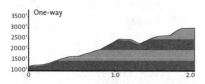

Map: Green Trails Bandera No. 206; **Contact:** Washington State Parks, (360) 902-8844, www .parks.wa.gov; **GPS:** N 47 26.519, W 121 40.332

Grand views, spectacular spring wildflowers, and easy access make this a great after-work outing or an early spring escape. The route follows an old logging road turned trail up a rock-rimmed mountain, providing hikers a good workout absent crowds.

GETTING THERE
From Seattle drive east on I-90 to exit 38. Turn right (south) onto old US 10 and after crossing the South Fork Snoqualmie River, turn right again into Olallie State Park/Twin Falls Section.

ON THE TRAIL
Find the access trail near the restroom building. This short spur trail cuts up to an old roadbed, which leads in turn to the Iron Horse Trail. Follow the Iron Horse rail-trail west a few hundred yards before turning left (south) onto an old gravel logging road. This two-track trail leads upward in long switchbacks, climbing the northern face of Mount Washington.

Much of the landscape has been logged at some distant point in the past, but as you climb, the cleared areas—now thick with green growth—offer grand views. The road/ trail winds up the steep face of the mountain, over and around rocky bluffs, craggy cliffs, and deep ravines. On sunny summer weekends you might find superhero wannabes doing Spiderman impersonations on many of the rock walls.

Your route climbs continuously from the Iron Horse. Any time you encounter a spur trail, stick to the main trail and continue up, up, up. At 2 miles you'll find grand views from a broad bench on the flank of the mountain. This area provides the best views found anywhere on the mountain. Enjoy them, and then head back the way you came.

EXTENDING YOUR TRIP
If you want more, push on up the old roadway, staying left at the next intersection and then hugging the main trail at subsequent intersections. Four miles after leaving the viewpoint you'll reach the 4040-foot summit of Mount Washington (6 miles from the trailhead).

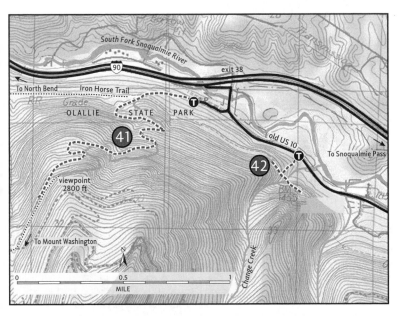

View from Mount Washington toward Rattlesnake Mountain

Climbers heading to the crags

42 Deception Crags

RATING/ DIFFICULTY	ROUND-TRIP	ELEV GAIN/ HIGH POINT	SEASON
**/1	1 mile	250 feet/ 1450 feet	Apr–Nov

One-way elevation profile: 1200' to 1500', distance 0 to 0.5

Map: Green Trails Bandera No. 206; **Contact:** Washington State Parks, (360) 902-8844, www.parks.wa.gov; **GPS:** N 47 26.285, W 121 39.666

 *This easy walk provides some unique opportunities to view the local wildlife—Craggius rattius, better known as crag rats.* These human creepy crawlers can be found hanging from their fingertips all along the rocky walls towering over the Iron Horse Trail near the Change Creek canyon. Of course, rock walls draw more than vertically oriented humans. An assortment of birds call these cliff faces home as well—swallows and swifts, hawks and falcons. Indeed, some of the most exciting wildlife moments come from swallows diving and swirling around the heads of climbers (who frequently will suck up close to the wall to avoid the "bombs" dropped by these small flyers).

GETTING THERE
From Seattle drive east on I-90 to exit 38. Turn right (south) onto old US 10 and, after crossing the South Fork Snoqualmie River, continue on this road as it veers left. About 0.7 mile from the freeway, find a parking area just before crossing Change Creek (if you find yourself on a rickety old bridge, you've gone a bit too far).

ON THE TRAIL
No multiday assaults on multipitch, big-wall routes here. The most common form of climbing you'll see is actually bouldering, or climbing "low." In bouldering, climbers stick to the rock and seldom get more than 10 feet off the flat ground. Instead, they'll plaster themselves onto the rock face, then traverse along it, staying a few feet above the ground. It's a great sport to watch, and a great way to practice climbing without fear of falling from heights.

The trail follows Change Creek, climbing steeply from the road to the Iron Horse Trail. Once on the Iron Horse, you'll immediately be in the midst of the climbing world. Before you is the Change Creek Wall. This tall face is usually streaked with white chalk scuffs, and on close inspection you'll see it is marred by countless steel bolts—climbers have drilled the wall and installed these permanent anchors through which they clip their ropes. The bolts improve safety, but are somewhat controversial among climbers, since they turn natural rock into gymlike, man-made climbing routes.

Still, hikers will barely notice the bolts (unless you hear a purist climber howl in protest). Hike east to cross Change Creek on a rustic trestle for views out over the South Fork Snoqualmie (I-90) Valley. After visiting the trestle, head back west and continue past the trail you came up on to explore the base of several climbing walls along this short 0.5-mile stretch of trail as well as views down into Olallie State Park.

THE BEAR ESSENTIALS

Usually a bear encounter will only involve catching a glimpse of the bear's behind. But occasionally the bruin may actually want to get a look at *you*. In very rare cases a bear may act aggressively. If you did everything right (see "Bear in Mind" in the introduction) and Yogi appears to be agitated, heed the following advice:

- Respect a bear's need for personal space. If you see a bear in the distance, make a wide detour around it, or if that's not possible (i.e., if the trail leads close to the bear) leave the area.
- If you encounter a bear at close range, remain calm. Do not run, as this may trigger a predator/prey reaction from the bear.
- Talk in a low, calm manner to the bear to help identify yourself as a human.
- Hold your arms out from your body, and if wearing a jacket hold open the front so you appear to be as big as possible.
- Don't stare directly at the bear—the bear may interpret this as a direct threat or challenge. Watch the animal without making direct eye-to-eye contact.
- Slowly move upwind of the bear if you can do so without crowding the bear. The bear's strongest sense is its sense of smell, and if it can sniff you and identify you as human, it may retreat.
- Know how to interpret bear actions. A nervous bear will often rumble in its chest, clack its teeth and "pop" its jaw. It may paw the ground and swing its head violently side to side. If the bear does this, watch it closely (without staring directly at it). Continue to speak low and calmly.
- A bear may bluff-charge—run at you but stop well before reaching you—to try to intimidate you. Resist the eager desire to run from this charge, as that would turn the bluff into a real charge and you will *not* be able to outrun the bear (black bears can run at speeds up to 35 miles per hour through log-strewn forests).
- If you surprise a bear and it does charge from close range, lie down and play dead. A surprised bear will leave you once the perceived threat is neutralized. However, if the bear wasn't attacking because it was surprised—if it charges from a long distance, or if it has had a chance to identify you and still attacks—you should fight back. A bear in this situation is behaving in a predatory manner (as opposed to the defensive attack of a surprised bear) and is looking at you as food. Kick, stab, punch at the bear. If it knows you will fight back, it may leave you and search for easier prey.
- Carry a 12-ounce (or larger) can of pepper spray bear deterrent. The spray—a high concentration of oils from hot peppers—should fire out at least 20 or 30 feet in a broad mist. Don't use the spray unless a bear is actually charging and is in range of the spray.

43 Dirty Harry

RATING/ DIFFICULTY	ROUND-TRIP	ELEV GAIN/ HIGH POINT	SEASON
***/3	5 miles	1300 feet/ 2600 feet	June–Oct

One-way

Map: Green Trails Bandera No. 206; Contact: Mount Baker–Snoqualmie National Forest, Snoqualmie Ranger District, North Bend office, (425) 888-1421, www.fs.fed.us/r6/mbs; Notes: Northwest Forest Pass required; GPS: N 47 26.030, W 121 37.952

Go ahead, hike this way. Okay, Clint Eastwood I'm not. But this hike is more entertaining than any Dirty Harry movie you'll see. It follows an old logging road up to a high bench overlooking the central section of the South Fork Snoqualmie River valley. The walking is fairly easy on this wide road-turned-trail, and the views are breathtaking. This previously unnamed peak was given its Hollywood-sounding name by wilderness advocate (and guidebook legend) Harvey Manning. The name is a backhanded memorial to Harry Gault, the logger who carved so many roads and clear-cuts into the mountains (including this one) of the Snoqualmie Valley. Dirty Harry indeed!

View of McClellan Butte from Dirty Harry's Balcony

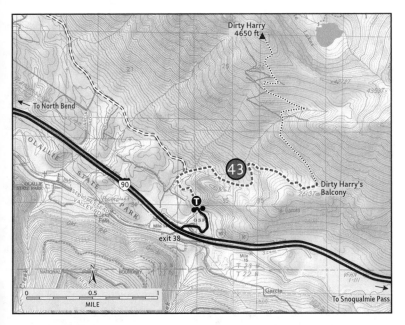

GETTING THERE

From Seattle drive east on I-90 to exit 38. After exiting, follow the signs to "State Fire Training Center." This will lead you under the freeway and, 0.25 mile later, to a gate. This gate is well marked: "Locked after 4 PM daily." Park just outside this gate unless you are absolutely sure you'll be back before 4:00 PM. If you are, continue about another 0.5 mile (crossing the South Fork Snoqualmie River) to a small gravel road on the right (you'll find it in the middle of a left-hand curve) at about 1350 feet elevation.

ON THE TRAIL

If, as recommended, you park outside the gate, walk the 0.5 mile up the road to the "Dirty Harry Logging Road" on the right. (Note that by walking up to this true starting point, you're far less likely to miss it.)

The next 1.5 miles of road walking is a little more exciting than the initial road, but not much. Roadside trees limit the views until you get higher, so just enjoy the exercise as you climb to 2500 feet elevation.

About 2 miles from the gate (and your car), look for a faint path on the right just at the apex of a switchback to the left. This 0.5-mile-long boot trail climbs 100 feet to a rocky ledge Mr. Manning dubbed Dirty Harry's Balcony. Marvelous views sweep across the rugged mountains to the south and east. Big Mac (McClellan Butte) rises to the south. On your east flank is Bandera Mountain, while to the west Mount Washington rises into the sun.

EXTENDING YOUR TRIP

Turn your 5-mile hike into an 11-mile trek (with an additional 2000 feet of elevation gain) by continuing up the road-turned-trail route to the 4650-foot summit of Dirty Harry.

44 Mount Gardner

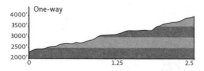

RATING/ DIFFICULTY	ROUND-TRIP	ELEV GAIN/ HIGH POINT	SEASON
***/4	5 miles	1500 feet/ 3800 feet	Apr–Nov

Map: Green Trails Bandera No. 206; **Contact:** Mount Baker–Snoqualmie National Forest, Snoqualmie Ranger District, North Bend office, (425) 888-1421, *www.fs.fed.us/r6/mbs*; **Notes:** High-clearance vehicle recommended; **GPS:** N 47 23.469, W 121 33.465

This is one of the finest places to view birds of prey in the South Fork Snoqualmie Valley. Hawks, falcons, kites, and occasionally eagles soar on the thermals that spin up off the sun-heated rocks on the face of Mount Gardner. You can also look across the valley to the high meadows and rocky top of Granite Mountain to see even more birds, circling ever higher on the rising air currents. But even if the birds don't come out to play, you'll enjoy your day on this seldom-visited mountain. Grand views and plenty of solitude await you here.

GETTING THERE

From Seattle drive east on I-90 to exit 39. Turn east onto old US 10 and drive 2 miles, paralleling I-90. At 2 miles turn right onto Forest Road

Male mountain goat sporting a thick fall coat

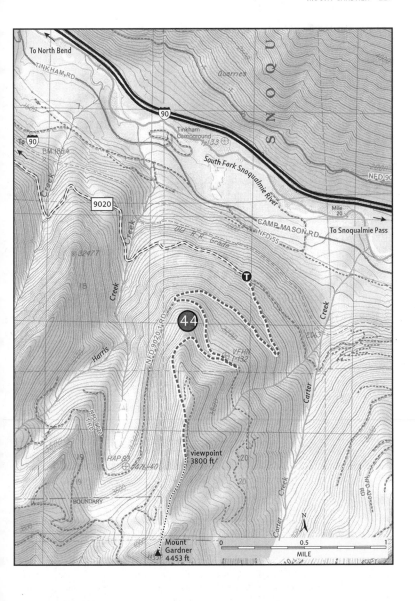

To North Bend

TINKHAM RD.

90

Quarries

SNOQU

To 90

BM 1884

Tinkham
Campground

133

South Fork Snoqualmie River

NFD 90

Mile
20

CAMP MASON RD.

NFD 55

To Snoqualmie Pass

OLD R R Grade

9020

32477

T

44

NFD 9020 RD.

VFHN
132

Harris   Creek

2063

Carter   Creek

NFD 9020
TRD

HAP 83

3476 40

viewpoint
3800 ft

20

20

Carter   Creek

NFD 40

RD

BOUNDARY

N

Mount
Gardner
4453 ft

0   0.5   1

MILE

View of I-90 from McClellan Butte

9020. In another mile this rough road crosses the Iron Horse Trail, then at 4.5 miles from the freeway exit you'll cross the McClellan Butte Trail (Hike 45). For the next 3.5 miles the road is rough (high-clearance vehicle recommended). At a fork in the road, about 8 miles from the freeway (elev. 2350 ft), find a place to park. The road continues, but it degrades the higher you climb, so better to trust your feet rather than your wheels from here on out.

ON THE TRAIL

Start up the road on your right, climbing toward the Carter Creek drainage before sweeping back to the west in a looping switchback turn about 0.5 mile out. In another 0.5 mile you'll enter a broad, open slope. This talus field is a massive slide of broken rock. Look for soaring raptors overhead. Look, too, for

the raptors' prey underfoot—ground squirrels and marmots scurry in these steeply sloped rock gardens.

At 1.5 miles the trail splits again. Here, endless views can be enjoyed. Peer north to Bandera Mountain, Granite Mountain, and west down the long sweep of the South Fork Snoqualmie River. Turn around here for a casual 3-mile day. Or press on, climbing another mile along the road as it angles back to the west before running straight south along the upper flank of the Harris Creek valley to a viewpoint at 3800 feet, just below the summit of Mount Gardner.

EXTENDING YOUR TRIP

The road disappears here, but a boot-beaten trail continues climbing due south and in another 0.5 mile reaches the 4453-foot summit.

45 McClellan Butte

RATING/ DIFFICULTY	ROUND-TRIP	ELEV GAIN/ HIGH POINT	SEASON
***/5	9 miles	3700 feet/ 5162 feet	July–Oct

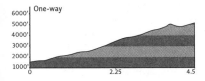

Map: Green Trails Bandera No. 206; **Contact:** Mount Baker–Snoqualmie National Forest, Snoqualmie Ranger District, North Bend office, (425) 888-1421, *www.fs.fed.us/r6/mbs*; **Notes:** Northwest Forest Pass required, avalanche danger when slopes are snow-covered; **GPS:** N 47 24.851, W 121 35.305

Sometimes, you hike the steep trails to get the best possible views. Other times, you hike the steep trails just because they are steep. McClellan Butte hikers generally fall into this later category. The trail is steep and physically demanding, while the views are less spectacular than you'll find on other nearby trails. But folks flock to this wonderful trail, using it as a warm-up for more serious alpine adventures later in the year. And unlike other "training" hills (Mount Si and Granite Mountain, for instance), McClellan Butte doesn't draw hundreds of people every day in the spring and summer. You're not going to hike in solitude, of course (every

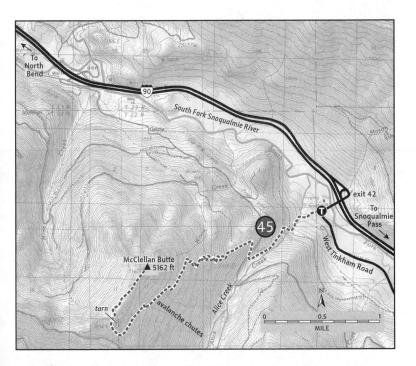

Summit block on McClellan Butte

trail in the I-90 corridor draws weekend boot traffic), but you might only see a few other people as you sweat your way to the summit.

GETTING THERE

From Seattle drive east on I-90 to exit 42 (West Tinkham Road). Turn right from the off-ramp and continue past the Department of Transportation office. The parking lot and trailhead are just past the office driveway on the right (west) side of the road.

ON THE TRAIL

Like much of the west side of the South Fork Snoqualmie Valley (the I-90 corridor), loggers got to his mountain before you. The trail leaves the parking area and ascends through dense second-growth timber for about a mile, crossing the Iron Horse Trail (rail-to-trail route) about 0.5 mile up the Alice Creek valley.

About 0.5 mile past that broad trail, the trail to McClellan pokes out onto a rough old logging road. You might find vehicles here, but don't worry. It's much better to park low and hike this far than to beat your vehicle to death on the long, roundabout rough road.

After that first warm-up mile, the trail turns steep while the forest opens up a bit, with a few majestic old-growth behemoths still gracing this mountain retreat. The trail climbs ever steeper, winding through an endless series of tight switchbacks. Finally, about 2.5 miles into your hike, the trail levels a bit and rolls east to a very steep avalanche chute. **Caution:** This area can be covered in snow until well into July some years. If there is snowpack on the steep slope, come back when the way is clear, since the snow can slide at any time.

Beyond that potential hazard zone, the trail gets back to the business of climbing, offering you more switchbacks to enjoy. At 4.1 miles you'll crest the mountain's southern ridge (elev. 4500 ft). Stop here (as if you had a choice after that blistering climb!) and enjoy the views. Peer down into the deep, green wilderness of the Cedar River watershed (off-limits to most humans) and across the way to Kent Mountain.

The next 0.5 mile of trail rolls down to a small tarn, then up along the ridge spine toward the summit. Grand views can be had from the ridgetop viewpoints, and anyone without well-honed rock scrambling skills should consider stopping here. The last 100 vertical feet to the top of the mountain requires use of hands and feet to move cautiously up to the 5162-foot summit.

46 Ira Spring Trail

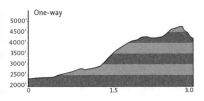

RATING/ DIFFICULTY	ROUND-TRIP	ELEV GAIN/ HIGH POINT	SEASON
***/4	6 miles	2550 feet/ 4750 feet	June–Oct

One-way

Map: Green Trails Bandera No. 206; **Contact:** Mount Baker–Snoqualmie National Forest, Snoqualmie Ranger District, North Bend office, (425) 888-1421, *www.fs.fed.us/r6/mbs*; **Notes:** Northwest Forest Pass required; **GPS:** N 47 25.543, W 121 35.057; **Status:** Rescued

⭐ Hikers owe an incredible debt of thanks to Ira Spring. This soft-spoken man and his trail-loving photography did more for trail protection in Washington than any other person in hiking history. Ira was a tireless advocate for trails, working both behind the scenes and as one of the most recognizable trails spokesmen in the country. He lobbied Congress, he influenced local land-management decisions, and he introduced several generations of hikers to the wonders of Washington's trail network through the hiking guide series he created with The Mountaineers Books. It is only fitting that this rehabilitated trail to Mason Lake bears his name. The fact that his namesake trail leads to a beautiful mountain lake is also appropriate, as Ira loved lakes of all kinds and sizes.

GETTING THERE

From Seattle drive east on I-90 to exit 45 (Forest Road 9030). Drive north, then stay left

Coral mushroom

on FR 9030. About 1 mile from the freeway, you'll encounter a fork. Stay left again, now on Mason Lake Road (FR 9031). At about 3.9 miles from the freeway, park where the road is blocked—the road continues on the other side, but only for foot traffic.

ON THE TRAIL

Start up the road and in just 0.5 mile cross Mason Creek. You'll enjoy a couple of miles of walking on this old roadbed-turned-trail, giving you ample time to stretch and loosen up muscles before starting the real climbing. The road ends at around 2 miles, and the new trail leads upward into the forest.

You'll find a trail junction near the Alpine Lakes Wilderness boundary at 2.25 miles out. Stay left here and continue climbing through the dense, young forest (regrowth that sprouted after a fire many decades ago). In just 0.5 mile you'll crest the ridge (elev. 4750 ft) and start a short but steep descent (losing 500 feet in elevation) to the forested basin of Mason Lake.

Mason Lake is a deep pool, home to some fine—though hard to hook—trout. Enjoy a dip in the cool waters, if you don't want to try your angling skills, and then relax under the shady forest fringe and reflect on the man who helped save these mountains for hikers.

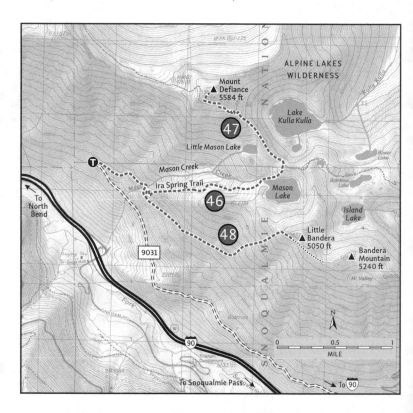

View of Lake Kulla Kulla and Mason Lake from Mount Defiance

47 Mount Defiance

RATING/ DIFFICULTY	ROUND-TRIP	ELEV GAIN/ HIGH POINT	SEASON
*****/5	11 miles	3384 feet/ 5584 feet	Aug–Oct

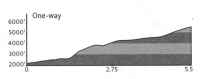

Map: Green Trails Bandera No. 206; **Contact:** Mount Baker–Snoqualmie National Forest, Snoqualmie Ranger District, North Bend office, (425) 888-1421, *www.fs.fed.us/r6/mbs*; **Notes:** Northwest Forest Pass required; **GPS:** N 47 25.543, W 121 35.057

Defiance is futile! This peak and its stunning views will amaze you. The long ridge spine to the north of the South Fork Snoqualmie River (the I-90 corridor) offers some of the steepest hiking trails in the Cascades, but also some of the best views. Mount Defiance gives you both, and lakeside rest areas make the thigh-burning climb well worth the effort. Plan your trip when the atmosphere is clear (right after or a few days before a storm—look for barometric pressure changes to clue in to weather changes). With clear skies and clean air around you, views will stretch across the breadth of Washington—from Mount Baker near the Canadian border to Mount Adams (and very faintly, Mount Hood) near the Columbia River and the Oregon border.

GETTING THERE

From Seattle drive east on I-90 to exit 45 (Forest Road 9030). Drive north, then stay left on FR 9030. About 1 mile from the freeway, you'll encounter a fork. Stay left again, now on Mason Lake Road (FR 9031). At about 3.9 miles from the freeway, park where the road is blocked—the road continues on the other side, but only for foot traffic.

ON THE TRAIL

Start climbing the Ira Spring Trail, following it as it ascends the old logging road and then the true trail toward Mason Lake (Hike 46). At about 2.7 miles, as you skirt above the shore of Mason Lake, turn left at a trail fork. Right leads down alongside Mason Lake and on toward Rainbow and Pratt Lakes.

This left-hand path climbs for 2 miles, running through forest and open slopes to an elevation of 5240 feet. You'll find yourself in a broad meadow packed with wildflowers and views. Those with no desire or skill to scramble can enjoy this wonderful wilderness garden, but those looking for a little more can push on.

A rough path runs steeply up the ridge to the summit of Mount Defiance at 5584 feet. From here, the views are as good as you'll find anywhere. Due north look for the snow-capped cone of Mount Baker and to its right and a little closer in, Glacier Peak. Turn and face west to see the South Fork Snoqualmie Valley running down into the Puget Sound lowlands and, beyond, the sawtooth ridges of the Olympic Mountains. Face south and enjoy the massive mountain that is Rainier and behind it, Mount Adams. To the west of these you might see the abbreviated summit of Mount St. Helens, and in the gap between Adams and St. Helens, look for the faint outline of Mount Hood (count yourself lucky if you see it). Finally, look east and take in the long ridge to Bandera and Pratt Mountains.

48 Little Bandera Mountain

RATING/ DIFFICULTY	ROUND-TRIP	ELEV GAIN/ HIGH POINT	SEASON
***/4	7 miles	2850 feet/ 5050 feet	June–Oct

Map: Green Trails Bandera No. 206; **Contact:** Mount Baker–Snoqualmie National Forest, Snoqualmie Ranger District, North Bend office, (425) 888-1421, www.fs.fed.us/r6/mbs; **Notes:** Northwest Forest Pass required; **GPS:** N 47 25.543, W 121 35.057

Bandera may be the most overlooked mountain in the Snoqualmie Pass region. Granite Mountain, Mount Defiance, and McClellan Butte all get more traffic, though the climb to Bandera offers all the same great features you'll find on those routes—with far fewer people to crowd you off the trail. Grand views, beautiful wildflowers, delicious berries, and a wonderful path through the wilderness await you here.

GETTING THERE

From Seattle drive east on I-90 to exit 45 (Forest Road 9030). Drive north, then stay left on FR 9030. About 1 mile from the freeway, you'll encounter a fork. Stay left again, now on Mason Lake Road (FR 9031). At about 3.9 miles from the freeway, park where the road is blocked—the road continues on the other side, but only for foot traffic.

ON THE TRAIL

Start climbing the Ira Spring Trail, following it as it ascends the old logging road, and then pass the true trail toward Mason Lake (Hike

Granite rock outcropping on Bandera Mountain

46). Continue along the old road as it traverses the slope until about the 2-mile mark, where the way turns steep. Follow this road-turned-trail as it runs straight up to the ridge spine leading toward Bandera Mountain.

Once on the ridge, the trail rolls up the spine through the high alpine forest and across granite slopes to the summit of Little Bandera at 5050 feet, nearly 3.5 miles out. Stop here for a long pause and enjoy the panoramic views. These are views equal to any you'll find in the region, sweeping in the entire western face of the Cascades north to south.

EXTENDING YOUR TRIP

If you're not a summit bagger, turn back at Little Bandera, satisfied that you've seen the best views of the route. Otherwise, continue about another mile of forested walking along the rolling ridgeline, reaching the true summit of Bandera Mountain at 5240 feet—don't expect views from the timbered summit, however.

49 Talapus and Olallie Lakes

RATING/ DIFFICULTY	ROUND-TRIP	ELEV GAIN/ HIGH POINT	SEASON
**/2	4 miles	1220 feet/ 3780 feet	June–Oct

Map: Green Trails Bandera No. 206; **Contact:** Mount Baker–Snoqualmie National Forest, Snoqualmie Ranger District, North Bend office, (425) 888-1421, *www.fs.fed.us/r6/mbs*; **Notes:** Northwest Forest Pass required; **GPS:** N 47 24.041, W 121 31.137

These easy-to-reach lakes receive a lot of visitors every sunny summer weekend, but don't let that keep you away. All those people can't be wrong—even if it means sharing. In fact, bring the kids—by mid-August the snow-fed lakes have warmed enough that you can take a swim without turning blue. Even if cool mountain lake swimming isn't your bag, there's still a lot to keep kids occupied. There are some trout (though they get a lot of fishing pressure), and other critters abound. Deer are frequent visitors, and gray jays (a.k.a. camp robber jays) have learned to congregate wherever hikers travel en masse. Indeed, these beautiful birds can be downright pesky. Keep a close eye on your gorp bag, or you might find a camp robber carrying it off.

GETTING THERE

From Seattle drive I-90 east to exit 45 (Forest Road 9030). Turn left under the freeway on FR 9030. In 1 mile bear right at the junction. Continue straight to the trailhead at the road's end.

ON THE TRAIL

From the parking area, head up the broad trail as it climbs through easy switchbacks for the first mile. As you cross into the Alpine Lakes Wilderness the route levels out through a broad bench that boasts a bit of a bog. As you move through this wet section, try to stay on the trail even if it's a bit muddy—better to dirty your boots than to erode more land around the trail.

The trail soon sweeps across a small bridge (crossing the lake's outlet) just below Talapus Lake, then climbs the last few yards to the lakeshore at 3250 feet. Forests push in along the shores of this pretty lake, with talus tapering down to the water's edge on the far side. Anglers can wet their lines in this lake first, and families can find fine swimming opportunities along its banks.

The trail climbs away from Talapus before

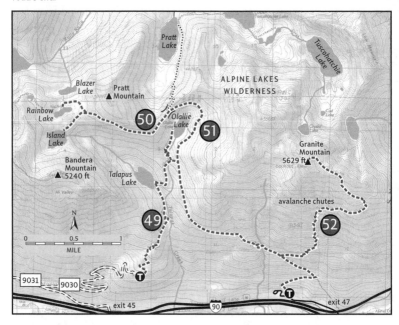

Olallie Lake overlook and Mount Rainier

traversing the valley wall, heading up the valley to Olallie. About 0.7 mile from Talapus, stay left at a small trail junction and proceed up-valley to the outlet of Olallie Lake. This pretty lake sits in a nice alpine basin, providing plenty of opportunities to enjoy cooling shade under the boughs of towering firs. It also offers sun lovers a chance to get warm while catching a few rays on the rocks along the shore.

50 Island and Rainbow Lakes

RATING/ DIFFICULTY	ROUND-TRIP	ELEV GAIN/ HIGH POINT	SEASON
****/4	10 miles	2000 feet/ 4400 feet	June–Oct

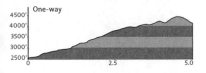

Map: Green Trails Bandera No. 206; **Contact:** Mount Baker–Snoqualmie National Forest, Snoqualmie Ranger District, North Bend of-

fice, (425) 888-1421, *www.fs.fed.us/r6/mbs*; **Notes:** Northwest Forest Pass required; **GPS:** N 47 24.041, W 121 31.137

If you want to shed the crowds while still exploring the wonderful routes of the western Snoqualmie Pass region, this might be the destination to consider. Sure, you'll have to share the first section of the route with the hordes, but most of the casual hikers will drop out at Talapus or Olallie Lake. By pushing on, you get higher and quieter country to explore as well as a much more scenic lake basin to enjoy.

GETTING THERE

From Seattle drive I-90 east to exit 45 (Forest Road 9030). Turn left under the freeway on FR 9030. In 1 mile bear right at the junction. Continue straight to the trailhead at the road's end.

ON THE TRAIL

Head up the trail toward Talapus and Olallie Lakes (Hike 49), looping through a couple of long switchbacks before crossing into the Alpine Lakes Wilderness at about 1 mile.

In a long 0.25 mile past that boundary you'll find yourself at Talapus Lake (elev. 3250 ft), and in another mile you'll swing around the Olallie Lake basin. Avoid the trail to the lakeshore of Olallie. Instead, turn right and cross the creek, then turn left at the next trail junction (just above the creek) to stay on the high trail as it sweeps along the hillside to the east of the lake.

The trail curves to the west along the headwall of the lake basin, and at 3.6 miles from the trailhead it reaches another trail junction. Stay left (Hike 51, Pratt Lake Basin, is to the right). Skirt the flank of Pratt Mountain for 1 mile to a high point above Island and Rainbow Lakes. Turn left here and drop 0.4 mile to Island Lake, or stay right and drop 0.5 mile to Rainbow. A small boot-beaten path through the woods links the two lakes.

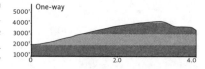

51 Pratt Lake Basin

RATING/ DIFFICULTY	ROUND-TRIP	ELEV GAIN/ HIGH POINT	SEASON
****/4	8 miles	2300 feet/ 4100 feet	June–Oct

Bobcat resting on a large boulder

Kaleeten Peak from the approach to Pratt Lake

Maps: Green Trails Bandera No. 206 and Snoqualmie Pass No. 207; **Contact:** Mount Baker–Snoqualmie National Forest, Snoqualmie Ranger District, North Bend office, (425) 888-1421, *www.fs.fed.us/r6/mbs*; **Notes:** Northwest Forest Pass required; **GPS:** N 47 23.874, W 121 29.163; **Status:** Rescued

⭐ *The path to Pratt Lake was once a braided super highway, at times more than 10 feet wide. Hardly the stuff of wilderness. But Washington Trails Association (WTA) volunteers stepped in and rebuilt the trail. Not only did they rebuild the tread to channel all hikers onto the proper path, they decommissioned all the unauthorized secondary trails, creating a new single track worthy of a pristine wild area. Hikers can now stroll easily up this picturesque trail to the pretty Pratt Lake basin.*

GETTING THERE

From Seattle drive east on I-90 to exit 47 (Asahel Curtis/Denny Creek). Turn north over the freeway, turn left at the T, and drive to the nearby Pratt Lake–Granite Mountain parking area.

ON THE TRAIL

The first mile of trail is busy. You're sharing this section with crowds headed for Granite Mountain (Hike 52). But don't worry: at the 1-mile mark most of your fellow hikers will peel off to the right as you push on straight ahead to Pratt Lake.

At around 3 miles out you'll find a fine viewpoint at 3400 feet. Pause to take pictures of the Snoqualmie Valley and the peaks above the Ollalie, Talapus, and Pratt Lake basins. Just beyond you'll enter the Alpine Lakes Wilderness, and then you'll encounter a side trail at

3.8 miles leading down to forest-rimmed Talapus Lake.

A scant 0.25 mile past this junction you'll reach a low saddle (elev. 4100 feet) separating the higher Pratt Lake basin from the Talapus and Olallie basins. This is a great place to stop for a rest and, in late August (most years), to harvest the abundant huckleberries. Turn around here unless you really need to reach the lake.

EXTENDING YOUR TRIP

If you're a lake bagger, push on the final 1.6 miles as the trail swings around the basin walls and slowly angles up to the shores of Pratt Lake (elev. 5099 ft).

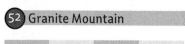

52 Granite Mountain

RATING/ DIFFICULTY	ROUND-TRIP	ELEV GAIN/ HIGH POINT	SEASON
*****/5	8 miles	3800 feet/ 5629 feet	June–Oct

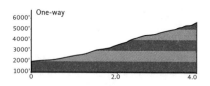

Map: Green Trails Snoqualmie Pass No. 207; **Contact:** Mount Baker–Snoqualmie National Forest, Snoqualmie Ranger District, North Bend office, (425) 888-1421, www.fs.fed.us/r6/mbs; **Notes:** Northwest Forest Pass required, avalanche danger when slopes are snow-covered; **GPS:** N 47 23.874, W 121 29.163

One look at the parking lot midday on any summer weekend, and the obvious will jump out and bite you: the Granite Mountain Trail is the most heavily traveled summit path in the Snoqualmie Pass corridor. Of course, there is a good reason for that: it's spectacular. But it's also steep. Mind numbingly, thigh-burning steep. You'll climb a heel-blistering 3800 feet in 4.3 miles to an old fire lookout at the 5600-foot summit, with awesome views in all directions. Pack plenty of water, as there is no good source along the trail.

GETTING THERE

From Seattle drive east on I-90 to exit 47 (Asahel Curtis/Denny Creek). Turn north over the freeway, turn left at the T, and drive to the nearby Pratt Lake–Granite Mountain parking area.

ON THE TRAIL

The trail starts out climbing. You'll hike away from the trailhead parking area through a lush old forest and gain a solid 800 feet in the first mile. At 1 mile the trail forks. Turn right off this relatively flat (!) trail for some serious climbing (Hike 51 to Pratt Lake goes left).

In the next 0.5 mile the switchbacks are easy, if a bit steeper. But as you near 2 miles the switchbacks get tighter, the trail gets steeper, and the breathing gets more difficult. At 4000 feet elevation you'll get a breather as the trail angles across a tricky avalanche chute.

Caution: Early in the year the upper mountain is covered in snow and ice, and the upper slopes are **VERY** avalanche prone. If you're here any time before mid-June (most years), pause before crossing the chute and look up the gully. If there is still snow above you, be extremely careful—slides can happen at any time.

Once across, the trail starts climbing again. If you time your trek just right, you'll find huckleberries alongside the trail all the way to the ridge top. You'll also break out of the trees and start exploring wide, steeply slanted meadows. Bulbous beargrass fills these meadows in

The impressive Granite Mountain lookout

early summer, and when those white blooms disappear, lupine and paintbrush color the slopes red and blue.

At 5200 feet you'll crest the summit ridge, getting a brief reprieve from the ruthless climbing as you cross a meadow. You still have another 0.5 mile or so to cover along the ridge crest and then up the summit crown, but the hardest work is behind you. Get to the top and enjoy the 360-degree views from the lookout—on some weekends, volunteers open it up to visitors.

53 Denny Creek

RATING/ DIFFICULTY	ROUND-TRIP	ELEV GAIN/ HIGH POINT	SEASON
***/1	4 miles	700 feet/ 3000 feet	June–Oct

Map: Green Trails Snoqualmie Pass No. 207; **Contact:** Mount Baker–Snoqualmie National Forest, Snoqualmie Ranger District, North Bend office, (425) 888-1421, *www.fs.fed.us/r6/mbs*; **Notes:** Northwest Forest Pass required; **GPS:** N 47 24.903, W 121 26.593

Denny Creek may be the most family-friendly trail in the region. The popular path leads to a series of waterfalls and to a smooth natural waterslide—a massive rock face over which the creek flows, providing a slippery summertime escape from the heat of the lowlands. Just beyond, hikers will

Denny Creek

find a couple more falls—most notably the beautiful Keekwulee Falls.

GETTING THERE

From Seattle drive east on I-90 to exit 47 (Asahel Curtis/Denny Creek). Turn left over the overpass and proceed to a T. Turn right and travel 0.25 mile to Denny Creek Road (Forest Road 58). Turn left and drive 2.5 miles, turning left on the paved road just after the Denny Creek Campground. The trailhead is at the road's end.

ON THE TRAIL

Head up the trail as it rolls north under the high viaduct that carries I-90 traffic west. The trail crosses a creek at about 0.5 mile, then winds through the forested valley before re-crossing the creek at base of the waterslide rock at about 1.3 miles.

Come mid-August, you'll certainly find hikers—young and old—sporting in the cold water of Denny Creek as it slides over the granite slabs. The creek is shallow enough to be safe, but strong enough to be fun. You'll want to stick close to the kids, though, as there is a small plunge pool at the end of the slab, and the cold water can be shocking.

After cooling off, keep moving up the trail. Just above the waterslide is a small stairstep falls, Keekwulee Falls. In another 0.5 mile (2 miles from the trailhead), is the small Snowshoe Falls. Turn around here for a 4-mile hike. Be sure to stop at the waterslide on your way out—its worth another round of water play before driving home.

EXTENDING YOUR TRIP

Should your waterplay leave you rejuvenated and energized, you can press on from Snowshoe Falls all the way to Melakwa Lake for a 9-mile round-trip (see Hike 54).

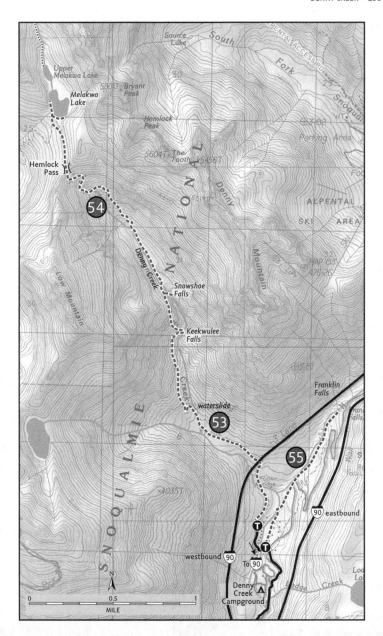

54 Melakwa Lake

RATING/ DIFFICULTY	ROUND-TRIP	ELEV GAIN/ HIGH POINT	SEASON
***/4	9 miles	2300 feet/ 4600 feet	June–Oct

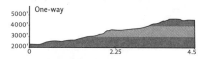

Crowds abate once past Denny Creek's waterfalls (Hike 53)—the hordes thinning to a respectable number of serious hikers looking for an alpine lake experience. And what an experience! The trail finally crests Hemlock Pass and descends moderately to Melakwa Lake, a broad alpine wonder with rocky slopes leading straight down into the crystal water. Those bright waters also reflect the craggy peaks that ring the lake: Chair and Kaleetan Peaks, most notably.

Map: Green Trails Snoqualmie Pass No. 207; **Contact:** Mount Baker–Snoqualmie National Forest, Snoqualmie Ranger District, North Bend office, (425) 888-1421, *www.fs.fed .us/r6/mbs*; **Notes:** Northwest Forest Pass required; **GPS:** N 47 24.903, W 121 26.593

GETTING THERE

From Seattle drive east on I-90 to exit 47 (Asahel Curtis/Denny Creek). Turn left over the overpass and proceed to a T. Turn right and travel 0.25 mile to Denny Creek Road (Forest Road 58). Turn left and drive 2.5 miles, turning

Mountains line the eastern shore of Melakwa Lake.

left on the paved road just after the Denny Creek Campground. The trailhead is at the road's end.

ON THE TRAIL

Hike up the trail as it rolls under the I-90 westbound viaduct to the Denny Creek waterslide at 1.3 miles. You'll pass Keekwulee Falls at 1.4 and Snowshoe Falls at 2 miles and will then climb the long, steep valley of Denny Creek. The path crosses the creek periodically and ambles through dense forest and across rocky avalanche chutes.

At about 3 miles the trail gets serious about climbing and weaves up a series of switchbacks to Hemlock Pass at 3.5 miles (elev. 4600 ft). The trail slides through the forested pass (yes, it's largely a hemlock forest), before dropping gradually over the next mile to the shores of Melakwa Lake.

Avoid walking though the fragile meadows as much as possible—there's enough rock and established trail that you won't need to further damage the already trampled heather and wildflower fields around the lake.

EXTENDING YOUR TRIP

The path continues another 3 miles, descending along the lake's outlet stream to Pratt Lake (Hike 51). This is a rough trail with far less traffic than the path to Melakwa.

Map: Green Trails Snoqualmie Pass No. 207; **Contact:** Mount Baker–Snoqualmie National Forest, Snoqualmie Ranger District, North Bend office, (425) 888-1421, *www.fs.fed .us/r6/mbs*; **Notes:** Northwest Forest Pass required; **GPS:** N 47 24.780, W 121 26.493

  Settlers heading for the Puget Sound lowlands had few route options: they could float down the Columbia River (portaging around the falls near The Dalles), they could take a ship through the Pacific—either from California, or all the way around from the Atlantic— or they could take the Snoqualmie Pass Wagon Road. This road was originally a trading path used by Native Americans, and later was a mule trail used by fur traders. Eventually, settlers and traders carried goods on wagons over this lowest of the Cascade passes. Today's interstate uses parts of the old wagon track, but in the Denny Creek area, where the interstate splits, the old wagon trace is still visible.

GETTING THERE

From Seattle drive east on I-90 to exit 47 (Asahel Curtis/Denny Creek). Turn left over the overpass and proceed to a T. Turn right and travel 0.25 mile to Denny Creek Road (Forest Road 58). Turn left and drive 3 miles, passing the Denny Creek Campground. Just past the campground, turn left onto FR 5830 and park before crossing the bridge.

ON THE TRAIL

The trail is well marked as it follows the old wagon track along the South Fork Snoqualmie River. There's also a continuation of the Denny Creek Road as it follows the old highway route up to the pass. If the kids get footsore on the mile-long hike up to the falls, let them skip down the road on the way back. But the trail is the better option, as it climbs through the

55 Franklin Falls

RATING/ DIFFICULTY	ROUND-TRIP	ELEV GAIN/ HIGH POINT	SEASON
***/1	2 miles	400 feet/ 2600 feet	June–Nov

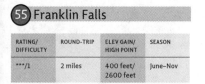

mossy forest, periodically crossing the old carved ruts of the wagon road—those steel-shod wooden wagon wheels cut deep.

The path reaches Franklin Falls at 1 mile, with the last 100 yards climbing steeply on rocky trail to the base of the falls. The tall falls pounds down a sheer rock face, providing a refreshing spray to cool hot hikers. Don't venture out into the falls water, however. It's coming down hard and frequently carries loose rocks down with the tumbling water.

56 Asahel Curtis Nature Trail

RATING/ DIFFICULTY	ROUND-TRIP	ELEV GAIN/ HIGH POINT	SEASON
***/1	0.5 mile	180 feet/ 2000 feet	May–Nov

Map: Green Trails Snoqualmie Pass No. 207; **Contact:** Mount Baker–Snoqualmie National Forest, Snoqualmie Ranger District, North Bend office, (425) 888-1421, *www.fs.fed .us/r6/mbs*; **Notes:** Northwest Forest Pass required; **GPS:** N 47 23.560, W 121 28.465

Great towering forests can still be found in the Snoqualmie Pass corridor, and this beautiful little interpretive loop offers a wonderful glimpse into the majesty of these fine old forests. The kids will love this walk through the woods. They can scamper over massive fallen logs, marvel at towering trees, and listen to the flitterings and callings of birds. The trail is named for perhaps the most renowned photographer in Washington history.

GETTING THERE

From Seattle drive east on I-90 to exit 47 (Asahel Curtis/Denny Creek). Turn right from the off-ramp and continue 0.25 mile, then turn left on Forest Road 5590. You'll find the parking area in 0.3 mile.

ON THE TRAIL

Minnesota-born Asahel Curtis moved to Washington in 1888 at the age of fourteen and started working in a family-owned photo studio when he was twenty. He soon became the

Footbridge over Humpback Creek
Opposite: Franklin Falls on the South Fork Snoqualmie River

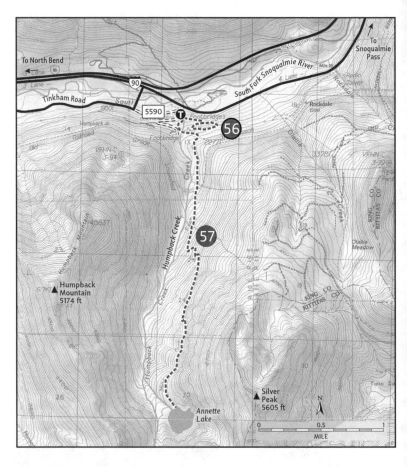

preeminent photographer in the Seattle area, documenting the natural landscape, the native people, and the historic elements of the Pacific Northwest right up until his death in 1941. The Washington State History Museum holds more than sixty thousand of his photographic images.

This trail named for Curtis gives a taste of what inspired him. It first meanders away from the trailhead, following Humpback

Creek through the refreshingly cool old forest. This moss-laden woodland felt the bite of axes in the early part of the twentieth century, but today the scars of logging are limited to old stumps—many now nursing new trees in the old, rotting cores. The short path loops through these old forests, exploring both natural and human history while providing a wonderfully peaceful walk through the forest primeval.

Springtime at Annette Lake

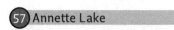

57 Annette Lake

RATING/ DIFFICULTY	ROUND-TRIP	ELEV GAIN/ HIGH POINT	SEASON
****/3	7.5 miles	1400 feet/ 3600 feet	June–Nov

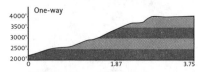

Map: Green Trails Snoqualmie Pass No. 207; **Contact:** Mount Baker–Snoqualmie National Forest, Snoqualmie Ranger District, North Bend office, (425) 888-1421, www.fs.fed .us/r6/mbs; **Notes:** Northwest Forest Pass required; **GPS:** N 47 23.560, W 121 28.465

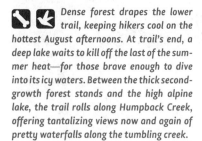 *Dense forest drapes the lower trail, keeping hikers cool on the hottest August afternoons. At trail's end, a deep lake waits to kill off the last of the summer heat—for those brave enough to dive into its icy waters. Between the thick second-growth forest stands and the high alpine lake, the trail rolls along Humpback Creek, offering tantalizing views now and again of pretty waterfalls along the tumbling creek.*

GETTING THERE
From Seattle drive east on I-90 to exit 47 (Asahel Curtis/Denny Creek). Turn right from the off-ramp and continue 0.25 mile, then turn left on Forest Road 5590. You'll find the parking area in 0.3 mile.

ON THE TRAIL
The trail begins alongside the Asahel Curtis Nature Trail (Hike 56) but continues to climb to the right when the gentle Asahel Curtis Loop goes left. You'll follow an ancient old logging road (mostly reclaimed by the fertile forest).

At about 1 mile out, you'll pass under a high-tension powerline and 0.25 mile later will cross the wide track of the Iron Horse Trail (the old railroad right-of-way). From this point, the trail gets serious. Serious about scenery, and serious about climbing.

The path switchbacks up the Humpback Creek valley for more than 1.5 miles until the last steep pitch puts you at about 3600 feet elevation. For the next mile, you'll traverse the slope above Humpback Creek, with occasional views across the valley to Humpback Mountain. The trail ends at the shores of Annette Lake, which lies in the cirque between Humpback Mountain, Abiel Peak, and Silver Peak.

Opposite: View of Annette Lake from the summit of Silver Peak

Say "Snoqualmie Pass" to just about anyone in Washington, and they'll think "Interstate 90." This low pass in the center of the Cascade Range has a long history. Native tribes used the path through the pass as a trade route. Early settlers upgraded the trail to a wagon road. Later, a railroad track was added to the wagon road, and the wagon road was upgraded into a motorway. Today, the freeway represents the core use of the Snoqualmie Pass corridor. But fast travel from east to west reveals only the veneer most people see when they look at Snoqualmie Pass. A closer look uncovers the pass as a gateway to one of the most spectacular wilderness areas in the country. The Alpine Lakes Wilderness, found just north of Snoqualmie Pass, draws backcountry recreationists like flies to honey—for good reason. High craggy peaks, crystal-clear alpine lakes, and lush forests and meadows await you in the Alpine Lakes and the surrounding mountains and valleys.

58 Commonwealth Basin

RATING/ DIFFICULTY	ROUND-TRIP	ELEV GAIN/ HIGH POINT	SEASON
****/4	10 miles	2700 feet/ 5350 feet	July–Oct

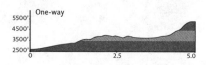

Map: Green Trails Snoqualmie Pass No. 207; **Contact:** Mount Baker–Snoqualmie National Forest, Snoqualmie Ranger District, North Bend office, (425) 888-1421, *www.fs.fed.us /r6/mbs*; **GPS:** N 47 25.722, W 121 24.806

There's nothing common about Commonwealth Basin. This deep canyon nestled in the shadows of Red Mountain and Kendall Peak offers a great opportunity to explore the wild heart of the Cascades with minimal driving and easy hiking. The trail starts just off the most heavily used highway in the Cascades, yet you'll soon find yourself caught deep in the wilderness experience as you stride into the fragrant forests, scrambling over the tumbling creeks of crystal-clear snowmelt waters and climbing through the rocky meadows in this mountain valley.

GETTING THERE
From Seattle drive I-90 to exit 52 (signed for Snoqualmie Pass west). At the bottom of the exit ramp, turn left (north) and cross under the freeway. In about 100 yards, turn right onto a dirt road leading into the Pacific Crest Trail (PCT) trailhead.

ON THE TRAIL
Start up the PCT as it climbs into the trees above the parking lot and makes a long, lazy sweep east before rounding a hairpin turn to return west across the lower end of an avalanche slope. The jumble of trees piled around the trail illustrate how powerful a little snow can be when it starts to slide downhill. The trail stays in the trees for 2.5 miles before reaching a fork. The PCT continues to climb (Hike 59), while your path angles off left, slicing up into the valley of Commonwealth Creek.

The trail continues up the creek for the next mile, climbing moderately to the headwall of the basin. Here, the going gets tough as the trail runs upward through a long series of tight, steep switchbacks. At nearly 4 miles the route levels a bit as the forest finally gives way to heather meadows.

At 4.5 miles you'll pass above Red Pond (elev. 4860 ft)—a short spur trail drops down to it. Huckleberries can be found in season around the pond basin, and a variety of wildflowers color the meadows above and below the pond.

The final 0.5 mile of trail gains 500 feet

View of Guye Peak heading into Commonwealth Basin

Crossing the Kendall Katwalk on the Pacific Crest Trail

as it rises up to the saddle of Red Pass on the ridge between Red Mountain and Lundin Peak. Grand views can be enjoyed from here.

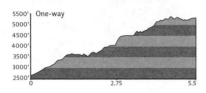

59 Kendall Katwalk

RATING/ DIFFICULTY	ROUND-TRIP	ELEV GAIN/ HIGH POINT	SEASON
*****/4	11 miles	2700 feet/ 5400 feet	July–Oct

One-way

(Elevation profile graph: y-axis 2500' to 5500'; x-axis 0 to 5.5, marked at 2.75)

Map: Green Trails Snoqualmie Pass No. 207; **Contact:** Mount Baker–Snoqualmie National Forest, Snoqualmie Ranger District, North Bend office, (425) 888-1421, *www.fs.fed.us /r6/mbs*; **GPS:** N 47 25.722, W 121 24.806

The Katwalk offers a remarkable hiking experience—striding on a narrow shelf hundreds of feet in the air. The trail, blasted into the cliff face by dynamite crews hanging suspended from ropes, is perfectly safe once the winter's snow has completely melted off. If snow lingers, don't attempt to cross—it's not the place to slip and fall. There is, of course, more to this hike than the just the Katwalk. The Pacific Crest Trail

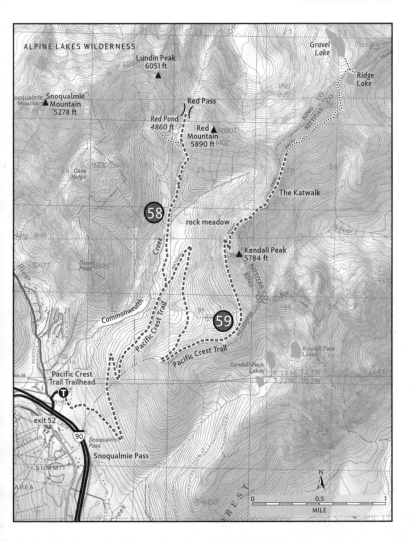

(PCT) climbs from Snoqualmie Pass through old-growth forests, dances through a log-littered avalanche slope (a perfect place to see just how powerful an avalanche can be), and traverses broad, steep-sloped wildflower meadows.

GETTING THERE

From Seattle drive I-90 to exit 52 (signed for Snoqualmie Pass west). At the bottom of the exit ramp, turn left (north) and cross under the freeway. In about 100 yards, turn right onto a dirt road leading into the PCT trailhead.

ON THE TRAIL

Climbing moderately for the first 2.5 miles, the trail runs through forests on the flank of Kendall Peak. At the junction with the Commonwealth Basin Trail (Hike 58), go right and continue up the PCT. Just past that junction, the trail steepens into a series of long switchbacks.

The forest thins as the trail gains elevation, and about 3.5 miles into the hike the forest starts to break up as small clearings and meadows appear. Soon, the trail angles across the open meadows below Kendall Ridge. Red Mountain fills the skyline ahead while wildflowers color the ground around your feet.

These wildflower fields—known to some as Kendall Gardens—continue as the trail crests the ridge and angles north through a jumble of boulders on the ridge top. Finally, at 5.5 miles, the gardens narrow to a mere path, and the path suddenly disappears onto a broad shelf on the east face of the ridge. This is the Katwalk. The timid can turn back on the near side, but most hikers prefer to cross the Katwalk before heading back to the gardens for a leisurely lunch and the return hike to the trailhead.

Kendall Peak as seen from north of the Kendall Katwalk

EXTENDING YOUR TRIP

Those who want to spend the night can continue another 2 miles on relatively level trail to a pair of lakes that border the trail just below Alaska Mountain—the best campsites are just south of Ridge Lake, but Gravel Lake (on the north side of the trail) also has a few good spots.

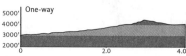

60 Snow Lake

RATING/ DIFFICULTY	ROUND-TRIP	ELEV GAIN/ HIGH POINT	SEASON
****/4	8 miles	1300 feet/ 4400 feet	July–Oct

One-way

Map: Green Trails Snoqualmie Pass No. 207; **Contact:** Mount Baker–Snoqualmie National Forest, Snoqualmie Ranger District, North Bend office, (425) 888-1421, *www.fs.fed.us /r6/mbs*; **GPS:** N 47 26.725, W 121 25.381; **Status:** Rescued

Snow Lake

⭐ If there's such a thing as a wilderness superhighway, this is it. The Snow Lake Trail is Washington's most heavily used trail within a designated wilderness area. On any given summer weekend, you can expect to share the area with upward of two hundred hikers. Fortunately, midweek the route is virtually deserted, and after Labor Day the number of weekend hikers drops to more reasonable levels. Why is it so popular? It's a combination of easy-to-access wilderness trail and a route to one of the most picturesque lakes in the water-rich Alpine Lakes Wilderness. Snow Lake is surrounded by high granite peaks and is visited by deer, mountain goats, and a host of small critters and birds. What's more, the lakeshores are lined with wildflowers in early summer and juicy huckleberries later in the year. All in all, the crowds are justified—few places that are so easy to reach offer such a stunning wilderness experience.

GETTING THERE

From Seattle drive east on I-90 to exit 52 (signed for Snoqualmie Pass west). Turn left (north), crossing under the freeway, and continue to the end of the road at the Alpental Ski Area parking lot.

ON THE TRAIL

Find the trail at the northeastern corner of the broad parking area (directly across from the ski lodge) and start up the long trail as it climbs a series of crib steps. These wooden "cribs" backfilled with dirt earn curses from some hikers, but they were necessary improvements. Volunteers added them in the late 1990s to reverse the ravages of erosion that plagued the trail. As you walk up the steps over the first 0.5 mile or so, take time to admire the workmanship and intensive effort that went into rescuing this trail from destruction. The steps may not match your stride perfectly, but the alternative would be a lost trail.

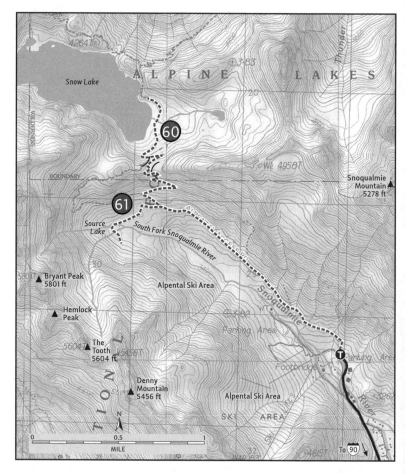

After that first 0.5 mile, the trail traverses the slope above the upper South Fork Snoqualmie River, rolling through forest and occasional alder-filled avalanche chutes for nearly 2.5 miles to a trail junction at that headwall of the valley. A secondary path leads off to the left, contouring around the headwall and leading to Source Lake (Hike 61).

The trail to Snow Lake goes right and climbs long, steep switchbacks up the head-

wall to a high saddle between Snoqualmie Mountain and Chair Peak. As you climb, you'll enjoy increasingly fine views of the craggy peaks of the Snoqualmie Pass area. The long ridge to the southwest starts with Chair Peak at the end of the ridge you're climbing, and south from there is Bryant Peak, The Tooth, and Denny Mountain.

At about 3.5 miles you'll crest the meadow-covered ridge (elev. 4400 ft) and start a moderately steep descent over the last 0.5 mile to the lakeshore. You can stroll all the way around the sprawling lake on boot-beaten trail, but please don't create new paths—or widen any of the other faint way trails that have been kicked into the heather by hikers' boots.

EXTENDING YOUR TRIP

If you want more adventure, continue along the eastern shore of the lake before climbing north along the ridgeline leading to Gem Lake, about 1.5 miles beyond the shores of Snow Lake.

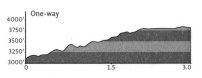

Map: Green Trails Snoqualmie Pass No. 207; **Contact:** Mount Baker–Snoqualmie National Forest, Snoqualmie Ranger District, North Bend office, (425) 888-1421, *www.fs.fed.us /r6/mbs*; **GPS:** N 47 26.725, W 121 25.381

It all starts at Source Lake—the mighty Snoqualmie River flows from this humble pond. But if the pond is humble and less than remarkable, the mountains surrounding it are anything but. The craggy peaks that form a granite fence around the headwaters of the South Fork Snoqualmie form an impressive skyline.

61 Source Lake

RATING/ DIFFICULTY	ROUND-TRIP	ELEV GAIN/ HIGH POINT	SEASON
***/3	6 miles	700 feet/ 3800 feet	July–Oct

Bryant and Chair Peaks above Source Lake

GETTING THERE

From Seattle drive east on I-90 to exit 52 (signed for Snoqualmie Pass west). Turn left (north), crossing under the freeway, and continue to the end of the road at the Alpental Ski Area parking lot.

ON THE TRAIL

The trail starts from the northeastern corner of the broad parking area (directly across from the ski lodge). Head up the Snow Lake Trail (Hike 60), taking a moment to silently thank the volunteers who worked countless hours to save this route from years of neglect. The trail winds upward through a long series of crib steps before turning north on a long, climbing traverse of the lower flank of Snoqualmie Mountain. The trails stays well above the South Fork Snoqualmie River, but crosses many seasonal creeks and seeps as it angles up the valley. Cool fir forest gives way to heat-drenched, alder-clogged avalanche chutes.

Denny Mountain reflected in Lodge Lake

At about 2.5 miles, as the trail sweeps across the headwall of the South Fork basin, stay left on the secondary trail as the main path leads upward to Snow Lake. The Source Lake Trail continues to swing around the headwall, climbing gently for another 0.5 mile. Enjoy a dip in the lake's cool waters while gazing out over the spires and peaks above: Chair Peak, Bryant Peak, The Tooth, Denny Mountain, and Snoqualmie Mountain tower overhead.

62 Lodge Lake

RATING/ DIFFICULTY	ROUND-TRIP	ELEV GAIN/ HIGH POINT	SEASON
**/3	3 miles	500 feet/ 3500 feet	June–Oct

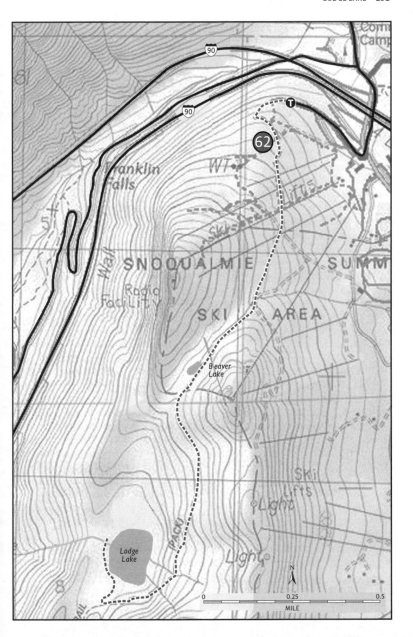

Map: Green Trails Snoqualmie Pass No. 207; **Contact:** Mount Baker–Snoqualmie National Forest, Snoqualmie Ranger District, North Bend office, (425) 888-1421, *www.fs.fed.us /r6/mbs*; **GPS:** N 47 25.640, W 121 25.226

Snoqualmie Pass grows ever more developed each year. Condos go up left and right, the ski area plans new ski lifts (or replacements for existing chairs), and hotels pop up east and west. But even with the development, these are still mountains and there is still stunning mountain scenery to enjoy, even on the fringes of the developed areas. Lodge Lake stands as proof.

GETTING THERE

From Seattle drive east on I-90 to exit 52 (signed for Snoqualmie Pass west). Turn right (south) and right again onto the dirt road leading around the westernmost parking lot of the ski area. Park at the far western end of the road, near the sign marking the Pacific Crest Trail.

ON THE TRAIL

The trail climbs gradually through scrubby forest for 0.5 mile as it makes its way from the freeway corridor. Abruptly, the path erupts out of the trees onto the smooth grassy slopes of the ski runs.

For the next 0.25 mile or so, the trail runs through the sun-filled slopes, crossing under ski lifts and around lift towers before cresting the ridge near the 3500-foot level, about 0.75 mile from the start of the hike.

The trail drops off the ridge in a gentle traverse to a photogenic pond—Beaver Lake—it makes a grand reflecting pool for the surrounding mountain peaks. From Beaver, the trail continues downhill, ending at 1.5 miles on the shores of the tree-lined Lodge Lake. The namesake lodge is long gone (it was a cabin built by The Mountaineers in the

early 1900s), but the lake remains a place for kids and dogs to play while parents enjoy the surrounding mountain scenery.

63 Iron Horse Trail: The Tunnel

RATING/ DIFFICULTY	ROUND-TRIP	ELEV GAIN/ HIGH POINT	SEASON
***/3	6 miles	0 feet/ 1100 feet	May–Oct

Map: Green Trails Snoqualmie Pass No. 207; **Contact:** Washington State Parks, (360) 902-8844, *www.parks.wa.gov*; **Notes:** Tunnel is closed Nov 1–May 1; **GPS:** N 47 23.581, W 121 23.568

Here's a trivia question to toss out during your next trail party: The Iron Horse Trail and Washington's other cross-state trail, the Pacific Crest Trail (PCT), intersect but never touch. Why not? Answer: Because the Iron Horse Trail runs through the 2.3-mile-long Snoqualmie Tunnel while the PCT rolls up and over the peaks south of Snoqualmie Pass. When you head out to explore this dark Iron Horse section, be sure you bring a flashlight—and a headlamp. In fact, make sure every person in your party has a primary light and a backup—this is not a hike you want to do without light. The tunnel is long enough that you'll be in deep, total darkness much of the way. And it's easy to get turned around inside. I've seen savvy hikers bouncing like pinballs inside the tunnel because they couldn't get themselves headed straight down the tunnel after losing their light.

GETTING THERE

From Seattle drive east on I-90 to exit 54. Turn east (left) on State Route 906, and in 0.5 mile turn right on Keechelus Lake Boat Launch Road. In about 200 feet turn right to access the trailhead parking area.

Inside looking out: the Snoqualmie Tunnel

ON THE TRAIL

Find the trail on the south side of the parking area, and turn west to hike along the open railroad trail until you reach the eastern portal to the tunnel. Stop and recheck your flashlight batteries before diving into the darkness.

You might also want to pull on your sweater before you go in so you don't have to fumble in the darkness. It can be 100 degrees Fahrenheit outside on a bright, sunny day, but underground the temperature drops into the 50s. The dampness makes it feel even colder.

Also, note that the tunnel is gated November 1 through May 1 for safety reasons. Giant icicles form in the tunnel during the cold

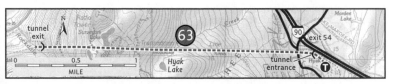

winter months, creating massive spears that could threaten the unwary.

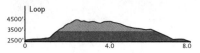

64 Tinkham and Silver Peaks

RATING/ DIFFICULTY	ROUND-TRIP	ELEV GAIN/ HIGH POINT	SEASON
***/3	8 miles	2600 feet/ 4500 feet	July–Oct

Map: Green Trails Snoqualmie Pass No. 207; **Contact:** Okanogan and Wenatchee National Forests, Cle Elum Ranger District,

(509) 852-1100, *www.fs.fed.us/r6/wenatchee*; **Notes:** Northwest Forest Pass required; **GPS:** N 47 21.804, W 121 25.347

Be prepared for animal encounters—the forest and dense underbrush along the lower sections of this route are perfect cover for a host of critters, from raccoons and possums to bobcats, coyotes, badgers, weasels, martens, mink, and more. Pretty alpine meadows also await you on the flanks of rocky Tinkham Peak; sparkling alpine tarns dot the ridgeline. And if you venture up the side trip to Silver Peak, glorious views from the grassy summit spread out like a picnic buffet before

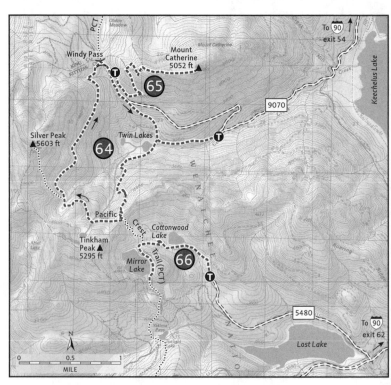

View from summit of Silver Peak

your feet—a veritable feast for the eyes as you look south to the Norse Peak Wilderness, north to the Alpine Lakes Wilderness, west through the gap of Snoqualmie Pass to Granite Mountain, and east into the receding Cascade foothills.

GETTING THERE

From Seattle, drive east on I-90 to exit 54 (signed "Hyak"). At the bottom of the ramp check your odometer, then turn right, followed by a left onto a gravel road leading into a broad parking lot at the base of the Hyak Ski Area. Stay left as you cross the parking lot and find a road (signed "Hyak Estates Drive") leading east out of the center of the parking lot. Continue east through a series of vacation homes and public works buildings. The road soon turns to gravel and becomes Forest Road 9070. Continue up the road to a hairpin turn to

the right, found about 3.5 miles from the interstate ramp (where you checked your mileage, remember?). There is parking at the apex of the corner, or you can move farther above or below the corner to park along the road. The Cold Creek Trail begins at the corner.

ON THE TRAIL

The trail angles off into a tight bramble of slide alder, fireweed, and lupine before climbing slowly into a stand of second-growth forest. The trail stays mostly in the shady forest for the next mile as it climbs gradually to Twin Lakes. The trail splits at the lake basin and you go left. The first 0.5 mile past the lakes leads into a steeply angled tangle of devil's club and stinging nettles. The trail stays above the worst of the pricking weeds, but it's a good idea to resist reaching out for handholds along this trail.

At 2.5 miles from the trailhead, the route reaches a junction with the Pacific Crest Trail (PCT) on the flank of Tinkham Peak. The PCT drops left (south) a mile to reach Mirror Lake (Hike 66), but you should go right and traverse through small meadows and past tiny tarns for a little more than 0.5 mile to reach a climbers path leading to the summit of Silver Peak (see Extending Your Trip).

Continue north around the loop on the PCT to Windy Pass, 5.3 miles from the trailhead. The last 0.6 mile of the route to Windy Pass slices through a relatively fresh clear-cut—the replanted trees are barely taller than most (two-legged) hikers. These types of clearcuts are great habitat for deer, as the absent forest canopy means lots of sun reaching the ground plants, bringing them into lush growth for the deer to munch on.

At Windy Pass the PCT strikes a road. Turn right onto this road and hike 0.6 mile to a trail that drops off the right side of the road. The trail descends the steep slope on a long traverse. The path is brushy for the first 0.5 mile before dropping into trees to roll another 0.6 mile to Twin Lakes and the junction with the Cold Creek Trail, which leads you back to the trailhead in 1 mile.

EXTENDING YOUR TRIP

If summit views are your aim, head up the side trail to Silver Peak. This trail can be difficult to spot—watch for a path leading into the thin forest clearings as the PCT turns almost due north. The scramble to the top of the mountain requires some routefinding skills, as it climbs nearly 1 mile through stands of forest and rocky meadows to the 5603-foot summit. The upper slopes of the peak are carpeted with colorful wildflowers, and the views are wonderful from the top.

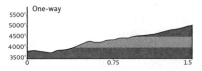

65 Mount Catherine

RATING/ DIFFICULTY	ROUND-TRIP	ELEV GAIN/ HIGH POINT	SEASON
**/3	3 miles	1300 feet/ 5052 feet	July–Oct

One-way

Map: Green Trails Snoqualmie Pass No. 207; **Contact:** Okanogan and Wenatchee National Forests, Cle Elum Ranger District, (509) 852-1100, www.fs.fed.us/r6/wenatchee; **Notes:** Northwest Forest Pass required; **GPS:** N 47 22.2080, W 121 26.658

Cross-country skiers and snowshoers have long enjoyed Mount Catherine, but hikers have pretty much ignored this Snoqualmie Pass peak since the middle of the twentieth century. The route is short, and the close-in views encompass sprawling clear-cuts, so perhaps hikers simply decided it wasn't worth a visit—even map makers have neglected to include the trail on their maps. But when the masses wrote off this route as unworthy, they actually made it more enjoyable for the rest of us. You'll find fine views from Mount Catherine once you lift your eyes above the logging scars on the slopes below. You'll also find broad thickets of huckleberries and an array of birds and animals that take advantage of that abundant juicy fruit.

GETTING THERE

From Seattle, drive east on I-90 to exit 54 (signed "Hyak"). At the bottom of the ramp

Opposite: The sun bursts through the forest fog.

check your odometer, then turn right, followed by a left onto a gravel road leading into a broad parking lot at the base of the Hyak Ski Area. Stay left as you cross the parking lot and find a road (signed "Hyak Estates Drive") leading east out of the center of the parking lot. Continue east through a series of vacation homes and public works buildings. The road soon turns to gravel and becomes Forest Road 9070. Continue up the road past the Tinkham–Silver Peak Trail (Hike 64) to a small parking area signed "Mount Catherine" (if gun nuts haven't blasted the sign to bits again), about 8.5 miles from the freeway.

ON THE TRAIL

The trail climbs east up the flank of Mount Catherine, utilizing an old logging track for the first 0.5 mile. After crossing an old berry-filled clear-cut the trail runs into the forest before climbing switchbacks for 0.7 mile. Most of the elevation gain comes with these hairpin turns. Visit in early August most years and you'll find a rich crop of huckleberries in the trail's first mile.

Once on the ridge top, the trail turns and runs steeply up the spine to the summit of the mountain. Along this section the trail pops in and out of forest, providing grand views as you hike. Tinkham Peak and Silver Peak can be seen to the south and, once atop Catherine, look north to the peaks of Snoqualmie Pass.

Map: Green Trails Snoqualmie Pass No. 207; **Contact:** Okanogan and Wenatchee National Forests, Cle Elum Ranger District, (509) 852-1100, *www.fs.fed.us/r6/wenatchee*; **Notes:** Northwest Forest Pass required. High-clearance vehicle recommended for last 0.5 mile to true trailhead, but can park and walk; **GPS:** N 47 20.645, W 121 25.477

Mirror, mirror, in the mountains: where's the fairest lake of all? Truth be told, the answer isn't Mirror Lake—there are far finer lakes in these lake-rich mountains. But Mirror Lake is arguably the fairest lake of all in the area south of Snoqualmie Pass. This region has been ravaged by logging, and the few pockets of undisturbed wildlands generally are unremarkable. But Mirror Lake sits in a deep basin alongside the Pacific Crest Trail (PCT). Forests line much of the water's edge, but there are plenty of clear banks where you can sit in the sunshine and enjoy the marvelous views over the lake and beyond to the mountains ringing the basin. Sit quietly and you might see kingfishers in the trees or diving on the resident trout. There's also a host of deer living in the region and they make frequent visits to the lake basin for water and rich forage.

GETTING THERE

From Seattle drive east on I-90 to exit 62 (signed "Kachess Lake"). At the bottom of the exit ramp turn right and drive southwest over the Yakima River. At 1.1 miles turn right (northwest) onto Forest Road 5480. Remain on this road as it continues along the shores of Keechelus Lake before climbing above Roaring Creek and then skirting the north shore of Lost Lake. The road continues up the hill above Lost Lake. At 7.1 miles from the freeway the rough gravel road turns into a very rough dirt track. Most hikers prefer to park here (elev. 3600 ft), though those with high-

66 Mirror Lake

RATING/ DIFFICULTY	ROUND-TRIP	ELEV GAIN/ HIGH POINT	SEASON
**/2	2 miles	800 feet/ 4200 feet	June–Oct

A black bear peers through the grass

clearance four-wheel-drives can push on the final 0.5 mile to the trailhead at 3750 feet.

ON THE TRAIL

From the lower parking area walk 0.5 mile up the gently climbing rough road to the true trailhead, found at the switchback in the road. The trail contours away from the road, climbing gradually through brushy forest and old clear-cuts for 0.5 mile before reaching the wading pond called Cottonwood Lake (this lake is too shallow for fish, but perfect for mosquito breeding—don't linger if you value your blood).

From Cottonwood continue upward, pushing north another 0.5 mile to a junction with the PCT at the shores of Mirror Lake. Turn left onto the PCT to walk the shoreline and to find the best reflections in the calm waters. Standing near the outlet stream you'll see Tinkham Peak in the lake's mirror finish.

EXTENDING YOUR TRIP

From Mirror Lake, the PCT continues north for another 200-plus miles. Hike as far north along the PCT as necessary to get your desired mileage in before returning the way you came.

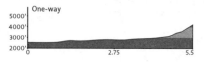

67 Gold Creek–Alaska Lake

RATING/ DIFFICULTY	ROUND-TRIP	ELEV GAIN/ HIGH POINT	SEASON
****/4	11 miles	1600 feet/ 4200 feet	July–Sept

One-way

Map: Green Trails Snoqualmie Pass No. 207;
Contact: Okanogan and Wenatchee National Forests, Cle Elum Ranger District, (509) 852-1100, www.fs.fed.us/r6/wenatchee; **Notes:** Northwest Forest Pass required; **GPS:** N 47 24.068, W 121 22.426

Early in the season, head here. This trail is haphazardly maintained and routefinding on its upper stretches can (and does) prove difficult. But for good routefinders and those who don't mind an occasional deadfall, it's a good early-season route to the high country of Alaska Lake. Even hikers who opt not to push on to Alaska Lake will enjoy the valley hike as it explores the creek basin and its multitude of beaver ponds and flower-filled clearings.

GETTING THERE

From Seattle drive east on I-90 to exit 54 (signed "Hyak"). Turn left (north) under the freeway and right on the frontage road

Gold Creek en route to Alaska Lake

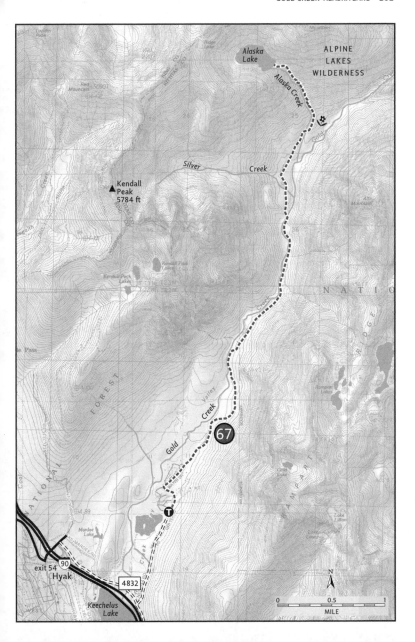

marked "Gold Creek." After about 0.5 mile turn left (north) on Gold Creek Road (Forest Road 4832), and in another 0.5 mile reach a junction. To the left is the Gold Creek Pond area—parking is available there if the road ahead is gated. If the gate is open continue straight ahead and stop at the next gate, about 0.7 mile farther on (steer clear of the private roads and driveways that branch off the main road).

ON THE TRAIL
The route follows the road as it heads north, deeper into the Gold Creek valley. Land on both sides of this road is privately owned, so don't wander off it for the first 0.5 mile. Past the end of the maintained road you'll find yourself on an old, abandoned miners track. This fading roadway peters out in another 0.25 mile, leaving you on a wide single-track trail. The path moves north along the floor of the valley, sometimes stretching out through thick forest, sometimes running along the foot of the slope in the dense vine maple brambles that clog avalanche chutes.

At 2 miles from the second gate the trail enters the Alpine Lakes Wilderness, and a mile farther on you'll cross Gold Creek via a rough-hewn footlog. Look for beaver activity along the creek—spring snowmelt frequently blows out the beaver dams, but they are rebuilt quickly, and the chisel-toothed animals have left their mark on plenty of alders and aspens along the creek shores.

The trail crosses Silver Creek at 3.5 miles. This creek tumbles down from the flanks of Kendall Peak to join Gold Creek. Above this point the trail is frequently brushy and sometimes hard to follow early in the year.

At 4.5 miles cross Alaska Creek and just beyond, in a flower-filled meadow, start the long, steep climb to Alaska Lake. If the climb proves too rough, turn back at the meadow. **Note:** The trail to the lake is frequently eroded by the ever-present water that rushes down from the heights, and dense vegetation—feeding on that same plentiful water—crowds the trail tread nearly into oblivion at times.

Opposite: The Cle Elum River valley as seen from the Paddy-Go-Easy Trail

snoqualmie pass corridor: east

One highway, one mountain pass, two different worlds. Few places in the country sit so closely together yet offer such stark contrasts. The wet west side of the Snoqualmie Pass corridor is filled with musky cedar, hemlock, and Douglas-fir forests. Ferns and mosses abound. Just east of the Cascade Crest, though, you enter a new world. Pines and larches fill the forests. The lush greenery of ferns and moss mostly disappears and hardier sun-loving plants such as huckleberries and heathers replace them. The trails east of Snoqualmie Pass offer sun-filled hikes on ridge tops and into fragrant pine forests. You'll find broad swathes of berry brambles and stunning views from high, open mountaintops.

68 Margaret Lake

RATING/ DIFFICULTY	ROUND-TRIP	ELEV GAIN/ HIGH POINT	SEASON
***/3	6 miles	1200 feet/ 5100 feet	June–Oct

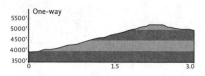

Map: Green Trails Snoqualmie Pass No. 207; **Contact:** Okanogan and Wenatchee National Forests, Cle Elum Ranger District, (509) 852-1100, *www.fs.fed.us/r6/wenatchee*; **Notes:** Northwest Forest Pass required; **GPS:** N 47 21.851, W 121 21.490

Who wants to hike in old clear-cuts? When they're packed with huckleberries, I do! If the huckleberries aren't ripe yet, you'll find paintbrush, lupine, columbine, and other wildflowers coloring the trail. Besides, the old clear-cuts found on the lower portion of this route peter out quickly as you climb the ridge before dropping into the picturesque lake basin.

GETTING THERE

From Seattle drive east on I-90 to exit 54 (signed "Hyak"). Turn left (north) under the freeway and right on the frontage road marked "Gold Creek." After about 0.5 mile turn left (north) on Gold Creek Road (Forest Road 4832) and drive east, parallel to the interstate briefly before the road angles upward. At 3.9 miles from the freeway turn left onto FR 4934, and in 0.25 mile look for the parking lot on the left.

ON THE TRAIL

Head up the gravel road leading past the parking lot and in 0.25 mile veer left onto a small dirt road. Hike around an old cable gate and climb the dirt road as it slants steeply upward into an old clear-cut. Don't let the ugly connotations of that label fool you, however. This field of stumps has been reclaimed by native flora—acres of huckleberries punctuated by an array of wildflowers. Beargrass, lupine, paintbrush, tiger lilies, fireweed, and more grace these slopes.

The road peters out in 0.5 mile and the narrow trail weaves upward, providing great views south over Keechelus Lake and back up toward Snoqualmie Pass. As you near the ridge Mount Rainier comes into view far to the south, too.

About 1.5 miles from the trailhead, the trail enters forest and, at 2 miles, reaches a junction near the ridgeline. To the left is Lake Lillian (Hike 69). Turn right instead to cross the ridge and descend a steep mile to Margaret Lake. The lake is a wonderful place to relax and enjoy a refreshing dip after lunch before heading back up and over the ridge.

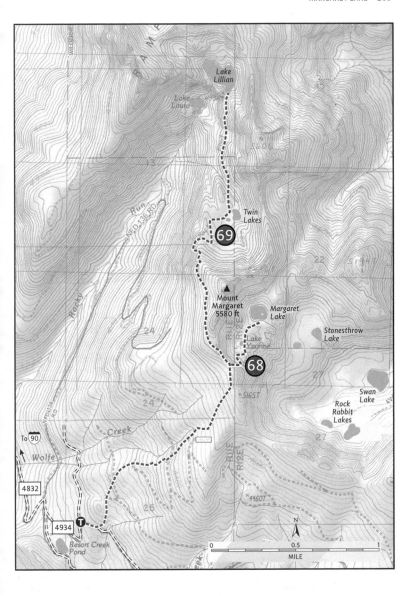

Hiker at Lake Margaret in thick morning fog

EXTENDING YOUR TRIP

Campsites ring the lake, and on the ridge below the pool you can see other small jewels glittering in the sun—Stonesthrow, Rock Rabbit, and Swan Lakes perch precariously on the slope under Margaret. Rough, boot-beaten trails lead down to these colorfully named alpine ponds.

69 Twin Lakes and Lake Lillian

RATING/ DIFFICULTY	ROUND-TRIP	ELEV GAIN/ HIGH POINT	SEASON
****/3	9 miles	1500 feet/ 5300 feet	June–Oct

One-way

[elevation profile: 3500'–5500', from 0 to 4.5 miles with marker at 2.25]

Opposite: Orange butterfly on a coltsfoot bloom

Map: Green Trails Snoqualmie Pass No. 207; **Contact:** Okanogan and Wenatchee National Forests, Cle Elum Ranger District, (509) 852-1100, *www.fs.fed.us/r6/wenatchee*; **Notes:** Northwest Forest Pass required; **GPS:** N 47 21.851, W 121 21.490

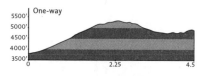 You'll run the gamut of scenery here, from clear-cuts, to ancient forests, to huckleberry fields, to alpine lakes. The route climbs up and over a forested ridge, rolls past an assortment of lakes, and provides great opportunities to see birds of prey hunting overhead and small mammals browsing underfoot. The best wildlife viewing comes in the clear-cuts thanks to the abundance of huckleberries growing in those man-made meadows. The lake basin also offers wildlife viewing, as beasts and birds flock to the pools to drink and to graze on

the lakeside vegetation. The lakes themselves are marvelous alpine wonders. Twin Lakes sparkle blue amid green and red heather, while Lake Lillian is a deep gem set in a granite cirque.

GETTING THERE
From Seattle drive east on I-90 to exit 54 (signed "Hyak"). Turn left (north) under the freeway and right on the frontage road marked "Gold Creek." After about 0.5 mile turn left (north) on Gold Creek Road (Forest Road 4832) and drive east, parallel to the interstate briefly before the road angles upward. At 3.9 miles from the freeway turn left onto FR 4934, and in 0.25 mile look for the parking lot on the left.

ON THE TRAIL
Walk up the road leading past the parking lot, then veer around an old cable gate and climb the dirt road as it slants steeply upward into an old clear-cut. The road peters out in 0.5 mile and the narrow trail weaves upward, providing great views south over Keechelus Lake and back up toward Snoqualmie Pass. As you near the ridge Mount Rainier comes into view far to the south.

About 1.5 miles from the trailhead the trail enters forest and, at 2 miles, reaches a junction near the ridgeline. To the right is Margaret Lake (Hike 68).

Go left and continue north 1.2 miles to Twin Lakes (elev. 4700 ft). These dual pools are shallow and sandy bottomed. They are popular with birds of all kinds, but look especially for nutcrackers and small songbirds—the shallow lakes and vegetation-rich meadows are full of insects for the birds to feed on.

From Twin Lakes the trail drops steeply, losing 150 feet in elevation, then climbs just as steeply back up 250 feet to reach the shores of Lake Lillian at 4.5 miles.

View down on Rachel Lake from Rampart Ridge

70 Rachel Lake

RATING/ DIFFICULTY	ROUND-TRIP	ELEV GAIN/ HIGH POINT	SEASON
****/4	8 miles	1600 feet/ 4600 feet	July–Oct

Maps: Green Trails Snoqualmie Pass No. 207 and Kachess Lake No. 208; **Contact:** Okanogan and Wenatchee National Forests, Cle Elum Ranger District, (509) 852-1100, *www .fs.fed.us/r6/wenatchee*; **Notes:** Northwest Forest Pass required; **GPS:** N 47 24.071, W 121 17.086; **Status:** Endangered

The condition of the trail to Rachel Lake and the lake's environs exhibit what can happen when too many nature-loving hikers are unleashed on a fragile landscape. Though you'll enjoy spectacular views at the lake and en route, closer examination reveals a web of way trails stomped into the fragile meadows around the lake. And heavy use and poor trail planning have left the trail in rough condition. You'll splash up a track marred by mud and water, with seasonal streams running down the middle of the trail at times. You'll also fight crowds for the right to that sloppy trail, which receives unbelievably heavy use every weekend in the summer. For maximum benefit visit midweek or after Labor Day.

GETTING THERE

From Seattle take I-90 east to exit 62 (signed "Kachess Lake"). Turn left from the exit ramp and drive northeast on Kachess Lake Road (Forest Road 49) toward Kachess Lake. Follow the signs to Lake Kachess Campground. Turn left on FR 4930, which leads about 4 miles to a large parking lot and the trailhead at the road's end.

ON THE TRAIL

The trail runs into the forest of the Box Canyon Creek, climbing gradually for the first mile before leveling out for another 1.5 miles. The path stretches along the flank of Hibox Mountain, with occasional views up the face of Hibox and across the valley to Alta Mountain.

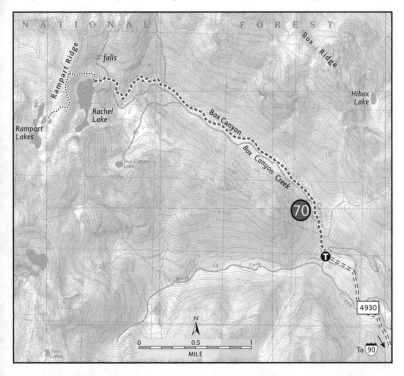

Mostly, though, the trail stays under the trees, keeping you cool and well shaded as you head for the head of the Box Canyon.

There, at about 2.5 miles, the trail starts upward, climbing steeply as it gains more than 1300 feet in the next mile. That cruel pace is made all the more difficult because of the trail's poor condition. Seasonal streams spring from the headwall slope, trickling down onto the trail until they merge into a muddy stream. Effort has been made to divert the water off the trail tread, but just as soon as one ribbon of water is siphoned off, another streams down to take its place.

At about 3.5 miles out, just as your legs are getting weak and your lungs are burning from the climb, the trail levels out and rolls through the splashing spray at the foot of a gorgeous and refreshingly cool fantail waterfall. Stop for pictures and a moment of rest before tiptoe-ing along the logs that cross the creek below the falls.

The next 0.5 mile of trail climbs more moderately before thrusting you out onto the sunlit shores of Rachel Lake. Try to stay on the primary trail around the lake—too many boots have stomped across the fragile heather and moss meadows, creating a web of way trails that are slow to heal.

Find a suitable rock on which to relax while enjoying the views of the broad lake and the towering wall of Rampart Ridge beyond.

HOW TO HELP THIS TRAIL

The best way to help protect this trail is to hike it, and then let the local ranger district know that you have visited and think the trail is a valuable part of the backcountry trail network in this area. But don't just call: put it in writing. Send a letter, describing your experience

Rampart Lakes area in autumn

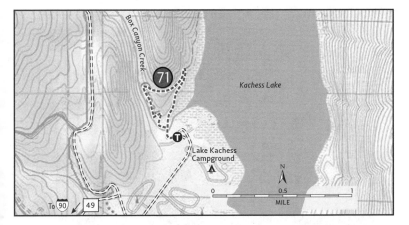

and where you see need for improvements (e.g., reconstruction of trail tread, brush cutting, log removal, etc.). Send the letter to the ranger and to the good folks at the Washington Trails Association, the leading volunteer trail-maintenance organization in the state.

EXTENDING YOUR TRIP
If you haven't worked enough, push on past Rachel Lake. The trail continues straight along the north shore of the lake, climbing 0.5 mile through a steep series of switchbacks to a saddle on Rampart Ridge (elev. 5100 ft). Once on the ridge, turn left and ramble along the ridge top for a bit over 1 mile to enter the pothole country of Rampart Lakes—a series of cool blue ponds nestled in depressions in the granite basin atop the ridge.

Kachess Lake

RATING/ DIFFICULTY	ROUND-TRIP	ELEV GAIN/ HIGH POINT	SEASON
***/1	1 mile	50 feet/ 2300 feet	July–Oct

Map: Green Trails Kachess Lake No. 208; **Contact:** Okanogan and Wenatchee National Forests, Cle Elum Ranger District, (509) 852-

1100, www.fs.fed.us/r6/wenatchee; **Notes:** Northwest Forest Pass required; **GPS:** N 47 21.522, W 121 14.763; **Status:** Endangered

This trail proves that not all hikes have to be epic outings to be enjoyable. Though short, this loop is a great learning adventure for folks of all ages. Preteen kids will especially love exploring its watery world of lakes and creeks, as well as diving deep into century-old forests.

GETTING THERE
From Seattle drive east on I-90 and take exit 62 (signed "Kachess Lake"). Turn left from the exit ramp and drive northeast on Lake Kachess Road (Forest Road 49) for 5 miles to a three-way intersection. Turn right and enter the Lake Kachess Campground. Just past the fee booth at the entrance (camping fee only), turn left and drive about 0.5 mile to the parking area for Little Kachess Trail No. 1312.

ON THE TRAIL
The hard-packed trail is open and accessible for all users, including folks in wheelchairs, making it perfect for anyone. Toddlers can bobble along, as can those who want a nature

Footbridge over Box Canyon Creek

adventure but can't walk far. The grade is gentle and the trail well maintained.

The trail loops over the pretty little Box Canyon Creek—stop on the bridge and peer down, trying to spot the small trout that dart through the clear waters in pursuit of aquatic insects. Once over the creek the trail climbs gently to a bench above the lake that provides views down on the creek and along the lakeshore.

The return portion of the loop rolls over a slab of moss-covered rock as big as a parking lot—note the many tall trees growing from this seemingly solid surface. Kids will marvel at the work of seeds and roots in forcing the rock open to allow the trees to grow.

HOW TO HELP THIS TRAIL

The best way to help protect this trail is to hike it, and then let the local ranger district know that you have visited and think the trail is a valuable part of the backcountry trail network in this area. But don't just call: put it in writing. Send a letter, describing your experience and where you see need for improvements (e.g., reconstruction of trail tread, brush cutting, log removal, etc.). Send the letter to the ranger and to the good folks at the Washington Trails Association, the leading volunteer trail-maintenance organization in the state.

72 Kachess Ridge

RATING/ DIFFICULTY	ROUND-TRIP	ELEV GAIN/ HIGH POINT	SEASON
****/3	6 miles	2200 feet/ 4600 feet	June–Oct

Map: Green Trails Kachess Lake No. 208; **Contact:** Okanogan and Wenatchee National Forests, Cle Elum Ranger District, (509) 852-1100, *www.fs.fed.us/r6/wenatchee;* **Notes:** Northwest Forest Pass required; **GPS:** N 47 16.032, W 121 10.424; **Status:** Endangered

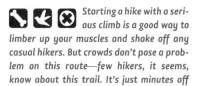 Starting a hike with a serious climb is a good way to limber up your muscles and shake off any casual hikers. But crowds don't pose a problem on this route—few hikers, it seems, know about this trail. It's just minutes off the interstate, with grand views of the three big lakes of the eastern Snoqualmie Pass corridor (Keechelus, Kachess, and Cle Elum). You'll also find panoramic views that encompass the peaks of the Cle Elum Valley and reach south to Mount Rainier.

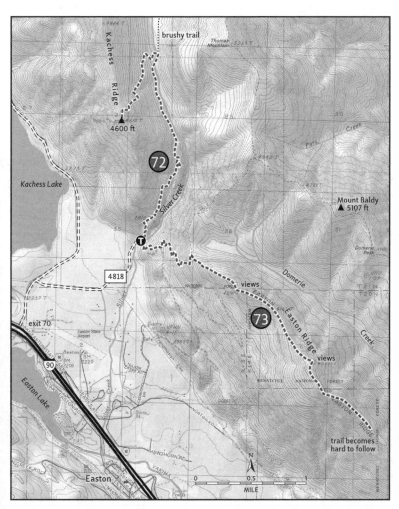

GETTING THERE

From Seattle drive I-90 over Snoqualmie Pass to exit 70. After exiting, turn left over the interstate and then turn left onto the frontage road. Continue a short distance before turning right onto Forest Road 4818 (signed "Kachess Ridge and Easton Ridge"). Drive about 1 mile, then turn right at the next road junction and continue another 0.5 mile to the trailhead.

ON THE TRAIL

From the trailhead, the hike to Kachess Ridge climbs to the left while a second path leads off to the right—south—along Easton Ridge (Hike 73). The trail wastes no time in starting to climb, running steeply up the nose of the tall face of Kachess Ridge. As you climb, the forest opens periodically to provide views south to Mount Baldy, Domerie Peak, and Easton Ridge.

Rather than continue straight up to the ridge top, the trail angle moderates just past 1 mile, running almost level for the next 0.75 mile as it follows the tumbling waters of Silver Creek upstream.

At 1.9 miles (elev. 3800 ft) the trail splits. The main trail continues right, up Silver Creek, paralleling the long spine of Kachess Ridge. Our route goes left, climbing through a couple of gentle switchbacks away from the creek.

Meadows along Kachess Ridge

The trail then straightens out for a long, climbing run up the ridge to a high knob (elev. 4600 ft) at the southern end of Kachess Ridge. This unnamed peak was used in the past as a base for an air-traffic beacon. Outstanding views await you, looking out on the deep basin of Kachess Lake, south to Mount Baldy, and west to Ambilis Mountain.

HOW TO HELP THIS TRAIL

The mile-long spur trail from the Kachess Ridge Trail to the Kachess Beacon site is rough and poorly maintained. After hiking it, write the Forest Service and ask them to devote some trail-maintenance resources to this endangered trail, and send a copy of your letter to the good folks at the Washington Trails Association, the leading volunteer trail-maintenance organization in the state.

73 Easton Ridge

RATING/ DIFFICULTY	ROUND-TRIP	ELEV GAIN/ HIGH POINT	SEASON
****/4	6 miles	2270 feet/ 4470 feet	June–Oct

One-way

```
5000'
4000'
3000'
2000'
     0            1.5           3.0
```

Map: Green Trails Kachess Lake No. 208; **Contact:** Okanogan and Wenatchee National Forests, Cle Elum Ranger District, (509) 852-1100, www.fs.fed.us/r6/wenatchee; **Notes:** Northwest Forest Pass required; **GPS:** N 47 16.032, W 121 10.424; **Status:** Endangered

Easton Ridge once sported a wonderful trail along its entire length. Hikers can still enjoy that long high route, but the trail disappears in the middle and the southern end is hard to ac-cess. Fortunately, the best of the trail is the northern end, where you'll find grand views, rich huckleberry brambles, and endless opportunities to enjoy wildlife—especially the feathered variety. The Easton area is home to one of the largest populations of turkey vultures in the state, and the massive birds of prey (or birds of opportunity, if you prefer) soar en masse over the thermal-producing faces of Easton and Kachess Ridges. Of course, those big birds of opportunity are here for a reason—the region has healthy populations of mammals, big and small, from marmots to mountain goats, beavers to bull elk. Keep your eyes open and you'll see a wide range of critters.

GETTING THERE

From Seattle drive east on I-90 to exit 70. After exiting, turn left over the interstate and then turn left onto the frontage road. Continue a short distance before turning right onto Forest Road 4818 (signed "Kachess Ridge and Easton Ridge"). Drive about 1 mile, then turn right at the next road junction and continue another 0.5 mile to the trailhead.

ON THE TRAIL

Find the trailhead near the parking area, then take the right-hand path (Trail No. 1308.2) as it climbs steeply (!) to the southeast, plunging straight up the steep face of the wall above Silver Creek (Hike 72 is the left-hand trail). The trail switchbacks for more than 0.75 mile, gaining 1000 feet, to reach the junction with the Easton Ridge Trail (elev. 3400 ft).

Turn right at the trail junction to head south along the ridgeline. In the next 2 miles you'll climb gradually to a 4470-foot viewpoint on the ridge. Peer down to the small community of Easton alongside Lake Easton. On the other side (to the east) look across the Domerie Creek valley to Domerie Peak and Mount Baldy.

Dennis Long hiking Easton Ridge in spring

HOW TO HELP THIS TRAIL

The best way to help protect this trail is to hike it, and then let the local ranger district know that you have visited and think the trail is a valuable part of the backcountry trail network in this area. But don't just call: put it in writing. Send a letter, describing your experience and where you see need for improvements (e.g., reconstruction of trail tread, brush cutting, log removal, etc.). Send the letter to the ranger and to the good folks at the Washington Trails Association, the leading volunteer trail-maintenance organization in the state.

Map: Green Trails Kachess Lake No. 208; **Contact:** Okanogan and Wenatchee National Forests, Cle Elum Ranger District, (509) 852-1100, *www.fs.fed.us/r6/wenatchee*; **Notes:** Northwest Forest Pass required; **GPS:** N 47 22.399, W 121 9.466; **Status:** Endangered

This loop offers outstanding rewards but demands serious effort in payment. The trail has suffered years of neglect, leaving the route rough. Add the strenuous climbs and you have a hike that taxes even the toughest hikers. In return, though, hikers will find views that are unmatched in this part of the state.

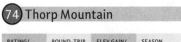

74 Thorp Mountain

RATING/ DIFFICULTY	ROUND-TRIP	ELEV GAIN/ HIGH POINT	SEASON
***/4	10 miles	2300 feet/ 5854 feet	June–Oct

From the fire-lookout cabin atop the heather-carpeted peak you can scan the horizon in every direction, picking out peaks and valleys throughout the Alpine Lakes Wilderness and south all the way to Mount Rainier (on clear days). The ridges rolling away from Thorp Mountain sport colorful flower meadows, and the blue pool of Kachess Lake sparkles in the deep valley at its foot.

GETTING THERE

From Seattle drive east on I-90 to take exit 80 (signed "Roslyn/Salmon la Sac"). Head north on Salmon la Sac Road (State Route 903) about 15 miles, passing through Roslyn and past Cle Elum Lake. Just past the upper end of the lake, turn left onto French Cabin Road (Forest Road 4308). Drive 3.25 miles up FR 4308 to FR 4312 on the right. Go right and drive 1.5 miles to another road junction, with FR 4312-121. This road is typically gated, so park here (don't block the gate).

ON THE TRAIL

Walk around the gate and walk 0.25 mile to a bridge over Thorp Creek. Cross the creek and turn left. The true trail starts 0.25 mile up this road on the left. The trail climbs steadily but modestly as it parallels tumbling Thorp Creek. Keep your eyes wide open and you might spot a lot of wildlife along the lower trail, especially as the path leaves the stands of forest and pops briefly into old, overgrown clear-cuts. These transition zones are popular places for

USFS worker John Morrow at the Thorp Mountain fire lookout

deer to hang out, since they provide good cover (the forest) as well as close proximity to good browse (in the clear-cuts).

About 1.5 miles from the gate the trail starts to climb more steeply, angling upward away from the creek. The forest thins with increasing elevation, providing more sun breaks and viewpoints.

At nearly 3 miles a small side trail drops 0.5 mile to Thorp Lake. If time permits this makes a nice side trip. Otherwise, continue climbing as the trail sweeps upward around the headwall of the Thorp Valley.

At 3.4 miles another junction is reached, this time with the Kachess Ridge Trail. Stay left as this trail angles west around the flank of Thorp Mountain, and in 0.2 mile go right to climb the steep 0.3-mile scramble trail to the top of the mountain and its awesome views.

To complete the loop, drop back down the 0.3 mile to the Kachess Ridge Trail and follow it northeast along No Name Ridge for 1.5 miles. At that point, about 5.9 miles from the gate, turn right onto a faint trail heading west and follow it to Little Joe Lake, at 8.5 miles.

This trail can be brushy and hard to follow at times. At Little Joe turn right and descend 1.5 miles back to the gate.

HOW TO HELP THIS TRAIL

The best way to help protect this trail is to hike it, and then let the local ranger district know that you have visited and think the trail is a valuable part of the backcountry trail network in this area. But don't just call: put it in writing. Send a letter, describing your experience and where you see need for improvements (e.g., reconstruction of trail tread, brush cutting, log removal, etc.). Send the letter to the ranger and to the good folks at the Washington Trails Association, the leading volunteer trail-maintenance organization in the state.

75 French Cabin Creek

RATING/ DIFFICULTY	ROUND-TRIP	ELEV GAIN/ HIGH POINT	SEASON
****/3	7 miles	1400 feet/ 5500 feet	June–Oct

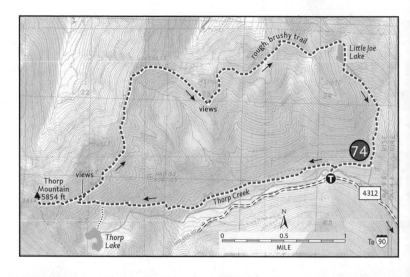

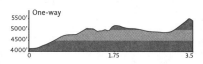

One-way

5500'
5000'
4500'
4000'
0   1.75   3.5

Map: Green Trails Kachess Lake No. 208;
Contact: Okanogan and Wenatchee National
Forests, Cle Elum Ranger District, (509) 852-
1100, www.fs.fed.us/r6/wenatchee; **Notes:**
Northwest Forest Pass required. High-
clearance vehicle recommended for last 0.5
mile to true trailhead, but can park and walk;
GPS: N 47 19.971, W 121 10.816

*A moderate hike leads
through open pine forests,
across sprawling fields of flowers, and to
glorious views of surrounding alpine peaks.
Lupine, shooting stars, beargrass—the
French Cabin Creek basin has them all. Birds
and beasts, including deer and elk, love the
meadows and open forests for the dense insect population and nutrient-rich forage.
Fortunately, the lack of standing water
means most of the bugs are creepy crawlers
rather than buzzing skeeters, which leaves
you free to enjoy the grand views and lush
flora and fauna without pesky biters and
blood suckers.*

GETTING THERE

From Seattle drive east on I-90 to take exit 80
(signed "Roslyn/Salmon la Sac"). Head north
on Salmon la Sac Road (State Route 903) about
15 miles, passing through Roslyn and past Cle
Elum Lake. Just past the upper end of the lake,
turn left onto French Cabin Road (Forest Road
4308). Drive 6.5 miles up FR 4308 to a small
dirt road, FR 4308-132 (marked with a sign for
French Cabin Creek Trail). Turn right onto this
road and drive 0.5 mile to the road's end. FR
4308-132 is narrow and rough. Those driving
low-clearance passenger cars should park at

French Cabin Basin

the bottom of the road and walk the 0.5 mile
to the trailhead.

ON THE TRAIL

The trail starts with a steady climb up a
steep, badly eroded trail through the forest.
For nearly 1 mile the route stays under the
overhanging branches, providing relief from
the sun but no views and little local scenery
to enjoy (occasional forest glades do provide
glimpses of tiny forest flowers, like avalanche
and glacier lilies).

At 1 mile the trail breaks out into a clearing
with views up to the spires of French Cabin
Mountain. In another 0.25 mile the scattered
clumps of trees and meadows give way to a
small section of clear-cut as the trail hooks
out into a section of private timberland.

Just inside the clear-cut, the trail splits.
Stay left and descend briefly before climbing

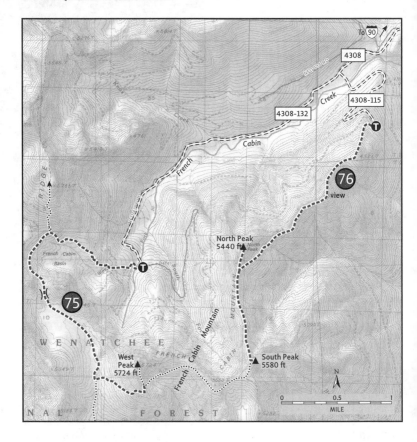

once more to reach a high pass (elev. 5000 ft) separating the forest and meadows of French Cabin Creek's basin from the sprawling meadows of Silver Creek basin. Stop and enjoy the views of the flower fields before you drop steeply into Silver Creek's meadows. Then for more than 1.5 miles you'll climb gently as you wander through grass and knee-high wildflowers in the sun-drenched meadows below French Cabin Mountain.

At 3.5 miles from the trailhead you'll find another trail junction. Heading left here leads you up to the flank of West Peak for great views of the Kachess Ridge and French Cabin peaks. Turn around and head back the way you came before the trail starts to descend the other side.

76 French Cabin Mountain

RATING/ DIFFICULTY	ROUND-TRIP	ELEV GAIN/ HIGH POINT	SEASON
****/5	6 miles	1750 feet/ 5580 feet	July–Oct

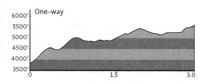

Map: Green Trails Kachess Lake No. 208; **Contact:** Okanogan and Wenatchee National Forests, Cle Elum Ranger District, (509) 852-1100, *www.fs.fed.us/r6/wenatchee;* **Notes:** Northwest Forest Pass required; **GPS:** N 47 21.041, W 121 8.185

Wildflowers near French Cabin Mountain

You'll climb in a long, steady push over the course of this 3-mile trail. No switchbacks, few turns, just a straight out and back to the South Peak of French Cabin Mountain— dropping briefly, then climbing steeply again to skirt just below the lower North Peak on the way. Near the southern summit the trail pierces sprawling wildflower meadows, with expansive views in all directions. Down near the start of the trail, you'll enjoy the cooling shade of pine forests. This is a lonesome path, with few visitors and no water, so make sure you pack everything you need.

GETTING THERE
From Seattle drive east on I-90 to take exit 80 (signed "Roslyn/Salmon la Sac"). Head north on the Salmon la Sac Road (State Route 903) about 15 miles, passing through Roslyn and past Cle Elum Lake. Just past the upper end of the lake, turn left onto French Cabin Road (Forest Road 4308). Drive 3.8 miles up FR 4308 and turn left onto FR 4308-115. Follow this rough road about 1.9 miles to the Domerie Peak trailhead, located at a sharp right-hand turn.

ON THE TRAIL
Start up the trail (No. 1308) as it climbs straight up the hillside above the road, without the benefit of switchbacks. You'll climb for the first 1.2 miles, pushing upward to a 5000-foot knoll, before dropping briefly and then climbing steeply onto the meadow-crowned top of North Peak at around 2 miles. You'll have to scramble off-trail a few hundred yards to attain the true 5440-foot summit.

Another mile or so of rolling up and down along the ridge leads to South Peak (elev. 5580 ft). The trail continues past this meadow-covered summit to a junction with the French Cabin Creek Trail (Hike 75). Stop at the top, though, for the best views: south to Mount Rainier, north to Thorp Mountain, east to Cle Elum Lake and the Sasse Mountain/Hex

Mountain ridgeline, and west to West Peak and the long line of Kachess Ridge.

77 Pete Lake

RATING/ DIFFICULTY	ROUND-TRIP	ELEV GAIN/ HIGH POINT	SEASON
***/3	9 miles	400 feet/ 3200 feet	May–Oct

Map: Green Trails Kachess Lake No. 208; **Contact:** Okanogan and Wenatchee National Forests, Cle Elum Ranger District, (509) 852-1100, www.fs.fed.us/r6/wenatchee; **Notes:** Northwest Forest Pass required; **GPS:** N 47 26.097, W 121 11.127

  With little elevation gain, plenty of scenery, and a broad, sun-warmed forest lake at the end of the valley, this hike makes a great warm-up outing for you and your kids. You can enjoy a refreshing swim in the lake before turning around and returning along the gentle forest trail.

GETTING THERE
From Seattle drive east on I-90 to take exit 80 (signed "Roslyn/Salmon la Sac"). Head north on Salmon la Sac Road (State Route 903) about 15 miles, passing through Roslyn and past Cle Elum Lake. Turn left (west) onto Forest Road 46 and drive 5 miles to Cooper Lake. Turn right onto FR 4616, crossing Cooper River, and continue 1 mile past the upper loops of the campground to the trailhead at the end of the road near the upper end of the lake.

ON THE TRAIL
This trail is essentially a continuation of the Cooper River Trail (Hike 78), as it follows the

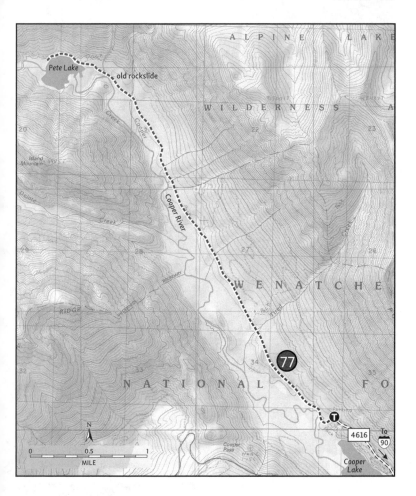

broad Cooper River valley upstream from Cooper Lake to its headwaters at Pete Lake. The trail begins in deep forest, with close views of the river during the early stretch. Watch for activity in the deeper pools, as beavers are making every effort to turn the river into a series of interconnected ponds.

The valley is blanketed with thick old-growth forest and the occasional river meadow, but few distant views. The lack of vistas, though, means you can focus on close-in scenery. Lush foliage and forest wildflowers line the trail. All that vegetation means good feeding for wildlife. Rabbits, weasels, fishers, and martens scurry around the bushes. Blacktail deer roam in great numbers through the area, and bobcats, coyotes, and cougars prowl around the lairs of those vegetarian beasts.

Pete Lake

As the trail nears the lake, around the 3-mile mark, it passes an old, massive rockslide. The slide covers the south side of the valley. The trail skirts the worst of the rubble, but provides good views of the pile of rock and displaced earth.

Pete Lake fills a broad basin near the upper end of the valley. The eastern shore of the lake offers good views of Big Summit Chief Mountain to the west and the surrounding ridges. The lake boasts a healthy population of rainbow trout—you might be lucky enough to pull a pan-sized fish out of the lake for a lunch-time protein burst.

78 Cooper River

RATING/ DIFFICULTY	ROUND-TRIP	ELEV GAIN/ HIGH POINT	SEASON
**/2	6 miles	400 feet/ 2800 feet	May–Oct

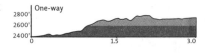

Map: Green Trails Kachess Lake No. 208; **Contact:** Okanogan and Wenatchee National Forests, Cle Elum Ranger District, (509) 852-1100, *www.fs.fed.us/r6/wenatchee*; **Notes:** Northwest Forest Pass required; **GPS:** N 47 24.264, W 121 5.947

This riverside trail offers no expansive views and doesn't explore any wildflower meadows or high alpine country. But it does track alongside a beautiful mountain river that sports a healthy population of hungry

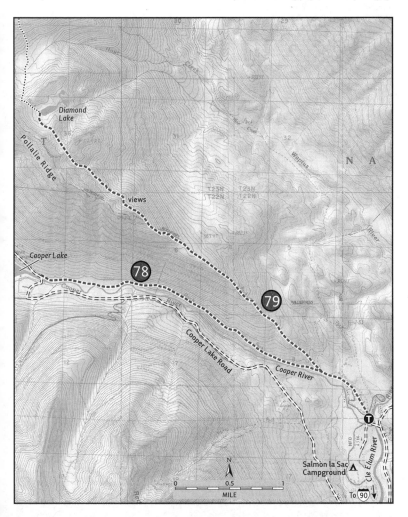

trout. It also provides ample opportunity to practice your bird-watching, as a number of avian species thrive here, including the river-loving water ouzel and the fish-loving kingfisher. The trip can be done as a one-way hike by shuttling vehicles or by hitching a ride back down the road from Cooper Lake.

GETTING THERE

From Seattle drive east on I-90 to take exit 80 (signed "Roslyn/Salmon la Sac"). Head north on Salmon la Sac Road (State Route 903) about 15 miles, passing through Roslyn and past Cle Elum Lake to Salmon la Sac. At the Y in the road near the Salmon la Sac Campground, take the left branch toward the campground. Cross

Cooper River gorge below the trail

the Cle Elum River bridge and turn right, away from the campground, and reach the trailhead parking area in another 0.5 mile.

ON THE TRAIL

The trail follows the pretty Cooper River valley upstream to Cooper Lake. The trail stays on the north side of the creek, and at times the valley narrows enough for you to hear (and possibly see) traffic on the road that runs on the other side of the valley. Ignore that interruption as you explore the dense old-growth forest around you.

The trail splits 0.7 mile from the trailhead. To the right is a path that climbs steeply up Polallie Ridge (Hike 79). Continue to the left instead, staying close to the river. If you're an angler keep an eye out for likely fishing holes. Take your time—the trail is gentle enough for you to adopt a mile-eating pace between fishing sessions.

About 2 miles from the trailhead the valley broadens a bit and the river begins to meander side-to-side across the gentle valley floor. You'll find some small patches of berries here, and occasional clumps of wildflowers along the river banks.

At 3 miles you'll encounter the Cooper Lake Road, which crosses Cooper River just below the lake outlet. Turn around here, or cross the road bridge to access the road leading back down to Salmon la Sac.

Map: Green Trails Kachess Lake No. 208; **Contact:** Okanogan and Wenatchee National Forests, Cle Elum Ranger District, (509) 852-1100, *www.fs.fed.us/r6/wenatchee*; **Notes:** Northwest Forest Pass required; **GPS:** N 47 24.264, W 121 5.947

Pack sunscreen, your wildflower guide, binoculars for bird-watching, and water—plenty of water! This trail climbs ceaselessly along an open ridge, providing some of the greatest panoramic views to be found in the eastern Cascades. This is also a bird-rich region, thanks to the plethora of wildflowers and their associated insect populations, and a popular grazing route for deer and even herds of mountain goats. This all adds up to a wonderful wilderness experience. All you have to do to enjoy it is plod upward, endlessly, on a sun-baked trail without a bit of water in sight.

GETTING THERE

From Seattle drive east on I-90 to take exit 80 (signed "Roslyn/Salmon la Sac"). Head north on Salmon la Sac Road (State Route 903) about 15 miles, passing through Roslyn and past Cle Elum Lake to Salmon la Sac. At the Y in the road near the Salmon la Sac Campground, take the left branch toward the campground. Cross the Cle Elum River bridge and turn right, away from the campground, and reach the trailhead parking area in another 0.5 mile.

ON THE TRAIL

The trail begins with a long climb up the eastern side of Polallie Ridge, ascending exposed switchbacks that weave through rock gardens. Pause frequently to enjoy the views across the Cle Elum Valley to Jolly and Sasse Mountains. In 3 miles the trail finally tapers to a more moderate pitch at around 5000 feet elevation. But the respite from the climbing is short lived.

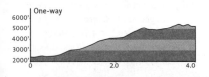

79 Polallie Ridge

RATING/ DIFFICULTY	ROUND-TRIP	ELEV GAIN/ HIGH POINT	SEASON
*****/5	8 miles	3000 feet/ 5300 feet	June–Oct

One-way

View of Mount Hinman from Polallie Ridge

A few hundred yards of easy ridgetop hiking is followed by a roll down to 4800 feet elevation, then a climb up to 5300 feet. Soon, it's down to 4900 feet, then up to 5200. The saving grace are the stellar views all along the way, with a jewel of a lake—Diamond Lake—nestled in a broad meadow about 4 miles up the trail.

EXTENDING YOUR TRIP

If you haven't worked enough, press on up the ridge. You can add another 2.5 miles of climbing to get to a 5422-foot knob above Tired Creek.

80 Davis Peak

RATING/ DIFFICULTY	ROUND-TRIP	ELEV GAIN/ HIGH POINT	SEASON
*****/5	11 miles	3900 feet/ 6426 feet	June–Oct

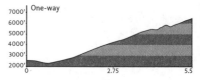

Map: Green Trails Kachess Lake No. 208; **Contact:** Okanogan and Wenatchee National Forests, Cle Elum Ranger District, (509) 852-1100, *www.fs.fed.us/r6/wenatchee*; **Notes:** Northwest Forest Pass required; **GPS:** N 47 24.913, W 121 04.860

Personal trainers charge hundreds of dollars for this kind of extreme exercise. The opportunity to sweat buckets goes for a premium in places like L.A. and New York. Yet you get to subject yourself to this brutal experience for free. What's more, while you exhaust yourself on this long, hot hike up a ruthlessly steep trail, you also earn great rewards: views that can't even be imagined by people chained to their treadmills. From Davis Peak you'll soak in sweeping views that include all of the splendid Alpine Lakes Wilderness and beyond.

GETTING THERE

From Seattle drive east on I-90 to take exit 80 (signed "Roslyn/Salmon la Sac"). Head north on Salmon la Sac Road (State Route 903) about 15 miles, passing through Roslyn and past Cle Elum Lake to Salmon la Sac. Go right at the Y to stay on the main road (rather than entering the campground), and in 1.6 miles look for the Paris Creek/Davis Peak trailhead parking area on the right.

ON THE TRAIL

From the parking area, hike across the road and follow the dirt road 0.5 mile to a bridge over the Cle Elum River. Continue along the trail for another 0.25 mile or so to where the path widens onto an old logging road for the next mile. By the end of this mile, the trail has turned vertical, entering a seemingly endless series of switchbacks. The trail bounces you back and forth so much you'll feel like a pinball—especially on the fast descent.

About 2.5 miles from the trailhead, you'll break out of the thinning forest cover, with the remainder of the climb—all 3 miles of it—under the full glare of the sun. Make sure your sunscreen is waterproof, or you'll sweat it off in no time. The sun-drenched, clear-cut "wildflower meadows" are a curse on hot summer days, but even then they are also a blessing, since with every plodding step upward you'll find ever-better views.

The Watpus River valley as seen from the Davis Peak Trail

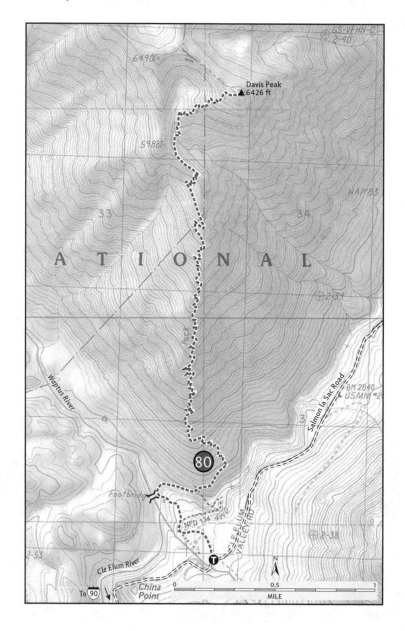

Western fence lizard exiting a hole in the ground

By the time you reach the crown of Davis Peak at 5.5 miles, you'll have earned the stellar views that ring you. Your panoramic vision stretches out 360 degrees, sweeping in the vast expanse of the Alpine Lakes Wilderness in all its glory. Mount Rainier also pokes up on the southern horizon. It's all stunning, and it's all yours—you earned it, so sit back and enjoy it!

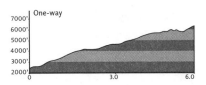

Map: Green Trails Kachess Lake No. 208; **Contact:** Okanogan and Wenatchee National Forests, Cle Elum Ranger District, (509) 852-1100, *www.fs.fed.us/r6/wenatchee*; **Notes:** Northwest Forest Pass required; **GPS:** N 47 24.264, W 121 5.947

81 Jolly Mountain

RATING/ DIFFICULTY	ROUND-TRIP	ELEV GAIN/ HIGH POINT	SEASON
***/5	12 miles	4000 feet/ 6440 feet	July–Oct

You'll feel jolly on top, but you'll jolly-well earn it. As you climb the trail you'll be questioning the value of *the views from the top—are they worth the thigh-burning, lung-popping workout of the ascent? But once you reach the top, you'll forget the sweat and tears of the trail as you soak in the mind-numbing, eye-pleasing panorama encircling you.*

GETTING THERE

From Seattle drive east on I-90 to take exit 80 (signed "Roslyn/Salmon la Sac"). Head north on Salmon la Sac Road (State Route 903) about 15 miles, passing through Roslyn and past Cle Elum Lake to Salmon la Sac. Look for the trailhead on the right, between Cayuse Horse Camp and the picnic area.

ON THE TRAIL

From the trailhead, find the trail behind the horse barn at the Forest Service workshop. The trail crosses Salmon la Sac Creek and starts upward immediately. The trail zigs and

zags for a steep 3.2 miles through forest, with occasional views into the Cle Elum Valley, to reach the first trail junction.

Stay right and climb the southern face of the valley's headwall. In another mile turn left at another trail junction, and climb even more steeply for another 0.5 mile to reach a third junction. This time, take the left fork and continue a long traverse around the north flank of Jolly Mountain.

The views now increase in frequency and magnificence. A half mile of traversing leads to the last trail junction at 6000 feet. On this north face of the mountain lingering snowfields are likely from this point on—the slippery snow may persist into August. Be careful crossing these slick patches of winter remembrances.

From the last trail junction at 6000 feet, turn right and climb a long, moderate mile to the summit of Jolly Mountain. The last 6 miles brought you up more than 4000 vertical feet.

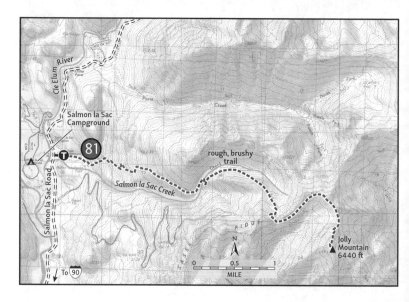

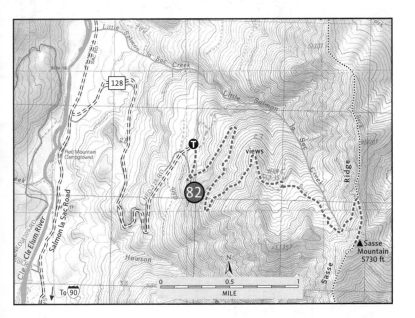

Congratulate yourself on a great achievement. Then look out from your lofty perch. On a clear day, enjoy views of everything within 100 miles as your fatigue falls away and the Jolliness of the summit takes over.

82 Sasse Ridge

RATING/ DIFFICULTY	ROUND-TRIP	ELEV GAIN/ HIGH POINT	SEASON
**/3	9 miles	2400 feet/ 5730 feet	July–Oct

Map: Green Trails Kachess Lake No. 208; **Contact:** Okanogan and Wenatchee National Forests, Cle Elum Ranger District, (509) 852-1100, www.fs.fed.us/r6/wenatchee; **Notes:** Northwest Forest Pass required; **GPS:** N 47 23.352, W 121 4.463

Sasse Ridge offers views nearly as good as those found from Jolly Mountain (Hike 81) without the muscle-ripping climb. You'll work hard for just over a mile, but then you have several miles of ridgetop meandering through meadows and over view-rich peaks. Few hikers visit this trail, so you can stride out and enjoy a quiet hike, stopping as often and for as long as you want to enjoy the fields of wildflowers on the dry (bring water), wind-swept ridge.

GETTING THERE

From Seattle drive east on I-90 to take exit 80 (signed "Roslyn/Salmon la Sac"). Head north on Salmon la Sac Road (State Route 903) about

Wildflowers cover the ridges along the Sasse Ridge Trail.

15 miles, passing through Roslyn and past Cle Elum Lake. Turn right onto Forest Road 128 and drive up the steep, winding road. You should be able to drive about 2.5 miles to a wide switchback turn (elev. 3400 ft). Beyond, the road gets very rough, so park here to save your vehicle from abuse. You might stop even lower.

ON THE TRAIL

The route follows the road to its end—if you park at the recommended switchback, you'll have about 2 miles of road walking. Fortunately, even though the road winds through old clear-cuts, the scenery is remarkably enjoyable. The old clearings provide grand views across the Cle Elum Valley toward Polallie Ridge and Davis Peak. And the clearings themselves are thick with wildflowers and, occasionally, thick brambles of huckleberry bushes.

Once you near the road end, look for the faint unmaintained trail as it climbs steeply away from the roadway. For the next mile the trail angles upward without benefit of switchbacks or respite, gaining more than 1100 feet to attain the crest of Sasse Ridge at 5500 feet.

When you hit the ridgeline, you'll find a trail junction. Turn right and stroll south along the ridge crest, hopping over rocks and tripping through flowers, which sometimes grow right in the middle of the seldom-used trail. In the next mile, you'll climb to the 5730-foot summit of Sasse Mountain. Stop and enjoy the vast vistas: Jolly Mountain, Elbow Peak and Hex Mountain fill the horizon to the north, east, and south. To the west, the blue chasm of Cle Elum Lake separates you from the tall summits of Domerie Peak and West Peak.

Note that this is a dry route—no water, but lots of sun and exposure. If you've brought Fido along, make sure to pack plenty of fluids for both of you to prevent dangerous dehydration. Also be aware that some small species of cactus grow here, so bring a pair of tweezers to pull spines from your dog's pads should he step on a spiny plant. (Better yet, teach him to walk in booties.)

EXTENDING YOUR TRIP

Walk south along the ridge before turning and heading back to the trailhead. The trail gets rough and hard to follow about a mile south of Sasse Mountain, however.

83 Scatter Creek

RATING/ DIFFICULTY	ROUND-TRIP	ELEV GAIN/ HIGH POINT	SEASON
****/3	9 miles	1500 feet/ 5300 feet	June–Oct

Map: Green Trails Kachess Lake No. 208; **Contact:** Okanogan and Wenatchee National Forests, Cle Elum Ranger District, (509) 852-1100, www.fs.fed.us/r6/wenatchee; **Notes:** Northwest Forest Pass required; **GPS:** N 47 30.391, W 121 03.553

This route explores a seldom-visited creek valley on the flank of the Wenatchee Mountains. The trail ascends through steeply sloped meadows into a broad wildflower basin at the head of the valley and eventually leads to a high pass on the ridge, affording awesome views of both the Cle Elum River valley and east into the Icicle Creek drainage.

GETTING THERE

From Seattle drive east on I-90 to take exit 80 (signed "Roslyn/Salmon la Sac"). Head north

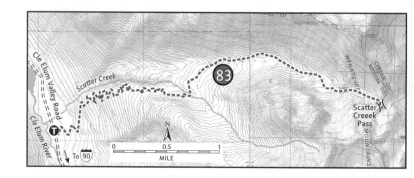

on Salmon la Sac Road (State Route 903) about 15 miles, passing through Roslyn and past Cle Elum Lake to Salmon la Sac. Go right at the Y to stay on the main road (rather than entering the campground), and continue up the Cle Elum Valley Road (FS 4330) another 9.5 scenic miles through beautiful meadows

to the trailhead on the right, just before the concrete-lined vehicle ford at Scatter Creek.

ON THE TRAIL

The trail leaves the road and climbs gradually through thin forest to start up the slope on the south side of Scatter Creek. For the next 2 miles

Mount Daniels and Cathedral Rock from upper Scatter Creek

the trail climbs 1500 feet through gentle switchbacks. The pine and fir forest is brightened by flower-filled glades—the bulbous beargrass blooms, sitting atop their tall stalks, are particularly noteworthy early in the summer.

At 2.3 miles find a trail intersection. To the right is the County Line Trail. Stay left instead, continuing up the Scatter Creek valley, and in 0.5 mile cross the creek. Once across the creek, the meadows slowly spread out until you're hiking in a rolling field of native grasses and wildflowers. The lightly used trail can be overgrown and brushy in places, but generally is easy to follow as it sticks close to Scatter Creek and hooks southeast into the basin at the head of the creek valley.

You could stop anywhere along here for a picturesque picnic site, with views out into the Cle Elum Valley—Goat Mountain can be seen on the far side of the valley—and flowers stretching out under your feet. If you want more exercise, continue up the trail as it climbs the steep wall at the head of the valley, reaching the crest of the Wenatchee Ridge at

Scatter Creek Pass, about 4.5 miles from the trailhead.

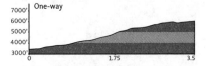

84 Paddy-Go-Easy Pass

RATING/ DIFFICULTY	ROUND-TRIP	ELEV GAIN/ HIGH POINT	SEASON
***/4	7 miles	2700 feet/ 6100 feet	July–Oct

Map: Green Trails Stevens Pass No. 176; **Contact:** Okanogan and Wenatchee National Forests, Cle Elum Ranger District, (509) 852-1100, *www.fs.fed.us/r6/wenatchee*; **Notes:** Northwest Forest Pass required; **GPS:** N 47 31.974, W 121 04.955

Starting in valley-bottom meadows, you'll enjoy open country start to finish. Oh, you'll dip into stands of trees now and again, but

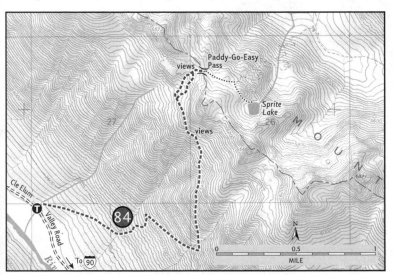

Hiker descending the Paddy-Go-Easy Pass Trail

other side of the ridge, over to the Wenatchee Mountains.

GETTING THERE

From Seattle drive east on I-90 to take exit 80 (signed "Roslyn/Salmon la Sac"). Head north on Salmon la Sac Road (State Route 903) about 15 miles, passing through Roslyn and past Cle Elum Lake to Salmon la Sac. Go right at the Y to stay on the main road (rather than entering the campground), and continue up the Cle Elum Valley Road (FS 4330) another 9.5 scenic miles through beautiful meadows to the trailhead on the right, just before the concrete-lined vehicle ford at Scatter Creek. About 0.5 mile past the Fish Lake Ranger Station, look for the Paddy-Go-Easy trailhead parking area in the meadows on the right.

ON THE TRAIL

The trail leaves the roadside meadows and heads into a stand of forest right off the bat. About 0.5 mile up the trail you'll cross a small creek and then start climbing with vigor. Within the next 0.5 mile the trail turns even steeper, leaving the last big section of forest just over 1 mile from the trailhead. Now you enter steep hillside meadows. The views, too, open up here. Look across the Cle Elum Valley to see Cathedral Rock (Hike 86) towering over the opposite valley wall.

Enjoy those views—they get progressively better—for the next mile. At 2.5 miles the trail splits. Both paths go to the pass. Take either, then come back on the other. For what it's worth, the left fork is a more direct route—I prefer it on the downhill return. So, go right to swing out past an old hard-rock mine (Gold? Silver? Not much of either was ever found here) and a small creek. The trails merge for the final 0.25 mile to the pass.

Paddy-Go-Easy Pass (elev. 6100 ft) is nestled below the 400-foot red-rock cliffs of an unnamed peak.

for the most part you'll be surrounded by wildflowers, alpine grasses, and low bushes. That low-growing vegetation means there's nothing but the distant mountains to prevent your views from stretching to the far horizon. And as you climb, the views get longer and longer. By the time you reach the pass you'll be peering out over the expanse of the Cle Elum River valley and, on the

EXTENDING YOUR TRIP
Press on another mile and you'll drop into the Sprite Lake basin. You'll find fabulous campsites around the lake.

85 Squaw Lake

RATING/ DIFFICULTY	ROUND-TRIP	ELEV GAIN/ HIGH POINT	SEASON
***/3	5 miles	1400 feet/ 4841 feet	July–Oct

Map: Green Trails Stevens Pass No. 176; **Contact:** Okanogan and Wenatchee National Forests, Cle Elum Ranger District, (509) 852-1100, *www.fs.fed.us/r6/wenatchee*; **Notes:** Northwest Forest Pass required; **GPS:** N 47 32.699, W 121 32.699

Start at a beautiful mountain stream and end at a gorgeous mountain lake. The trail climbs moderately from start to finish, but is well maintained and stays in the cool shade of the forest. Squaw Lake is a great family destination. The lake boasts shallow, warmer sections perfect for swimming, but anglers will appreciate the depths that remain cool enough for cold-water-loving trout to thrive. If neither water sport floats your boat, no worries. Simply sit back and, after a bit of quiet reflection, watch small songbirds to fish-loving raptors flit around the lake basin.

GETTING THERE
From Seattle drive east on I-90 to take exit 80 (signed "Roslyn/Salmon la Sac"). Head north on Salmon la Sac Road (State Route 903) about 15 miles, passing through Roslyn and past Cle Elum Lake to Salmon la Sac. Go right at the Y to stay on the main road (rather than entering the campground), and continue up the Cle Elum Valley Road (FS 4330) to the end of the road. Just before entering the Tucquala Meadow Campground, turn left into a wide trailhead parking lot.

Squaw Lake

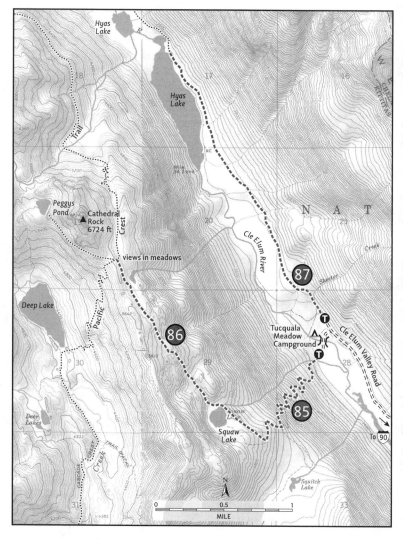

ON THE TRAIL

From the parking area, hike down a short dirt road to the Cle Elum River, and find the trailhead at a bridge over the river. Head up the trail on the far side of the river and climb

modestly for the first 2 miles (gaining just 1000 feet in the process) to a junction with Trail No. 1332 on the right.

Stay left as the trail turns north along a long ridge crest. The forest on the ridge is broken and offers frequent views out across the Cle Elum River valley to the Wenatchee Mountains on the opposite side of the valley.

At 2.5 miles the trail reaches Squaw Lake. Skirt the lake to find your ideal lunch spot—grassy slopes in the shade or rocky shelves in the sun. Sit on a log and dip your feet, or wade out through a squishy mud beach for a therapeutic foot bath. Take your time relaxing around the alpine pool before heading back down the trail to your waiting car.

86 Cathedral Rock

RATING/ DIFFICULTY	ROUND-TRIP	ELEV GAIN/ HIGH POINT	SEASON
****/4	9 miles	2200 feet/ 5600 feet	July–Oct

Map: Green Trails Stevens Pass No. 176; **Contact:** Okanogan and Wenatchee National Forests, Cle Elum Ranger District, (509) 852-1100, www.fs.fed.us/r6/wenatchee; **Notes:** Northwest Forest Pass required; **GPS:** N 47 32.699, W 121 32.699

Meadows, river, and lakes. Smooth trails, gentle climbs, and lots of grassy pastures in which to rest and relax. This route offers a taste of some of the finest meadows, prettiest lakes, and craggiest mountains in the Alpine Lakes Wilderness, all in a moderate hike along a picturesque ridge.

GETTING THERE
From Seattle drive east on I-90 to take exit 80 (signed "Roslyn/Salmon la Sac"). Head north on Salmon la Sac Road (State Route 903) about 15 miles, passing through Roslyn

Cathedral Rock from near the Pacific Crest Trail

and past Cle Elum Lake to Salmon la Sac. Go right at the Y to stay on the main road (rather than entering the campground), and continue up the Cle Elum Valley Road (FS 4330) to near the end of the road. Just before entering the Tucquala Meadow Campground, turn left into a wide trailhead parking lot.

ON THE TRAIL
From the parking area, hike down a short dirt road to the Cle Elum River, and find the trailhead at a bridge over the river. At 2.5 miles the trail passes Squaw Lake (Hike 85). This is a popular camping destination for families with small children or for folks who want to escape the noise and crowds without working excessively hard—the hiking distance isn't too great, and the shallow lake is perfect for wading or swimming.

THIS IS COUGAR COUNTRY

While eastern Washington is clearly cougar country (home to Washington State University), so are the central Cascades. But the cougars that roam these hills don't don red and gold—they're wild cats. And they're proliferating. Cougar populations throughout the state have been increasing. No surprise, so have sightings. Cougar encounters are still rare. But it's important to know how to react just in case you do have a run-in with this elusive predator.

Cougars are curious animals. They may appear threatening when they are only being inquisitive. By making the cougar think you are a bigger, meaner critter than it is, you will be able to avoid an attack (the big cats realize that there is enough easy prey out there that they don't have to mess with something that will fight back). Keep in mind that fewer than twenty fatal cougar attacks have occurred in the United States since the early twentieth century (on the other hand, more than fifty people are killed, on average, by deer each year—most in auto collisions with the deer).

If the cat you encounter acts aggressively:

- Don't turn your back or take your eyes off the cougar.
- Remain standing.
- Throw things, provided you don't have to bend over to pick them up. If you have a water bottle on your belt, chuck it at the cat. Throw your camera, wave your hiking stick, and if the cat gets close enough, whack it *hard* with your hiking staff (I know of two cases where women delivered good, hard whacks across the nose of aggressive-acting cougars, and the cats immediately turned tail and ran away).
- Shout loudly.
- Fight back aggressively.

You can minimize the already slim chances of having a negative cougar encounter by doing the following:

- Don't hike or run alone (runners look like fleeing prey to a predator).
- Keep children within sight and close at all times.
- Avoid dead animals.
- Keep dogs on leash and under control. A cougar may attack a loose, solitary dog, but a leashed dog next to you makes two foes for the cougar to deal with—and cougars are too smart to take on two aggressive animals at once.
- Be alert to your surroundings.
- Use a walking stick.

Moving past the lake, the trail follows the ridge north, alternating through grassy meadows and thin forest, with a few small tarns dotting the meadows along the way. At 4.5 miles the trail ends at a junction with the Pacific Crest Trail (PCT).

At this point you're directly under the towering spire of Cathedral Rock. Look closely and you might see some Spiderman wannabes scaling its rocky walls—Cathedral is quite popular with rock climbers. Find a place in the meadows for a leisurely lunch in the shadow of this monolith.

EXTENDING YOUR TRIP

At the junction with the PCT, hikers have three options to extend their adventures. Turn left and hike south, descending to Deep Lake—a beautiful blue-water lake fed by waterfalls off the south flank of Mount Daniel. Or you can turn right and follow the PCT north along the flank of Mount Daniel toward Deception Pass. Finally, you can cross the PCT and follow a faint climbers track to the northwest, skirting the steep southwest face of Daniel to a picturesque little cirque holding a small alpine pool known as Peggys Pond.

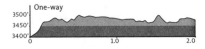

87 Hyas Lake

RATING/ DIFFICULTY	ROUND-TRIP	ELEV GAIN/ HIGH POINT	SEASON
**/2	4 miles	100 feet/ 3500 feet	July–Oct

One-way

Map: Green Trails Stevens Pass No. 176; **Contact:** Okanogan and Wenatchee National Forests, Cle Elum Ranger District,

Hyas Lake

(509) 852-1100, *www.fs.fed.us/r6/wenatchee*;
Notes: Northwest Forest Pass required; **GPS:**
N 47 32.714, W 121 05.906

*A flat hike through old forests leads to a
wide expanse of water. Hyas Lake is actually
a pair of pools in the middle of the Cle Elum
River. The lower pool is a broad but shallow
lake that sprawls nearly all the way across
the valley floor and stretches more than a
mile from one end to the other. The upper
pool is a smaller, even shallower lake. In re-
ality, it's the same lake, but the waters have
been divided by a hearty growth of marsh
grasses—as the grasses grew, they trapped
more and more sediment, until finally a small
band of muddy ground stretched across the
upper end of the long Hyas Lake, leaving the
smaller fragment just a few dozen yards
above the lower lake. Plan to venture at least
as far as the middle of the lower lake—and
the best rest stops are at the upper end of
the lake.*

GETTING THERE

From Seattle drive east on I-90 to take exit 80
(signed "Roslyn/Salmon la Sac"). Head north
on Salmon la Sac Road (State Route 903)
about 15 miles, passing through Roslyn and
past Cle Elum Lake to Salmon la Sac. Go right
at the Y to stay on the main road (rather than
entering the campground), and continue up
the Cle Elum Valley Road (FS 4330) another 12
miles to the end of the road. Just past the Tucquala Meadow Campground find the trailhead
parking area.

ON THE TRAIL

Heading up the Cle Elum River Trail you'll
wander along for a flat mile as the trail weaves
through the trees, well back from the river. As
you hike, listen for the twitter of birds—the
songs of small flittering birds will be your first
indication that you're nearly to the lake.

The lower section of Hyas Lake is a broad
grassland. About 1.1 mile from the trailhead
you'll finally see the open waters of the lake.
For the next mile, the trail gradually trends toward the lakeshore.

The best places to stop are about 2 miles
from the trailhead. You'll find campsites
that serve perfectly as picnic sites, too.
Wade out into the refreshingly cool water,
and look up on the towering peaks of Mount
Daniel and Cathedral Rock (Hike 86) before
heading for home.

Opposite: Mount Stuart and the Stuart Range dominate the view from Longs Pass.

teanaway country

Sunshine, wildflowers, wild animals, and remote trails. That's the Teanaway Country in a nutshell. The long, scenic Middle Fork and North Fork Teanaway River valleys provide access to some of the most wonderful, and unique, hiking opportunities in Washington. The trails climb long ridges through open forests and meadowlands populated with mule deer, elk, and mountain goats. Black bear are common here too, in part because of the abundance of Purple Gold (fat, juicy huckleberries!). And birds of all shapes, sizes, and colors call the Teanaway home, making these trails a paradise for bird-watchers. Then there are the flowers. Pick a trail, any trail, in the Teanaway Country, and you have a great chance of seeing a wide assortment of wildflowers in bloom. Lupine, columbine, shooting stars, tiger lilies, paintbrush, penstemon, buckwheat, aster, daisies… the list goes on and on. In short, regardless of what you want from your wildland trail, you'll find it here.

88 Middle Fork Teanaway River

RATING/ DIFFICULTY	ROUND-TRIP	ELEV GAIN/ HIGH POINT	SEASON
***/2	7 miles	300 feet/ 3000 feet	May–Oct

Maps: Green Trails Kachess Lake No. 208 and Mount Stuart No. 209; **Contact:** Okanogan and Wenatchee National Forests, Cle Elum Ranger District, (509) 852-1100, *www.fs.fed .us/r6/wenatchee*; **Notes:** Northwest Forest Pass required; **GPS:** N 47 17.868, W 120 57.744

Mountain rivers are magical, crystal-clear ribbons that inundate your senses. They can be cool massages for your feet. They offer delicate music for your eyes, sparkling flashes in the alpine sunlight. When properly treated, they offer needed refreshment for thirsty hikers. The Middle Fork Teanaway River offers all this and more. as it tumbles through a gorgeous mountain valley, home and habitat to a variety of birds, beasts and, yes, bugs. This riverside trail passes through rich valley meadows, grand old forests, and comfortable campsites for those who can't resist the chance to stay longer than a single day.

GETTING THERE
From Seattle drive east on I-90 to East Cle Elum, exit 85. Cross over the freeway overpass

Middle Fork Teanaway River

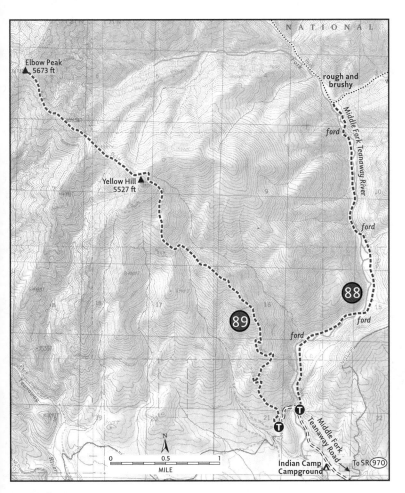

and turn right (northbound) on State Route 970. Cross the Teanaway River bridge, and in another mile turn left onto Teanaway Road. At the Teanaway Campground turn left onto the Middle Fork Teanaway Road and drive about 4.5 miles to the Indian Camp Campground. Continue 0.5 mile farther to the trailhead on the right, found near a sharp left turn in the road.

ON THE TRAIL

The Middle Fork Teanaway Trail (No. 1393) climbs gradually along the pretty river for an easy and fast hike if that's what you want. But I recommend enjoying it as an easy and slow hike. Bring the kids and stroll up the trail, letting the youngsters explore as you walk.

The trail leaves the trailhead with a fording of the river. Proceed upstream for 0.25 mile to

Wildflowers line the trail toward Elbow Peak.

the point where the river valley narrows into a steep-walled canyon. At this point the trail runs on a bench above the river, but within the next 0.5 mile the trail slides closer to the river and occasionally gets too close—the tread disappears periodically in small washouts.

Unfortunately, the trail receives only occasional maintenance, so the tread may be rough—or missing—in places. Fortunately, the gentle slope of the land makes scrambling through these rough sections fairly easy.

As you near the 1-mile mark the trail crosses

the river once more via a shallow ford. You'll cross the river again in about another 0.25 mile, then go back across yet again at just past 2 miles. Between fords, the trail alternates between cool forests and sun-streaked forest clearings. Look for wildlife—both ground-based critters such as deer and airborne beasts such as nuthatches and gray jays—in the margin areas where the forests open onto the clearings.

At 3 miles from the trailhead you'll come to yet another ford. About 0.5 mile past this last crossing you'll find a side stream—Way Creek—tumbling down to join the Middle Fork. In addition to the creek junction, you'll also find a trail junction. Continue a few dozen yards past the trail junction to find a broad campsite near the river. Stop here for lunch before turning back to complete your 7-mile hike.

EXTENDING YOUR TRIP

If you still have energy and a need for more wildlands, press on up the river trail. It continues another 3.5 miles. But beyond Way Creek the trail gets brushier and even rougher than what you've experienced so far.

89 Elbow Peak

RATING/ DIFFICULTY	ROUND-TRIP	ELEV GAIN/ HIGH POINT	SEASON
****/4	10 miles	2800 feet/ 5673 feet	June–Oct

Maps: Green Trails Kachess Lake No. 208 and Mount Stuart No. 209; **Contact:** Okanogan and Wenatchee National Forests, Cle Elum Ranger District, (509) 852-1100, *www.fs.fed .us/r6/wenatchee*; **Notes:** Northwest Forest

Pass required, trail open to motorbikes; **GPS:** N 47 17.719, W 120 57.898

The Teanaway Country is home to an assortment of birds and animals, as well as some truly magnificent wild country. It's not protected as wilderness, so you might hear or see motorcycles along the trails, but the grandeur of the country is worth that risk—fortunately, when you encounter motorcycles they disappear quickly from sight, even if the exhaust fumes and ringing in your ears linger for a time. This trail, though open to motors, offers hikers a rewarding excursion up a beautiful mountain in one of the most stunning parts of the Cascades, and Elbow Peak provides grand views and glorious wildflower-viewing opportunities.

GETTING THERE

From Seattle drive east on I-90 to East Cle Elum, exit 85. Cross over the freeway overpass and turn right (northbound) on State Route 970. Cross the Teanaway River bridge, and in another mile turn left onto Teanaway Road. At the Teanaway Campground turn left onto the Middle Fork Teanaway Road and drive about 4.5 miles to the Indian Camp Campground. Continue 0.7 mile farther to the trailhead on the left, found just past the Middle Fork Teanaway River trailhead (Hike 88).

ON THE TRAIL

The trail starts on road. Some gung-ho four-wheelers might drive farther up the rough dirt access road, but rational folks will realize a mile of hiking the old road is easier—and

Balsamroot covers open meadows on Elbow Peak.

likely faster—than creeping up in a car.

At the end of this road section the trail climbs steeply up the face of the ridge, ignoring the need for switchbacks on its straight-up run. At 1.5 miles you'll crest a bench on the long ridge climb where you'll find the first fine views. Look out over the Middle Fork Teanaway country as you catch your breath.

Once you're breathing freely again, push on up the trail as it moderates its pitch. You'll climb more gently along a traverse of the flank of Yellow Hill at around 2 miles out. In another mile you'll push up the steep final pitch to the summit of Yellow Hill (elev. 5527 ft).

The summit provides your first clear views of Mount Rainier to the south. Elbow Peak towers upvalley, nearly in your grasp. If you want a short hike, stop at Yellow Hill. Mile-hungry hikers, though, should pause just long enough to snap a picture or two—the views are very photogenic—before dipping back down to the ridge to start up the long slope toward Elbow Peak.

Over the next 1.5 miles you'll swing around Yellow Hill and roll up and down along the ridgeline up the southeast face of Elbow. Every step brings great views. Jolly Mountain looms just past Elbow Peak. Mount Stuart stands as an impressive sentinel to the northeast. And of course, mighty Mount Rainier rises to the south.

The last 0.5 mile of hiking requires a scramble through the rocks atop Elbow. Finally, at 5 miles, the faint trail crosses the summit. From the top of Elbow Peak (elev. 5673 ft), enjoy outstanding views over all the Teanaway Country and beyond.

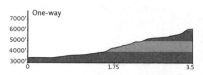

Map: Green Trails Mount Stuart No. 209; **Contact:** Okanogan and Wenatchee National Forests, Cle Elum Ranger District, (509) 852-1100, *www.fs.fed.us/r6/wenatchee*; **Notes:** Northwest Forest Pass required; **GPS:** N 47 23.326, W 120 52.339

Koppen Mountain offers incredible views of the Stuart Range and the jagged peaks of the Teanaway Country. Such views are found on many other trails in this area, but what those other routes don't have is the quiet and solitude found at Koppen. Enjoy this largely forgotten trail and you'll be able to selfishly soak in those views without having to share.

GETTING THERE

From Seattle drive east on I-90 to East Cle Elum, exit 85. Cross over the freeway overpass and turn right (northbound) on State Route 970. Cross the Teanaway River bridge, and in another mile turn left onto Teanaway Road. Drive north on Teanaway Road, veering right as it becomes first the North Fork Teanaway Road and then unpaved Forest Road 9737 at 29 Pines Campground. Drive 4 miles to Beverly Campground and then continue on to Forest Road 9737-120. Turn left and follow it to the abandoned De Roux Campground and the trailhead.

ON THE TRAIL

Start up the trail as it parallels De Roux Creek heading west. After nearly 1 mile of forest hiking, the trail forks. Go left to leave De Roux Creek and start a steep climb out of the valley (the right fork goes to Hike 92, Esmeralda

90 Koppen Mountain

RATING/ DIFFICULTY	ROUND-TRIP	ELEV GAIN/ HIGH POINT	SEASON
****/4	7 miles	2300 feet/ 6031 feet	July–Oct

Cross-shaped tree snag along the ridge of Koppen Mountain

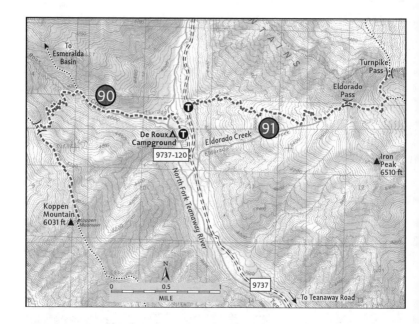

Basin). You'll soon be sweating as you ascend switchbacks for just over 0.5 mile to a 5040-foot pass on the shoulder of Koppen Mountain. You'll find fine views here, but don't stop now—the scenery and the views get better as you go higher.

At the pass the trail splits. Follow the wide boot-beaten path to the left as it climbs the north shoulder of Koppen Mountain. This trail was actually built before World War II when Koppen was home to a fire lookout station. Since the trail was built for fire spotters rather than recreationists, it tends to be steep and straight—these men truly believed that the fastest way from point A to point B was a straight line, even if that line ran vertically! Fortunately, the slope isn't too steep, and the trail is enjoyable.

The path rolls upward through grassy meadows to the open summit of Koppen Mountain (elev. 6031 ft), about 3.5 miles from the trailhead. Drop your pack and lie down in the cool grass. Look skyward to watch the resident raptors soar on the afternoon thermals. Look to the north to gawk at towering Mount Stuart beyond Iron Peak. Look northwest to Hawkings and Esmeralda Peaks. Look down to the long valley of the North Fork Teanaway River. Look out, or you might become so lost in the spectacular scenery that you'll lose track of time and end up spending the night!

EXTENDING YOUR TRIP

From the top of Koppen Mountain, you may choose to add mileage to your day by continuing south along the long, view-rich ridge that separates the North Fork and the Middle Fork Teanaway River valleys.

91 Eldorado and Turnpike Passes

RATING/ DIFFICULTY	ROUND-TRIP	ELEV GAIN/ HIGH POINT	SEASON
****/4	8 miles	2200 feet/ 6100 feet	July–Oct

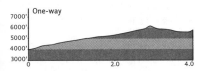

Map: Green Trails Mount Stuart No. 209; **Contact:** Okanogan and Wenatchee National Forests, Cle Elum Ranger District, (509) 852-1100, *www.fs.fed.us/r6/wenatchee*; **Notes:** Northwest Forest Pass required; **GPS:** N 47 25.296, W 120 56.243

Mount Stuart from the ridge on Iron Peak

If you're looking for a workout, with some great views along the way, this is the route for you. But the workout is worth it, especially if you like wild country full of wildflowers and wildlife. Deer, elk, mountain goats, marmots, pikas, black bears, porcupines, bobcats, and coyotes all live here. Then there are the flowers. Vast meadows of lupine, shooting star, columbine, phlox, paintbrush, daisies, and buckwheat, among countless others, sprawl over the ridge tops. Topping it all off, you can expect to encounter few other folks here—not many hikers extend themselves along these trails, though horse riders love this rugged, remote route.

GETTING THERE

From Seattle drive east on I-90 to East Cle Elum, exit 85. Cross over the freeway overpass

Dennis Long takes in a front-row view of Hawkins Mountain.

and turn right (northbound) on State Route 970. Cross the Teanaway River bridge, and in another mile turn left onto Teanaway Road. Drive north on Teanaway Road, veering right as it becomes first the North Fork Teanaway Road and then unpaved Forest Road 9737 at 29 Pines Campground. Continue north another 9 miles or so to the Eldorado trailhead, found about 0.5 mile past the High Country Outfitters Horse Camp.

ON THE TRAIL

From the trailhead, climb the steep, switchbacking Eldorado Creek Trail through forest for the first mile. Forest gives way to clearings and then broader meadows the farther up you go.

You'll dip into the headwater basin of Eldorado Creek at just past 2 miles, then climb the valley headwall through a very tight, very rugged series of switchbacks to the high saddle (elev. 6100 ft) below Iron Peak at 3 miles. Here, from Eldorado Pass, you'll enjoy grand views north to the Stuart Range and southwest to Koppen and Malcolm Mountains.

You could end your hike at this point, after resting up and enjoying the views. Or, press on as the trail drops over the back side of the ridge and descends 500 feet over the next 0.5 mile to a junction with the Beverly-Turnpike Trail.

Turn left and climb another 0.5 mile to a second pass, Turnpike Pass, this one separating the Beverly Creek and Turnpike Creek basins. Here, the views are as good as you'll find anywhere—Ingalls Peak towers to the northwest, Mount Stuart fills the northern skyline, and the long cut of Ingalls Creek valley rolls away to the east.

92 Esmeralda Basin

RATING/ DIFFICULTY	ROUND-TRIP	ELEV GAIN/ HIGH POINT	SEASON
****/3	7 miles	1750 feet/ 5960 feet	July–Oct

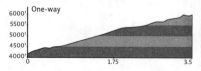

Map: Green Trails Mount Stuart No. 209; **Contact:** Okanogan and Wenatchee National Forests, Cle Elum Ranger District, (509) 852-1100, *www.fs.fed.us/r6/wenatchee*; **Notes:** Northwest Forest Pass required; **GPS:** N 47 26.203, W 120 56.230

Sometimes we need to re-adjust our perspectives to fully enjoy our outdoor experiences. Hiking in the Pacific Northwest typically means traveling through some of the most scenic mountains in the world. The high, jagged crest of the Cascades—punctuated by the glistening cones of the great volcanoes—

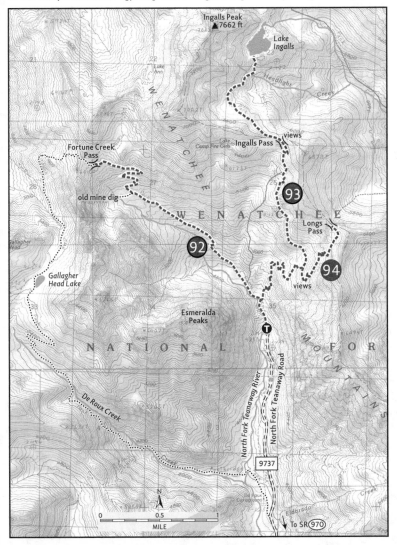

dominates the views. The attraction of those majestic scenic vistas, though, can prevent us from appreciating the scenery closer at hand—or foot. In the Esmeralda Basin you'll find your eyes straying, not to the distant views, but to the local wonders along the trail—an array of flower species, flittering birds, and even a dead forest sheared off 6 to 10 feet above the ground by a powerful avalanche.

GETTING THERE

From Seattle drive east on I-90 to East Cle Elum, exit 85. Cross over the freeway overpass and turn right (northbound) on State Route 970. Cross the Teanaway River bridge, and in another mile turn left onto Teanaway Road. Drive north on Teanaway Road, veering right as it becomes first the North Fork Teanaway Road and then unpaved Forest Road 9737 at 29 Pines Campground. Continue to the road's end.

View east from Fortune Creek Pass

ON THE TRAIL

Start on a three-in-one trail along an old miners road for 0.25 mile to a trail junction. Go left, while hikers seeking higher paths go right to Longs Pass (Hike 94) or Lake Ingalls (Hike 93).

The trail climbs gradually through forest and clearings for 1 mile, frequently within sight and sound of the gentle stream that is the North Fork Teanaway River. You'll pass through one broad field of shooting stars—gorgeous purple and white flowers that typically bloom in mid-July.

Over the next mile the trail climbs, skirting an avalanche slope, and passes more meadows. As you climb through that avalanche slope, take a look at the trees. Many of the stumps are 6 to 10 feet tall—the depth of the consolidated snowpack when the big slide occurred. That dense snowpack stayed in place, protecting the lower parts of the trees, while the snow above slid, sheering off the tops.

The trail reaches a junction of sorts near 2

miles, when the old miners track veers away to the left while the main trail continues up and to the right to reach the valley headwall. Here, you'll start a serious climb to the 5960-foot Fortune Creek Pass at 3.5 miles from the trailhead. Sweet views of the surrounding mountains await you, but even as you soak them in your eyes will be drawn downward to the brilliant wildflowers at your feet.

EXTENDING YOUR TRIP

To make a long (15-mile) loop, continue down the far side of the pass to a junction with a rough road. Turn left and hike the road/trail to Gallagher Head Lake, and just beyond it turn right onto the De Roux Creek Trail. Descend the De Roux Creek valley about 4 miles to the North Fork Teanaway Road (FR 9737). You'll have to walk the road nearly 2 miles upstream to your car at the road's end.

93 Lake Ingalls

RATING/ DIFFICULTY	ROUND-TRIP	ELEV GAIN/ HIGH POINT	SEASON
*****/5	9 miles	2600 feet/ 6500 feet	July–Oct

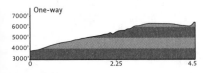

Map: Green Trails Mount Stuart No. 209; **Contact:** Okanogan and Wenatchee National Forests, Cle Elum Ranger District, (509) 852-1100, *www.fs.fed.us/r6/wenatchee*; **Notes:** Northwest Forest Pass required; **GPS:** N 47 26.203, W 120 56.230

Sometimes you just want to get high—physically, not psychedelically—and the Lake Ingalls Trail lets you do that while still exploring some of the grandest wild-

Donna Meshke relaxes on sandstone rocks around Lake Ingalls.

flower displays in the Cascades. You'll climb, descend, and climb again, crossing through no less than three distinct ecosystem types, each with its own species of wildflowers to entice and enchant you.

GETTING THERE

From Seattle drive east on I-90 to East Cle Elum, exit 85. Cross over the freeway over-pass and turn right (northbound) on State Route 970. Cross the Teanaway River bridge, and in another mile turn left onto Teanaway

Road. Drive north on Teanaway Road, veering right as it becomes first the North Fork Teanaway Road and then unpaved Forest Road 9737 at 29 Pines Campground. Continue to the road's end.

ON THE TRAIL

As with the Longs Pass Trail (Hike 94) you'll start out on the old miners road leading up the Teanaway Valley. Within the first 0.25 mile the wide roadbed fades to a true trail. It also splits, the path to the left heading to Esmeralda Basin and Fortune Creek Pass (Hike 92).

Go right to start your climb out of the Teanaway Valley. You'll be hiking through the first flora stratum you'll encounter on this hike, with huckleberry bushes, a few lilies, and other lesser known flowers, such as pipsissewa and wintergreens.

At 2 miles go left at another trail junction (right leads to Longs Pass). The trail angles upward, climbing steadily and at times steeply. As you near Ingalls Pass the trail meanders through a rock-strewn meadowland. Along the long, slow climb to the pass you'll enter a drier ecosystem full of alpine firs. Bitterroot, white paintbrush, penstemon, and spreading stonecrop (a pretty little succulent plant) grow in profusion.

The final 0.3 mile switchbacks up to Ingalls Pass, about 3 miles from the trailhead. Here you'll enjoy spectacular views of Ingalls Peak across the Ingalls Creek valley in front of you, and Esmeralda Peaks across the Teanaway River valley behind you.

The trail now descends briefly before contouring around the upper flank of Headlight Basin. As you crest the pass and descend into the rocky basin, you'll enter rich heather meadows filled with bistort, paintbrush, and—in one spring-fed ravine—a 10-acre spread of shooting stars. This lush valley sports many fine campsites alongside small

tarns and creeks in the open heather and flower fields. Of course, an abundance of rich foliage and plenty of water means birds and animals frequent this basin. Move silently and watch carefully for the best chances to see deer, mountain goats, marmots, coyotes, and countless bird species.

After gawking, pop your eyes back into your head and push on—the next mile swings around the upper edge of the basin, crossing a few creeks and weaving around some nice ponds. As you leave the flowers you'll traverse a broad granite slope and climb up and over a tangle of granite slabs and boulders before dropping to rock-rimmed Lake Ingalls. Views are hard to come by here—rock hard, that is.

Swing out to the left as you reach the lake and drop down to rest on the long rock slabs that taper down into the water. From here, look across the mirror-finish lake to the magnificent face of mighty Mount Stuart to the north, while the craggy top of Ingalls Peak towers directly over the lake on the west.

94 Longs Pass

RATING/ DIFFICULTY	ROUND-TRIP	ELEV GAIN/ HIGH POINT	SEASON
*****/4	5 miles	2100 feet/ 6250 feet	July–Oct

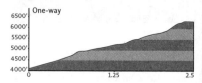

Map: Green Trails Mount Stuart No. 209; **Contact:** Okanogan and Wenatchee National Forests, Cle Elum Ranger District, (509) 852-1100, *www.fs.fed.us/r6/wenatchee*; **Notes:** Northwest Forest Pass required; **GPS:** N 47 26.203, W 120 56.230

If you want the best possible views with the shortest hiking distance, this trail is for you. Few 5-mile hikes offer the quality of views you'll find here. You'll cross steeply sloped alpine meadows, explore cool pine forests, climb through granite rock gardens laced with heather and huckleberries, and stare in awe at the jagged skyline created by the massive hulk of Mount Stuart. All in all, this is one of my favorite hikes in one of my favorite parts of the Cascades—the magical Teanaway Country.

GETTING THERE

From Seattle drive east on I-90 to East Cle Elum, exit 85. Cross over the freeway overpass and turn right (northbound) on State Route 970. Cross the Teanaway River bridge, and in another mile turn left onto Teanaway Road. Drive north on Teanaway Road, veering right as it becomes first the North Fork Teanaway Road and then unpaved Forest Road 9737 at 29 Pines Campground. Continue to the road's end.

ON THE TRAIL

The trail starts out on an old miners road marked Esmeralda Basin (I've always wondered: was Esmeralda a young sweetheart of one of the old miners?). A short distance from the trailhead, the wide roadbed fades to a true trail. It also splits, with one path departing to the left into the lovely wildflower meadows of Esmeralda Basin and Fortune Creek Pass (Hike 92).

For Longs Pass go right. The path winds upward more steeply now, slicing through thinning forests to the 2-mile mark, where the route forks once more. To the left is a steep ascent to Ingalls Pass and beyond to Lake

Mount Stuart view from Longs Pass

A wave of cloud on Annapurna in the Stuart Range

Ingalls (Hike 93). Once more, go right. But first take a long drink of water and strip off any extra clothing you might be wearing—you will be sweating very soon.

The Longs Pass Trail leaves the junction and rolls upward in a brutal series of switchbacks through old rock-lined meadows. As you're working hard you'll also be baked by the sun beating down on you and reflecting up at you. Fortunately, the climb is just 0.5-mile long, though it gains about 600 feet in that distance.

At Longs Pass (elev. 6250 ft) stop and catch your breath before lifting your eyes to the views before you. Mount Stuart looms large in front of you—a massive granite slab reaching into the sky just across the Ingalls Creek valley, which sprawls beneath you on the far side of the pass.

95 Iron Peak Loop

RATING/ DIFFICULTY	ROUND-TRIP	ELEV GAIN/ HIGH POINT	SEASON
*****/5	14.5 miles	3600 feet/ 6387 feet	July–Oct

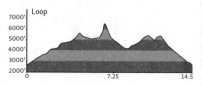

Map: Green Trails Mount Stuart No. 209; **Contact:** Okanogan and Wenatchee National Forests, Cle Elum Ranger District, (509) 852-1100, *www.fs.fed.us/r6/wenatchee*; **Notes:** Northwest Forest Pass required, portions of trail may be brush-covered and hard to follow, map-and-compass navigation skills essential; **GPS:** N 47 23.326, W 120 52.339

Scrambling along open ridge tops draped in grass and wildflowers, hikers here easily lose the trail as it fades under the rich plant life and disappears between jumbles of rock. Further complicating things, the glorious views prevent hikers from devoting their full attention to the trail—there's just too much beauty and natural splendor to enjoy. Great meadows stretch out all around, and on every horizon stand picture-perfect mountain ranges, with the hulking presence of Mount Stuart to the north dominating all others. Enjoy these sights, but make sure you give plenty of attention to the route too, and don't be afraid to turn back and hike out the way you came if you lose the loop.

GETTING THERE

From Seattle drive east on I-90 to East Cle Elum, exit 85. Cross over the freeway overpass and turn right (northbound) on State Route 970. Cross the Teanaway River bridge, and in another mile turn left onto Teanaway Road. Drive north on Teanaway Road, veering right as it becomes first the North Fork Teanaway Road and then unpaved Forest Road 9737 at 29 Pines Campground. Continue north for just under 4 miles before turning right (east)

Whitebark pine near the Iron Peak summit, with Mount Stuart behind it

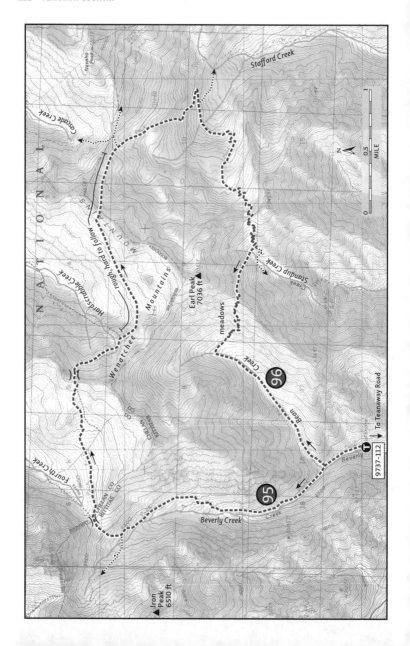

onto Forest Road 9737-112, signed for Beverly Creek. Drive 1.4 miles to the road end and trailhead.

ON THE TRAIL

The trail angles northwest along Beverly Creek for 0.5 mile before the path diverges (the right is your return route). Go left to stay alongside Beverly Creek, and in the next 2.2 miles climb the steep, narrow valley of this creek to a junction with a small trail on the left.

Leave the creekside here and climb steeply to the right (north) to reach a pass (elev. 5600 ft) separating Beverly Creek basin from Fourth Creek basin, 3.3 miles from the trailhead. This pass sits on the spine of the Wenatchee Mountains, below the craggy rock summit of Iron Peak. One look at the mountain's reddish hue explains the name—the iron-rich rocks have oxidized (rusted) to a russet orange.

From the pass, turn right and follow a long traverse to the east, looping around the head of Fourth Creek basin and climbing slowly to a high pass (elev. 6387 ft) between Fourth Creek and Hardscrabble Creek valleys. The trail then drops to a junction with the Hardscrabble Creek Trail at 5.1 miles from the trailhead. The trail to the left descends Hardscrabble Creek, and while it can be narrow and brushy, it is generally easy to see.

Straight ahead, though, our path plays hide and seek in the broad fields of rock and wildflowers. The trail can be hard to follow, but by maintaining an easterly heading and staying at the 5900-foot elevation, scramblers can work their way across the 2-mile stretch of trail between the Hardscrabble and the Cascade Creek Trails. Enjoy the views down into Ingalls Creek valley and across that valley to Mount Stuart and the jagged line of the Stuart Range.

Once you reach the junction with the Cascade Creek Trail at about 7.2 miles, turn right and hike south, descending into the Stafford

Creek valley. After about 1 mile you'll encounter the Standup Creek Trail. Turn right once more and follow this path up and over the ridge between Stafford and Standup Creeks, and cross the pass on the flank of Earl Peak.

At 5800 feet the trail splits, about 10.5 miles from the start. The main, easily followed trail drops along Standup Creek, but the faint, hard-to-follow path you want cuts west along the flank of Earl Peak and drops steeply into the Bean Creek basin, where you'll find a junction with the Beverly Creek Trail. Turn left on the Beverly Creek Trail and follow it 0.5 mile downstream back to your car.

96 Bean Creek Basin

RATING/ DIFFICULTY	ROUND-TRIP	ELEV GAIN/ HIGH POINT	SEASON
****/3	5 miles	2000 feet/ 5300 feet	June–Oct

Map: Green Trails Mount Stuart No. 209; **Contact:** Okanogan and Wenatchee National Forests, Cle Elum Ranger District, (509) 852-1100, www.fs.fed.us/r6/wenatchee; **Notes:** Northwest Forest Pass required; **GPS:** N 47 23.326, W 120 52.339

Mount Stuart dominates the eastern half of the Alpine Lakes Wilderness, towering so high above its surrounding peaks that it can be seen from trails throughout the region. Bean Creek is one of those trails affording views of the spectacular rock slabs of Stuart. But there's more to this trail than mountain views. Indeed, there are splendid views of Ingalls Peak and other summits in the Stuart Range.

But it's the little things that make Bean Creek special. A plethora of blooming plants—wildflowers of all varieties—grace the valley. And an army of wild critters calls the basin home, from mule deer to deer mice, from gray jays to pileated woodpeckers.

GETTING THERE

From Seattle drive east on I-90 to East Cle Elum, exit 85. Cross over the freeway overpass and turn right (northbound) on State Route 970. Cross the Teanaway River bridge, and in another mile turn left onto Teanaway Road. Drive north on Teanaway Road, veering right as it becomes first the North Fork Teanaway Road and then unpaved Forest Road 9737 at 29 Pines Campground. Continue north for just under 4 miles before turning right (east) onto Forest Road 9737-112, signed for Beverly Creek. Drive 1.4 miles to the road end and trailhead.

UNDERSTANDING ELK

Elk. Such a small, simple word for such a massive, majestic beast. I much prefer the Shawnee Indian name of *wapiti,* meaning "white rump." But a name is just a name and, wapiti or elk, these animals earn the respect and appreciation of anyone fortunate enough to see them in the wild.

But not all elk are created equal. Indeed, Washington boasts two distinct species of elk. Roosevelt elk, named for Theodore Roosevelt, are found on the Olympic Peninsula (hence their nickname, Olympic elk). In the Cascades—and points east—Rocky Mountain elk reign supreme.

Rocky Mountain elk are somewhat smaller than their Roosevelt cousins (a big Roosevelt bull may weigh more than a half ton), but they generally sport broader, heavier antler sets. A large part of this antler difference stems from the different habitats of each subspecies. Roosevelt elk tend to be in the foliage-rich rain forests of the Olympic Peninsula, so broad, heavy antlers become more problematic. Rocky Mountain elk thrive in the drier, more open forests of the Cascades, but they also move out over the plains of the eastern Cascade foothills and even out onto the desert steppes of the Columbia River basin. Indeed, Rocky Mountain elk once existed in vast herds on the Great Plains, alongside the mighty American bison.

Elk of both types feed by browsing on a variety of vegetation, from grasses to berries to evergreen needles. The most impressive time to experience elk is autumn, when the herds are in rut—in other words, mating season. Like most ungulates, the elk males (bulls) fight among themselves to establish dominance and decide which bull gets to mate with the female elk (cows).

As part of the ritual, the bulls challenge each other by issuing ringing calls. Known as bugling, these calls can be an eerie trumpet tone that sends chills down the spine. Listening to the undulating high-pitched calls as twilight falls over a forest glade will get even the most unimaginative hiker thinking that they're lost in the forest primeval.

The best bet for experiencing wapiti in the Snoqualmie region are along the trails in the Teanaway Country and in the Chinook Pass area.

A clump of bitterroot (Lewisia rediviva) in bloom

creek can be fast and tough to wade early in the year when melting snows swell the flow.

At 2 miles the trail leaves a stand of forest and erupts onto a broad swath of green, speckled with reds, blues, purples, yellows, and whites—that is, a vast grassy meadow filled with the odoriferous heads of blooming wildflowers.

At this point the trail forks. Stay left to climb into the flower fields of Bean Creek basin. The trail leads to a wonderful camp along the creek, and then angles up into a garden of color, dotted with alpine firs and stunted pines. As you ascend the 0.5-mile from this last trail junction, you'll find the meadows growing larger and the stands of trees growing smaller, until finally the meadow wins out and takes over all the basin before you. Here, at around 5300 feet, you'll be standing amid flowers that stretch across scores of acres.

Above the meadows tower the jagged tops of Earl Peak, Mount Stuart, and Iron Peak. Break out lunch, then enjoy a nap in the sun before heading for home.

97 Navaho Pass

RATING/ DIFFICULTY	ROUND-TRIP	ELEV GAIN/ HIGH POINT	SEASON
*****/3	11 miles	3000 feet/ 6000 feet	July–Oct

ON THE TRAIL
Cross Beverly Creek on the stout bridge near the trailhead and climb creekside on an old, overgrown roadbed. At 0.5 mile turn right at the first trail junction and start up Bean Creek valley (Hike 95 goes left). The trail drives upward through the tight valley, lined lightly with trees and carpeted with beargrass, buckwheat, and other blooming plants under the waving branches of the pines and firs.

Many of the trees that used to dot the hillsides can be seen rotting in piles at the bottom of the steep valley—dropped by a violent avalanche some years before. The trail continues a steep climb for nearly a mile, crossing the creek to access more cool forest and small forest meadows higher up the valley. The

Maps: Green Trails Mount Stuart No. 209 and Liberty No. 210; **Contact:** Okanogan and Wenatchee National Forests, Cle Elum Ranger District, (509) 852-1100, *www.fs.fed.us/r6 /wenatchee*; **Notes:** Northwest Forest Pass required; **GPS:** N 47 21.983, W 120 48.160; **Status:** Rescued

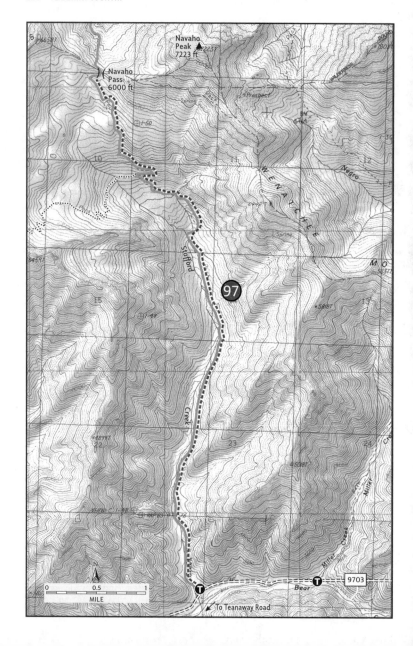

Approach trail to Navaho Pass, with view of Earl Peak

This route covers some of the best of the Teanaway Country, offering high alpine splendor and lush riparian habitats. Visit early for acres of wildflowers, or late for autumn colors—the vine maples are brilliant red, the cottonwoods and alders bright yellow, and the few scattered larches are glowing spires of gold. Beyond the trees, you'll gawk at vast walls of granite towering on all sides. Deer graze the valley bottoms, while mountain goats prance on the ridge tops. Overhead, turkey vultures, eagles, and hawks soar on the mountain thermals. What more could any hiker want?

GETTING THERE

From Seattle drive east on I-90 to East Cle Elum, exit 85. Cross over the freeway overpass and turn right (northbound) on State Route 970. Cross the Teanaway River bridge, and in another mile turn left onto Teanaway Road. Drive north on Teanaway Road, veering right as it becomes first the North Fork Teanaway Road and then unpaved Forest Road 9737 at 29 Pines Campground. At the first road junction after crossing the bridge over Stafford Creek, turn right onto Forest Road 9703 (signed "Stafford Creek") and drive 2.5 miles to the Stafford Creek trailhead, found just after crossing Stafford Creek.

ON THE TRAIL

The Stafford Creek Trail climbs alongside the stream, passing through pretty, fragrant pine forest. Ponderosa pines down low are followed by whitebark pines and a few lodgepole pines. Intermingling with the pines are spruces, hemlocks, a few larches, and even a smattering of massive old Douglas-firs. Throughout the evergreen forests you'll also find a few deciduous species, including some stands of cottonwood, the random aspen or two, and a few alders.

The trail sticks to the east side of the creek—floodwaters once devoured parts of the trail, but volunteer trail crews working with Forest Service professionals restored or replaced the flood-damaged sections.

The trail climbs moderately for 4 miles, where it merges with the Standup Creek Trail. Go left at the junction as the trail turns steeper. Trudge for more than 1 mile up switchbacks that climb the headwall of the Stafford Creek valley. The thigh-burning climb is made tolerable, and indeed, enjoyable, by the vast expanse of wildflowers spread before and around you. The whole upper basin is blanketed in wildflower meadows—somewhat swampy meadows, as the shallow bench serves as a catch basin for snowmelt runoff, creating this uniquely rich environment for water-loving wildflowers at 5600 feet elevation.

A half mile past these meadows, the trail crests Navaho Pass (elev. 6000 ft). Trails lead off in multiple directions from the pass, running east around Navaho Peak, west toward Earl Peak and Beverly Creek, and straight north down into the Ingalls Creek valley. The pass, though, is the perfect end of your hike. From here you'll enjoy a northern skyline dominated by Mount Stuart and the granite wall of the Stuart Range. To the south, look out over the long valley of the North Fork Teanaway to Mount Rainier and Mount Adams far in the distance.

98 Miller Peak

RATING/ DIFFICULTY	ROUND-TRIP	ELEV GAIN/ HIGH POINT	SEASON
****/3	8 miles	3200 feet/ 6400 feet	July-Oct

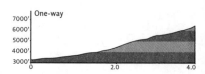

Maps: Green Trails Mount Stuart No. 209 and Liberty No. 210; **Contact:** Okanogan and Wenatchee National Forests, Cle Elum Ranger District, (509) 852-1100, *www.fs.fed.us/r6 /wenatchee*; **Notes:** Northwest Forest Pass required. Trail open to motorbikes; **GPS:** N 47 22.112, W120 47.146; **Status:** Endangered

  There's something special about the Teanaway Country. Fragrant pine forests. Sprawling wildflower fields. Grand views. Wildlife of all kinds and sizes. Miller Peak has all this, and more. The long climb along an exposed, sun-baked ridge provides unmatched views, reaching south to Mount Adams and north over the ragged teeth of the Stuart Range. That open ridge also offers up the risks of sunburn and heat exhaustion, so pack plenty of sunscreen and carry more water than you think you might need. Also, be prepared to encounter motorcycles along this trail. Though their use is sporadic and chances are you won't see the dirt bikers, their presence is felt even when they aren't around—the motorcycles gouge deep ruts into the trail tread and grind the soil into dust.

GETTING THERE

From Seattle drive east on I-90 to East Cle Elum, exit 85. Cross over the freeway overpass and turn right (northbound) on State Route 970. Cross the Teanaway River bridge, and in another mile turn left onto Teanaway Road. Drive 13 miles to 29 Pines Campground, where the pavement ends. Veer right, and continue about 1 mile. At the first road junction after crossing the bridge over Stafford Creek, turn

Wildflower-covered slopes on the summit of Miller Peak

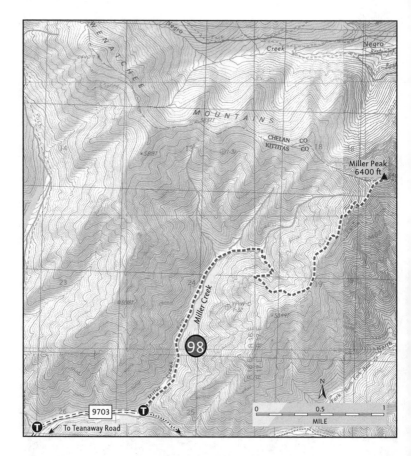

right onto Forest Road 9703 (signed "Stafford Creek") and drive 4 miles to road's end.

ON THE TRAIL

As you leave the trailhead, go left up the Miller Creek Trail (to the right is the Bear Creek Trail). You'll climb at a moderate rate for nearly 2 miles, crossing the creek a couple times in the first mile. The trail was built to multiuse standards, meaning it's open to hikers, mountain bikers, and motorcyclists. Since those wheeled users need gentle grades, the

climb is easy on hikers' legs.

At 2 miles the trail climbs out of the creek basin, ascending easy switchbacks up the valley wall for 0.5 mile to the crest of the ridge that runs north to the top of Miller Peak. The trail runs up this ridge, climbing through forest and meadow for the next mile to a trail junction just below the summit of Miller Peak.

Go straight, through the junction, and follow a faint path 0.5 mile to the 6400-foot summit of Miller and expansive views. To the west is the Teanaway Range and north of that, the mighty Stuart Range, dominated by the hulk of Mount Stuart. Around your feet, locoweed and bitterroot grow throughout the rough scree slopes, and pikas cheep and chirp all around you.

HOW TO HELP THIS TRAIL
After your visit, write to the land manager and mention any damage you encountered that was caused by motorcycles. Provide photos if possible, and send a copy of your letter to the good folks at the Washington Trails Association, the leading volunteer trail-maintenance organization in the state.

Hiking along the Teanaway Ridge Trail

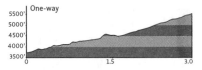

99 Teanaway Ridge

RATING/ DIFFICULTY	ROUND-TRIP	ELEV GAIN/ HIGH POINT	SEASON
***/3	6 miles	1900 feet/ 5489 feet	July–Oct

Map: Green Trails Liberty No. 210; **Contact:** Okanogan and Wenatchee National Forests,

Cle Elum Ranger District, (509) 852-1100, *www.fs.fed.us/r6/wenatchee*; **Notes:** Northwest Forest Pass required. Rough road for final 0.5 mile to trailhead. Trail open to motorbikes; **GPS:** N 47 21.258, W 120 43.101; **Status:** Endangered

❌ *Because of this route's high trailhead, much of your elevation gain is done before you start walking, meaning you can enjoy a high ridge route with relatively modest effort. The trail rambles along the ridge, rolling up and down with wildflowers underfoot and views stretching for hundreds of miles—as far south as Mount Rainier*

and north to Mount Stuart. The big rock of Diamond Head stands to the east. This trail is open to motorcycle use, so visit midweek to minimize the chance of running into these noisy beasts.

GETTING THERE

From Seattle drive east on I-90 to East Cle Elum, exit 85. Cross over the freeway overpass and turn right (northbound) on State Route 970. Turn left (north) on US 97 and drive 2.5 miles beyond Mineral Springs Resort to Iron Creek Road (Forest Road 9714). Turn left (west) and follow Iron Creek Road for 3.6 miles to the road end and trailhead. The road's final

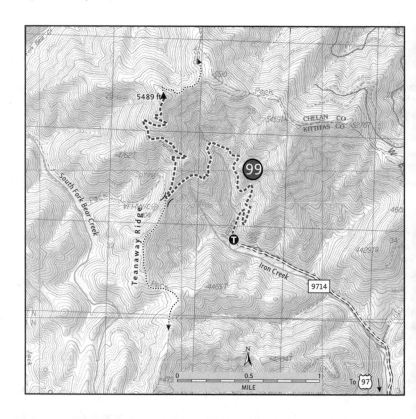

Thunderstorms building from behind the Stuart Range, as seen from Teanaway Ridge

0.5 mile is very rough. If you fear for your car's undercarriage, park lower and hike the last leg of the road.

ON THE TRAIL

The trail climbs steeply away from the trailhead, switchbacking up through rocky wildflower gardens. The path weaves upward for 1 mile, gaining 800 feet to reach a trail junction at the pass separating Iron Creek and Bear Creek valleys. One trail drops to the west into Bear Creek valley, another turns left onto the southern arm of the Teanaway Ridge, and the trail you want goes right to climb along the ridge to the north.

You'll continue to climb, now working along the rocky crest of the Teanaway Ridge. For the next 2 miles you'll roll upward. At times you'll run straight up the ridge spine. Occasionally you'll follow switchbacks as they weave up steep sections. Between climbs the trail traverses the edge of the ridge, crossing spectacular wildflower fields and climbing through

an old forest-fire area with silver skeletons of fire-killed trees. Views abound, but as grand as the scenery and the panoramas are, the best are found at the end of the hike.

At 3 miles from the trailhead the trail crosses the summit of an unnamed knob, the highpoint of the ridgeline (elev. 5489 ft). From here, 360-degree views greet you. To the east, Tronsen Ridge (Hike 100) stretches across the horizon. To the northwest, ever-present Mount Stuart looms large. And the mighty snow cone of Mount Rainier punctuates the southern sky.

HOW TO HELP THIS TRAIL

Motorcycles tend to chew up trail tread, turning compact—and thus stable—dirt into dust. That dust is highly susceptible to erosion from both the wind and rain, leading to deep ruts and mudholes in the trail. After your visit, write to the land manager and mention any damage you encountered that was caused by motorcycles. Provide photos if possible, and send

Lupines along the Tronsen Ridge Trail

a copy of your letter to the good folks at the Washington Trails Association, the leading volunteer trail-maintenance organization in the state.

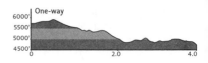

100 Tronsen Ridge

RATING/ DIFFICULTY	ONE-WAY SHUTTLE	ELEV GAIN/ HIGH POINT	SEASON
****/2	8 miles	1000 feet/ 5800 feet	June–Oct

Map: Green Trails Liberty No. 210; **Contact:** Okanogan and Wenatchee National Forests, Cle Elum Ranger District, (509) 852-1100, *www.fs.fed.us/r6/wenatchee*; **Notes:** Northwest Forest Pass required, high-clearance vehicle required to access northern trailhead; **GPS:**

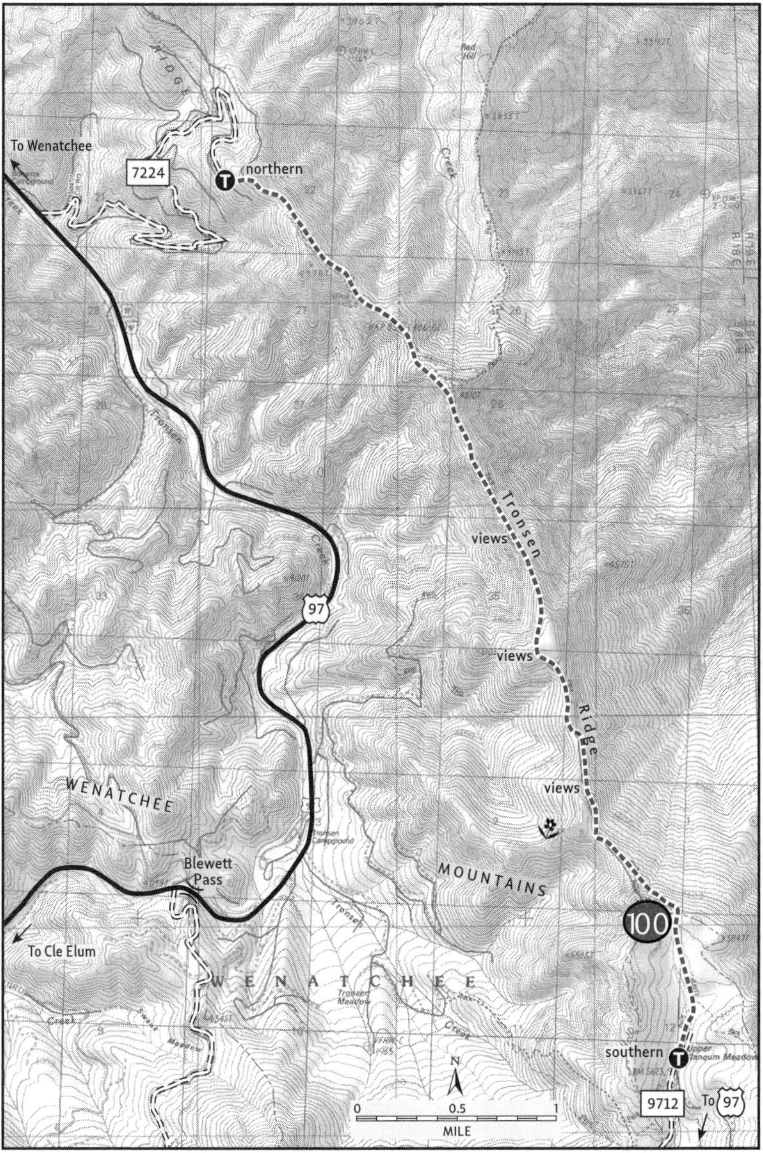

To Wenatchee

7224

T northern

Tronsen

views

views

Ridge

views

WENATCHEE

97

Blewett
Pass

To Cle Elum

MOUNTAINS

100

W E N A T C H E E

southern **T**

9712   To 97

N

0   0.5   1
MILE

southern trailhead N 47 19.361, W 120 31.590, northern trailhead N 47 23.052, W 120 34.488

👪 🪓 🐾 *Start high, stay high, and enjoy the endless bounty of the wild country between the Cascade Crest and the dry, open deserts of eastern Washington. Tronsen Ridge provides a little of both worlds. Long, dry ridges topped with open meadows and wildflower fields resemble the desert gardens of the Yakima Plateau, but dense stands of fir and ponderosa pine offer up the flavor of the mountains. The glorious meadows and forests atop the long ridge are wonderful playgrounds for wildlands enthusiasts. At various points, Tronsen Ridge grants peekaboo views out to Mount Adams, Mount Rainier, Mount Stuart, and countless other lesser peaks nestled in the eastern Cascades.*

GETTING THERE

From Seattle drive east on I-90 to East Cle Elum, exit 85. Cross over the freeway overpass and turn right (northbound) on State Route 970. Turn left (north) on US 97, and drive to Blewett Pass and turn right (southeast) onto Forest Road 9716. In 3.7 miles turn left onto FR 9712 and continue 5 miles to Haney Meadows and the Ken Wilcox Horse Camp. Drive another mile past the camp and, crossing Naneum Creek, find the southern trailhead in the Upper Naneum Meadow at a sharp right-hand switchback in the road. Hikers with high-clearance vehicles can also access the northern trailhead: continue north on US 97 for 5 miles past Blewett Pass, turn right onto Five Mile Road (FR 7224), and drive 3.5 miles to an undeveloped campsite and trailhead.

ON THE TRAIL

The trail heads north through the Upper Naneum Meadow, climbing gradually (a mere 100 feet) in the first 0.5 mile before sloping downward for a slow, soft descent along the ridge for the next 4 miles. The high point of the ridge, a grassy knob 0.5 mile into the hike, provides unmatched views of the eastern Wenatchee Mountains area and beyond.

After leaving this knob, the trail heads into a roller coaster ride to the north, climbing short peaks and ridge knolls, then dropping into low saddles. The net elevation change over the next 4 miles is a loss of 1000 feet.

Many of the ridge's high points are grassy bumps full of wildflowers, while the low saddles often are thinly timbered. Look for wildlife all along the ridge, but especially in the transition zones between forest and meadows.

EXTENDING YOUR TRIP

For additional adventures, with map and compass in hand (and good navigation skills) you can explore off-trail onto rocky promontories with awesome views of Mount Stuart, Mount Rainier, and the Wenatchee Mountains.

Opposite: Open hiking along the eastern end of American Ridge

chinook pass area

Some call Chinook the "forgotten pass." State Route 410, leading from Enumclaw to Yakima over Chinook Pass, draws far less traffic than any other mountain pass in the Cascades, yet the trails along this corridor offer as much if not more in the way of hiking. The trails west of the pass include some of the most spectacular views you'll find anywhere in Washington's backcountry—the view of Mount Rainier from the Noble Knob Trail is truly awestounding—while the routes east of Chinook Pass provide a level of solitude not usually found in the Cascades. Also east of the pass is the William O. Douglas Wilderness. This unique, sprawling wilderness area in the heart of the Cascades boasts an impressive mix of mountain peaks, massive meadowlands, acres of lakes, and scenic rivers. The William O. is not to be missed.

101 Flaming Geyser State Park

RATING/ DIFFICULTY	ROUND-TRIP	ELEV GAIN/ HIGH POINT	SEASON
**/1	3 miles	100 feet/ 425 feet	Year-round

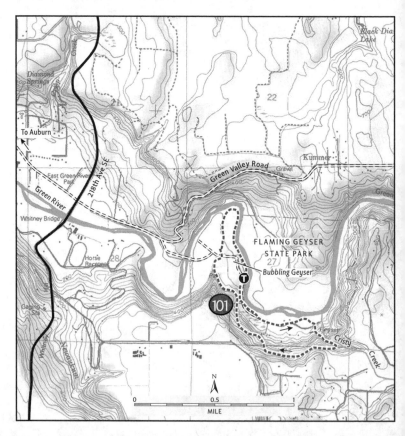

What's left of the historic "flaming geyser"

Map: Green Trails Enumclaw No. 237; **Contact:** Washington State Parks, (360) 902-8844, *www.parks.wa.gov*; **GPS:** N 47 16.625, W 122 1.878

Don't get your hopes up: there's no geyser here, and just a flicker of a flame. The park's geyser is a flame that burns the remnants of a methane-gas pocket, located nearly 1000 feet below the surface. The gas was discovered by early-1900s coal miners, who drilled a test hole and struck gas and salt water all at once. Next thing they knew, they had giant gushes of water and flames 25 feet high blasting from their test hole, which made for excellent dinner conversation, if not coal profits. Today, that "geyser" is a flame several inches tall in a rock-rimmed basin. Despite the misnomer, however, Flaming Geyser State Park sports some impressive features, including miles of trail through wonderful forest and along a gorgeous river. And it's accessible all year.

GETTING THERE

From Auburn head east on State Route 18. Just before crossing the Green River, take the Auburn–Black Diamond Road exit. At the bottom of the ramp go right and, almost immediately, go right again onto SE Green Valley Road. Drive 7 miles, and turn right to cross the Green River and enter Flaming Geyser State Park. At the first junction turn right to drive up the river to the large picnic area.

ON THE TRAIL

A variety of trails are available—more than 10 miles of hiking is possible by linking the numerous paths—but the best bet for a quiet afternoon is the Perimeter Loop. From the parking lot near the picnic area, find the path along the riverbank and follow it to a side stream, Cristy Creek. Turn right to head up the path alongside the creek. This trail takes you past the flaming gas leak and into a moss-laden forest of hemlock and big-leaf maple.

Winding up through the forest, you'll pass

another "geyser," this one the Bubbling Geyser—a small mud hole that bubbles, thanks to natural releases from that same underground gas pocket. Follow the trail uphill, sometimes on wooden stairs, to cross the creek and loop around the slope above the Green River valley.

The trail continues across the slope, then drops down into the tall-grass fields near the entrance to the park. Here, the trail is a simple mowed swath through the chest-high grasses. Follow the path upstream to reach your car.

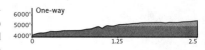

Map: Green Trails Enumclaw No. 237; **Contact:** Mount Baker–Snoqualmie National Forest, Snoqualmie Ranger District, Enumclaw office, (360) 825-6585, *www.fs.fed.us/r6/mbs*; **Notes:** Northwest Forest Pass required; **GPS:** N47 1.912; W121 49.612

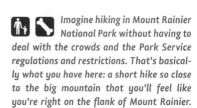

Imagine hiking in Mount Rainier National Park without having to deal with the crowds and the Park Service regulations and restrictions. That's basically what you have here: a short hike so close to the big mountain that you'll feel like you're right on the flank of Mount Rainier.

102 Summit Lake

RATING/ DIFFICULTY	ROUND-TRIP	ELEV GAIN/ HIGH POINT	SEASON
****/2	5 miles	1200 feet/ 5400 feet	June–Oct

Mount Rainier rises over Summit Lake

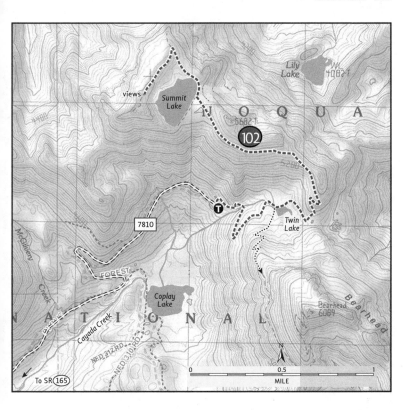

But as you trek up the easy trail, you'll seldom be bothered by any other hikers, especially when visiting on weekdays. Summit Lake, a picturesque little alpine lake with glorious views of Rainier, is the reward.

GETTING THERE

From Enumclaw drive west on State Route 410 (Chinook Pass Highway) to SR 165. Proceed on SR 165 to the Carbon River Road/Mowich Lake Highway junction. Turn left onto Carbon River Road and follow it to Cayada Creek Road (Forest Road 7810), just before the national park entrance. Turn left (north) and drive about 6.8 miles to the trailhead at the end of FR 7810.

ON THE TRAIL

The trail climbs through a brush-filled clear-cut before diving under the thick canopy of dense second-growth forest. You'll continue to climb, swinging wide across a steep hillside before reaching a trail junction and a small tarn at 1 mile. The pond, Twin Lake (why is a single lake named twin?), is little more than a mosquito nursery much of the summer, so you won't want to linger.

Go left at the trail junction to loop around the western side of the lake basin before climbing the wall to the north of the lake. After 1 mile of climbing, the trail traverses west along the ridge, breaking out of the forest periodically for nice views south to Mount Rainier.

At 2.5 miles the trail slides along the shore of Summit Lake (elev. 5400 ft). This lake is a true alpine lake—wide, cold, and crystal clear. On calm, clear days the lake is a mirrorlike surface that reflects massive Mount Rainier. Wildflowers dot the lakeshores, providing color from the moment the snow melts off (avalanche and glacier lilies) to late summer (spreading phlox and paintbrush). In between you'll find beargrass, lupine, and others too numerous to name.

There are campsites around the lake and additional trail miles above the lake bowl for those who just can't bring themselves to leave the lovely basin.

103 Clear West Peak

RATING/ DIFFICULTY	ROUND-TRIP	ELEV GAIN/ HIGH POINT	SEASON
***/1	2 miles	900 feet/ 5400 feet	June–Oct

Map: Green Trails Enumclaw No. 237; **Contact:** Mount Baker-Snoqualmie National Forest,

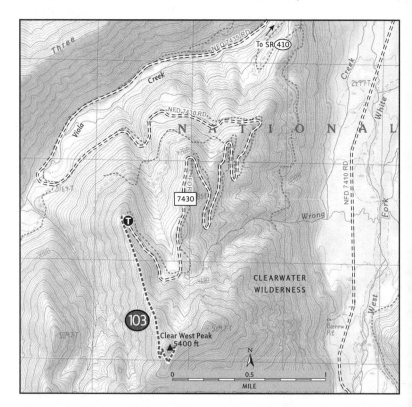

Watching morning formations of lenticular clouds from Clear West Peak

Snoqualmie Ranger District, Enumclaw office, (360) 825-6585, *www.fs.fed.us/r6/mbs*; **Notes:** Northwest Forest Pass required; **GPS:** N 47 01.446, W 121 44.036

Bring the kids, and the dog. This short trail allows ample time to explore the local forest ecology before it presents you with grand views of the oft-forgotten Clearwater Wilderness and the surrounding country. The trail climbs gradually, making it suitable for short legs and old-timers. It's a bird-watchers paradise, too, since it starts in a clear-cut, runs through forest, and opens onto clearings. Birds love the variety of ecosystems, which provide both cover (forest) and food (in the clear-cuts and clearings).

GETTING THERE

From Enumclaw drive east on State Route 410 (Chinook Pass Highway) for nearly 22 miles before turning right (south) onto West Fork Road (Forest Road 74). Drive this road 7.2 miles and turn left onto FR 7430. Continue 7.3 miles to the road end and trailhead.

ON THE TRAIL

The trail leaves the brushy clear-cut that surrounds the trailhead, rolling up into dense forest. You'll amble along on the straight-line trail as it angles up the flank of Clear West Peak. The clear-cut gives way to forest, which gives way to mountaintop clearing.

Look for hummingbirds and insect-eating gnatcatchers in the clear-cut. There are grouse roosting in the forest and jays, nutcrackers, and an array of raptors on the mountaintop. I even spotted an owl in a tree-top at the summit. Deer are also common. and if you hike in the twilight you might duplicate this experience: I watched a bobcat stalking a ground squirrel in the clear-cut.

After 1 mile the trail reaches the summit of Clear West Peak, where you'll find views of Mount Rainier and, to the east, the peaks of the Norse Peak Wilderness, including Arch Rock, Norse Peak, and Dalles Ridge.

104 Greenwater and Echo Lakes

RATING/ DIFFICULTY	ROUND-TRIP	ELEV GAIN/ HIGH POINT	SEASON
***/3	14 miles	1600 feet/ 4100 feet	June–Oct

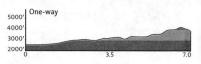

Map: Green Trails Lester No. 239; **Contact:** Mount Baker–Snoqualmie National Forest, Snoqualmie Ranger District, Enumclaw office, (360) 825-6585, *www.fs.fed.us/r6/mbs*; **Notes:** Northwest Forest Pass required; **GPS:** N 47 6.335, W 121 28.475

Lush old-growth forest; dark, mysterious forest lakes; and a wonderful chance to meet and see wildlife await hikers here. The trail sticks to a deeply forested river valley where it passes a wonderfully clear, cool lake—Greenwater—with good fishing. The route eventually reaches Echo Lake in a long 7 miles, but these miles fly by as you stride through the cool forest. Footsore hikers will love the soft, duff-rich trail tread, and Echo itself is a wonderful place to rest and relax before hiking back down the pretty trail. But for all that, few people visit, perhaps because the trail doesn't offer sweeping panoramas. The distant views may be missing, but the route is remarkably scenic and solitude is a high probability.

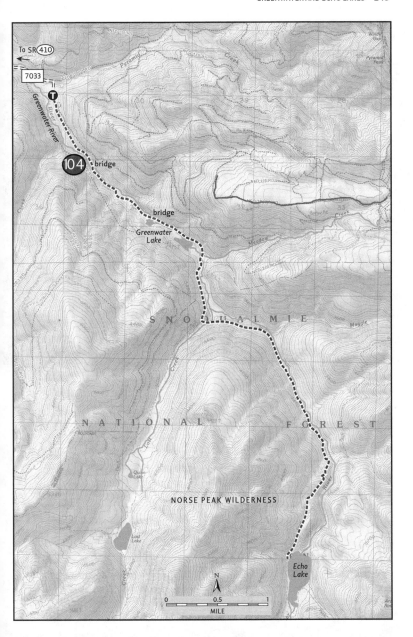

To SR 410

7033

T

Greenwater River

104 bridge

bridge

Greenwater Lake

S N O Q U A L M I E

N A T I O N A L   F O R E S T

NORSE PEAK WILDERNESS

Lost Lake

Quinn Lake

Echo Lake

N

0   0.5   1

MILE

Footlog bridge over the Greenwater River

GETTING THERE

From Enumclaw drive east on State Route 410 (Chinook Pass Highway) to the small town of Greenwater. About 1 mile east of the Greenwater Fire Station (at the eastern end of the community), turn left (north) onto Greenwater River Road (Forest Road 70). Drive about 9 miles, crossing the Greenwater River, and turn right just past the bridge onto FR 7033. Drive up this narrow road about 0.5 mile to the large trailhead parking lot.

ON THE TRAIL

Leave the trailhead and hike into the moss-laden forest, following the Greenwater River upstream. The trail is quiet and damp—even in summer—providing soft footing for those hiking in shoes other than boots. As you hike up the trail watch for any sign of critters. Deer and elk browse through this valley, and where there are deer and elk there may be cougar, coyotes, and bobcats.

The trail crosses the Greenwater River three or four times before reaching the long, shallow Greenwater Lake at about 2 miles. Then for the next 3 miles the route maintains a slow, easy ascent of the valley.

At 5 miles the climb steepens substantially. For 1.5 miles the path switchbacks up the valley wall before tapering off into a smooth, level glide into the Echo Lake basin at 7 miles.

This pretty forest lake offers great swimming, sunning, and general wilderness R & R. Enjoy the relaxing atmosphere of the beautiful basin before heading back down the trail.

105 Arch Rock

RATING/ DIFFICULTY	ROUND-TRIP	ELEV GAIN/ HIGH POINT	SEASON
****/2	12 miles	500 feet/ 5200 feet	June–Oct

One-way

Map: Green Trails Lester No. 239; **Contact:** Mount Baker–Snoqualmie National Forest, Snoqualmie Ranger District, Enumclaw office, (360) 825-6585, *www.fs.fed.us/r6/mbs*; **Notes:** Northwest Forest Pass required, rough road for last mile to trailhead; **GPS:** N 47 5.578, W 121 24.292

Following the Pacific Crest Trail (PCT) south from the broad fields of Government Meadow, this route explores one of the most solitary sections of the nation's premiere trail. Hikers can experience deep forests and rock bluffs, and dogs can walk with their humans without worrying about encountering too many other hikers along the way. The trail starts on an old wagon road that crossed the Cascades at nearby Naches Pass (now used extensively by four-wheel-drive fanatics).

GETTING THERE
From Enumclaw drive east on State Route 410 (Chinook Pass Highway) to the small town of Greenwater. About 1 mile east of the Greenwater Fire Station (at the eastern end of the community), turn left (north) onto Greenwater River Road (Forest Road 70). Drive about 15 miles to the trailhead at the road's end in an old clear-cut. The last mile of road is dusty,

Blue grouse along the Pacific Crest Trail

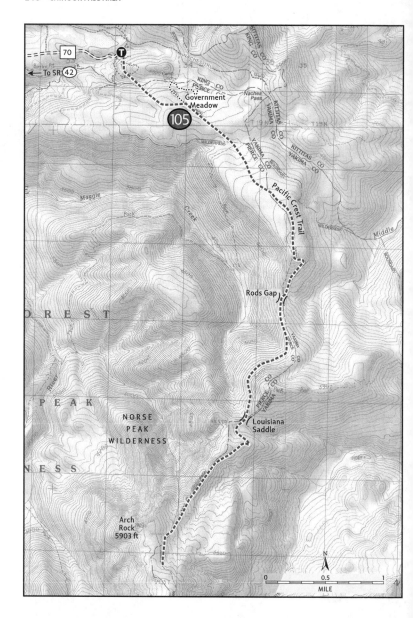

rough and at times, deeply rutted. Use care when traveling it, especially in low-clearance vehicles.

ON THE TRAIL

The trail leaves the clear-cut on an old logging road that leads into the trees. In 0.5 mile the broad connector trail ends at a junction with the PCT. Turning left leads you to Government Meadow in about 0.5 mile (see "Extending Your Trip"). Take this side trip now, or leave it for your return trip.

A right turn at the PCT junction leads along a fairly flat trail for the next few miles, weaving through the thick, old forests. About 1 mile from the trailhead a secondary trail leads off to the right. Stay left and in about 3 miles you'll find your first chance at a view. Just before the trail starts to descend into a few switchbacks down to Rods Gap you'll find a small clearing on the left side of the trail. Looking south and east, take in the rolling hills and gray-green forests spread out before you. But beware the dangers of looking northeast, where you'll see huge scars on the land beyond the wilderness boundary.

Rods Gap is a small forested saddle on the ridge separating the Greenwater River valley from the Naches River valley. From the gap the trail turns upward and climbs during the next 5 miles. Just 1 mile past Rods Gap you'll cross Louisiana Saddle near a junction with Trail No. 945 on the left. Continue upward on the PCT and you'll encounter a few clearings along the ridge where views of the nearby peaks present themselves. To the southeast you'll see the rocky top of Ravens Roost, while directly ahead is the prominent peak of Arch Rock.

The trail reaches the open slope below Arch Rock about 6 miles from the trailhead. Stop here and enjoy the views to the east—Ravens Roost cuts the sky just across the south Naches River basin.

The Pacific Crest Trail passing through meadows near Arch Rock

EXTENDING YOUR TRIP

On your way back to the trailhead, make the 1-mile round-trip detour to Government Meadow. These broad, marshy meadows are a haven for deer and elk and are worth a visit if you have the time and inclination to go look for critters.

106 Snoquera Falls

RATING/ DIFFICULTY	ROUND-TRIP	ELEV GAIN/ HIGH POINT	SEASON
**/2	6 miles	2800 feet/ 5000 feet	Mar–Nov

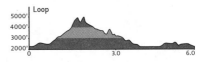

Map: Green Trails Greenwater No. 238; **Contact:** Mount Baker–Snoqualmie National

Forest, Snoqualmie Ranger District, Enumclaw office, (360) 825-6585, *www.fs.fed.us/r6/mbs*; **Notes:** Northwest Forest Pass required; **GPS:** N 47 1.968, W 121 33.471

This lush, moss-laden forest is reminiscent of Olympic Peninsula rain forests, for good reason. The western foothills of the Cascades can get twice as much annual rainfall as the Puget Sound area, making the low forests of these regions wet, mossy, and rich in plant (and animal) life. In short, a rain forest. This trail is short, but scenic—perfect for late-season hikes when the days are short and hiking time is at a premium. The trail leads past the base of a small cascade on Snoquera Creek, best viewed in late spring and early summer when the deep snowpack is melting, forcing impressive amounts of water over the rocky falls.

GETTING THERE

From Enumclaw drive east on State Route 410 (Chinook Pass Highway) through the

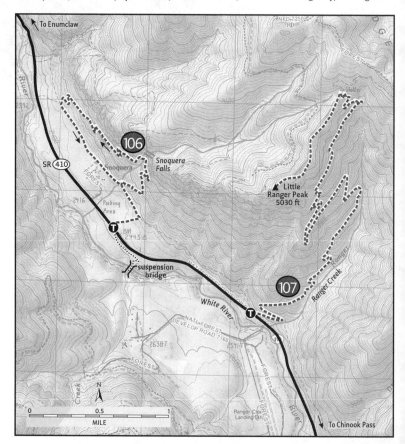

Snoquera Falls

town of Greenwater. Continue past the Dalles Campground and find a small parking area on the left (north) side of the highway, just a few yards south of the Camp Sheppard Boy Scout Camp.

ON THE TRAIL

The trail angles into the forest on the northeast side of the highway, climbing gradually through the nearly dripping cedar and hemlock forest and sweeping carpets of moss—in the spring spotted with splashes of yellow and white (skunk cabbage and trillium), and in the fall with garlands of red and umber (Oregon grape and drying ferns).

The trail steepens after the first 0.5 mile as it veers right at a trail junction. From the junction, the trail slants up the lower slope of Little Ranger Peak. Big-leaf maples and a few scrub oaks now fill the spaces between the hemlocks and Douglas-firs.

At 1.2 miles the trail drops into a little rocky basin, filled with maples, and crosses a small stream below the fantail waterfall on Snoquera Creek. This pretty falls can be roaring in the spring as the winter's snowpack melts,

View up the White River valley from Little Ranger Peak

but it can turn off, leaving just a trickle, later in the fall. For the full experience, plan to visit at least twice to see the difference in water levels and how it affects the whole basin.

From the waterfall basin, the trail continues north, rolling along the base of a steep, rocky slope for 1.5 miles before descending a few short switchbacks to a junction with the lower valley trail. Turn left and follow this trail south 1.3 miles, passing the Boy Scout camp before returning to your starting point.

EXTENDING YOUR TRIP

After your hike, if you have an extra hour, cross the highway and find a trail leading into the woods. Hike south 0.5 mile on this trail to a long, steel-cabled suspension bridge over the White River. This bouncy bridge provides access to the Skookum Flats Trail on the far side of the river.

107 Little Ranger Peak

RATING/ DIFFICULTY	ROUND-TRIP	ELEV GAIN/ HIGH POINT	SEASON
***/3	6 miles	1500 feet/ 5010 feet	June–Oct

One-way

[elevation profile chart: 5000', 4000', 3000' on vertical axis; 0, 1.5, 3.0 on horizontal axis]

Map: Green Trails Greenwater No. 238; **Contact:** Mount Baker–Snoqualmie National Forest, Snoqualmie Ranger District, Enumclaw office, (360) 825-6585, *www.fs.fed.us/r6/mbs*; **Notes:** Northwest Forest Pass required; **GPS:** N 47 01.458, W 121 32.213

 *Answer honestly now: how many of you have heard of Little Ranger Peak? This little-known summit trail offers great early season hiking, though it can also be enjoyed all summer and well into autumn. The south-facing trail*

melts out early, but the abundance of deciduous foliage (vine maples, alders, big-leaf maples) makes this is a nice fall-color hike. The trail climbs moderately, and as it tops the peak hikers find fantastic views of Mount Rainier and the mountains of the White River valley. But perhaps the best reason to visit Little Ranger Peak: the outstanding opportunity for some wildland solitude.

GETTING THERE

From Enumclaw drive east on State Route 410 (Chinook Pass Highway) for 30 miles. The White River trailhead will be on the right. To find the trail to Little Ranger Peak, cross to the north side of the highway.

ON THE TRAIL

Follow the White River Trail south, parallel to the highway, for 0.25 mile to find the start of the Ranger Creek Trail (No. 1197). The trail now climbs gently through majestic old-growth forest. The moss-laden living cathedral fills the Ranger Creek valley.

Wildlife is plentiful here, though with all the wonderful cover the critters can be hard to see. Squirrels scurry through the trees high overhead, and grouse rumble in the Oregon grape and salal underfoot. Owls are also common, though you have to be hiking around twilight to really see and hear them.

The trail climbs the creek valley for more than 2 miles, until at about 2.5 miles from the trailhead you encounter a trail junction. Turn left, heading up the valley wall in a few looping switchbacks.

The trail runs below the true summit Little Ranger Peak (elev. 5010 ft) at 3 miles out. Don't worry about scrambling up the steep slope to the true summit. The views from the trailside viewpoint are as good or better than from the precarious perch above. Look out over the White River valley to Mount Rainier before heading back down.

Hikers descending from the Norse Peak summit

108 Norse Peak

RATING/ DIFFICULTY	ROUND-TRIP	ELEV GAIN/ HIGH POINT	SEASON
****/4	10.6 miles	2800 feet/ 6858 feet	July–Oct

Map: Green Trails Bumping Lake No. 271;
Contact: Mount Baker–Snoqualmie National
Forest, Snoqualmie Ranger District, Enumclaw
office, (360) 825-6585, *www.fs.fed.us/r6/mbs;*

Notes: Northwest Forest Pass required; **GPS:**
N 46 57.862, W 121 28.974

Hike here in summer and you'll
want to pack several quarts of
water, then toss in two more once you've got
all you think you'll need. And you'll want to
be hydrated and feeling good, because the
scenery along these parched slopes will be
something you'll want to see and remember
for a long time. When you tire of the rainbow
of wildflowers on the ground, you can look up
to find breathtaking vistas around every corner. Herds of elk frequent the meadows, and
mountain goats dance and prance around the

rocks at the ridge top. Hawks and golden eagles soar overhead, and small snakes and alligator lizards live on the sun-heated slopes underfoot.

GETTING THERE

From Enumclaw drive east on State Route 410 (Chinook Pass Highway) about 34 miles and turn left (east) onto Crystal Mountain Road (Forest Road 7190) leading to the Crystal Mountain Ski Area. Drive about 3 miles to a large horse camp on the left (at a junction with FR 7190-410). Park in the lot at the upper end of the horse camp and find the trailhead on the left (east) side of the parking area.

ON THE TRAIL

The trail parallels FR 7190-410 for more than 0.5 mile before turning uphill for a steep, hot climb through open, rocky meadows. In the first mile the views are few, but as you pause periodically for a rest, glance south to see Mount Rainier rising over the ridge of Crystal Mountain. Each switchback in the trail brings more of the mighty mountain into view. By the time you reach the first trail junction at 4 miles (elev. 6300 ft), the entire peak towers over the ski area and its namesake mountain.

Go right at this junction on Trail No. 1191A to continue your sweaty climb toward the summit of Norse Peak. In just another 1.3 miles you'll be standing atop the 6858-foot peak with 360-degree views.

Because the former lookout site towers over the surrounding ridges and peaks, your views extend east past the Norse Peak Wilderness to Fifes Peaks and Gold Hill. To the west you'll see the sprawling patchwork forests of the central Cascades. This is checkerboard country—1 square mile is Forest

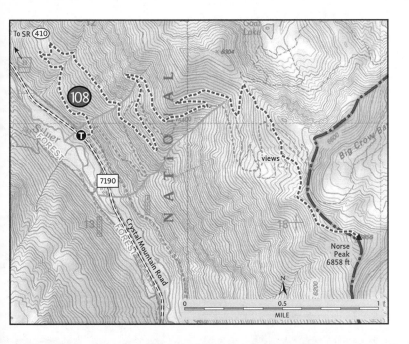

Service land, the next is private timber company land. The squares, unfortunately, are easily discernible, since most of the private holdings have been scraped bare by clearcutting. Fortunately, that's just one small part of the view.

Return the way you came.

109 Bullion Basin

RATING/DIFFICULTY	ROUND-TRIP	ELEV GAIN/HIGH POINT	SEASON
***/3	7 miles	1500 feet/6300 feet	July–Oct

Map: Green Trails Bumping Lake No. 271; **Contact:** Mount Baker–Snoqualmie National Forest, Snoqualmie Ranger District, Enumclaw office, (360) 825-6585, *www.fs.fed.us/r6/mbs*; **Notes:** Northwest Forest Pass required; **GPS:** N 46 56.270, W 121 28.476

Sure, it's a ski area, but it's not only for powder hounds. This alpine ramble leads through steep flower-filled meadows, over narrow ridge spines, and under shady forest canopies. Views sweep over the dry, pine valleys of the eastern Cascades, the glacier-covered summit of massive Mount Rainier, and the craggy peaks of the central Norse Peak Wilderness to the north. Best of all, despite the modest level of difficulty (not too long, nor too steep) the trail isn't

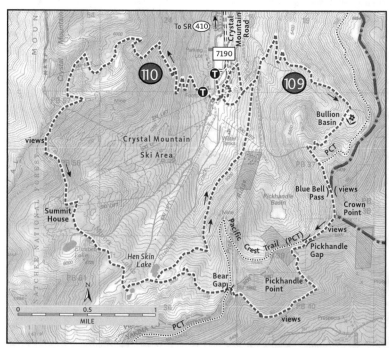

Bullion Basin

heavily used, so it's possible to find a quiet place for a peaceful lunch high on the ridge.

GETTING THERE

From Enumclaw drive east on State Route 410 (Chinook Pass Highway) about 34 miles and turn left (east) onto Crystal Mountain Road (Forest Road 7190) leading to the Crystal Mountain Ski Area. Drive about 5 miles to the end of the road at the ski resort. Park on the left (east) side of the upper lot and find a faint trail behind the ski school building.

ON THE TRAIL

The trail (No. 1156) climbs northwest away from the main ski lodge toward some cabins on the east wall of the valley. In just a few hundred yards, you'll encounter a dirt access road. Continue up this to the trailhead on left.

In the first 0.5 mile the trail climbs gradually through open forests and meadows as it slants northeast before switching back to head up the Bullion Creek valley into the heart of Bullion Basin. The basin, a flower-filled meadow in a shallow cirque, is reached in just less than 2 miles. After crossing the creek, the path enters a deep thicket of woods and then jumps back into the sunshine as it climbs steeply for 0.5 mile to reach the junction with the Pacific Crest Trail (PCT) at 6300 feet.

Turning south on the PCT you'll follow the ridge down to Blue Bell Pass, around Crown Point, and through Pickhandle Gap in the next 2 miles to reach Bear Gap (elev. 5882 ft). These 2 miles are all well above tree line and offer constant views of the wildflower pastures at your feet and of the panoramic vistas beyond—each pass and peak has its own special view. From Bluebell, look east to Fifes Peaks. From Crown Point, look southwest to Mount Rainier. From Pickhandle, look southeast to American Ridge. From Bear Gap, look north to

Elephants head in Bullion Basin's boggy meadows

Norse Peak, south to Rainier, east to Fifes, and west to Crystal Mountain.

Leave the PCT at Bear Gap by taking the right fork at the four-way trail junction and head toward Hen Skin Lake on Trail No. 1163. A gentle descent of 200 feet in 0.75 mile leads to the shallow, muddy-bottomed pond. You'll find a junction with Hike 110 (Crystal Mountain Loop) coming in from the left. There are a few small trout swimming in the lake, but also a whole lot of mosquito larvae early in the summer—keep moving and most of the little biters will miss you.

Turn right at the lake onto Trail No. 1192 and make a long, slow descent into the ski area. In 2 miles you'll cross a creek near a couple of rustic cabins and burst out onto an open ski slope. Angle down the open slope to reach the parking lot and your starting point.

110 Crystal Mountain Loop

RATING/ DIFFICULTY	ROUND-TRIP	ELEV GAIN/ HIGH POINT	SEASON
***/3	8 miles	2450 feet/ 6552 feet	July–Oct

Loop

[elevation profile chart showing elevation from 4000' to 7000' over 0 to 8.0 miles]

Map: Green Trails Bumping Lake No. 271; **Contact:** Mount Baker–Snoqualmie National Forest, Snoqualmie Ranger District, Enumclaw office, (360) 825-6585, *www.fs.fed.us/r6/mbs*; **Notes:** Northwest Forest Pass required; **GPS:** N 46 56.197, W 121 28.588

Okay, you're hiking through the heart of the ski area: so what? Once you pass the first ski lift you'll forget that you're in a developed basin. The trail rolls up through forest, across alpine meadows, and past a couple of fine little lakes before erupting onto a high, wind-swept ridge that is rich with views.

GETTING THERE

From Enumclaw drive east on State Route 410 (Chinook Pass Highway) about 34 miles and turn left (east) onto Crystal Mountain Road (Forest Road 7190) leading to the Crystal Mountain Ski Area. Drive about 5 miles to the end of the road at the ski resort. Stay right as you enter the parking lot area and park in the lower right-hand lot.

ON THE TRAIL

The trail initially follows a dirt road (a ski area service road), passing under a cluster of powerlines and then climbing through a broad clear-cut. The road gives way to trail as the route heads up the tree-studded ridge. You'll be in and out of trees, but mostly climbing in sun-drenched rock meadows.

At 3 miles you'll crest the ridge. After you pull your jaw off the ground, grab your camera to capture Mount Rainier filling the western horizon. It's close enough to touch—almost. If the climb exhausted you, turn around here for a modest 6-mile round-trip.

The better option is to continue along the ridge. At times you'll tiptoe along a knife edge, while at other times the ridge spreads out and sports a thick crop of wildflowers and—glory be!—huckleberries. After ambling about 2.5 miles along the ridge top (with Rainier always by your side), you'll find yourself at the Summit House—a restaurant atop the Rainier Express ski lift. From here descend along a dirt road about 0.3 mile before finding Trail No. 1163 on the left.

This path leads you quickly to the shores of tree-lined Hen Skin Lake, where you'll encounter Hike 109 (Bullion Basin) coming in from the right. Then it's down along Silver Creek and, in another 0.5 mile, out to the Crystal Mountain Ski Area lodge. Walk (or hitchhike) the final 2 miles down the road to your starting point.

111 Noble Knob

RATING/ DIFFICULTY	ROUND-TRIP	ELEV GAIN/ HIGH POINT	SEASON
****/3	7 miles	500 feet/ 6011 feet	July–Oct

Pika standing watch

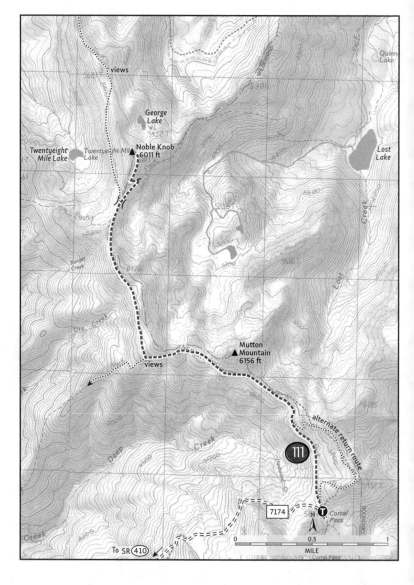

Opposite: Wildflowers and views of Mount Rainier along the trail to Noble Knob

Map: Green Trails Lester No. 239; **Contact:** Mount Baker–Snoqualmie National Forest, Snoqualmie Ranger District, Enumclaw office, (360) 825-6585, www.fs.fed.us/r6/mbs; **Notes:** Northwest Forest Pass required; **GPS:** N 47 0.839, W 121 0.838

Hike through meadows nestled more than a mile above sea level, but climb only 500 feet to get there. What could be better? Perhaps meadows punctuated with stunning horizons capped by the snow-clad Mount Rainier. Add in a large resident herd of elk, some pretty doe-eyed mule deer, and a few hundred birds. Too much to ask? Maybe, but that's exactly what you get on Noble Knob.

GETTING THERE

From Enumclaw, drive east on State Route 410 (Chinook Pass Highway) about 31 miles and turn left (north) onto Corral Pass Road (Forest Road 7174). Drive 6 miles to the trailhead on the left, near where the road hooks south (elev. 5700 ft). If you reach the road end, you've driven about 0.25 mile too far.

ON THE TRAIL

The trail angles north around the flank of Mutton Mountain, gaining only a few feet in the first mile. From the start the trail slides through lush wildflower meadows with incredible views of the rocky top of this mountain and back south to Castle Mountain.

A few hundred feet down the trail, a rough side trail leads to the right; this boot-beaten path rejoins the main trail in about a mile. Stay left on the mail trail to avoid this rough path. About 1.5 miles from the car, another trail split is reached. Stay right to continue contouring through meadows below the jagged spine of Dalles Ridge. At nearly 2.5 miles the trail crosses a low saddle (elev. 5900 ft) with phenomenal views over the surrounding

meadows. Soak it in, before pushing on, dropping a couple hundred feet in the next mile to another trail junction.

This time the left fork drops to above Twentyeight Mile Lake (see "Extending Your Trip"). Stay right and in 0.25 mile find a third junction, this one offering you three trails to choose from. Look left (George Lake), look right (Lost Lake), and go down the middle. Or rather, up the middle, as the center trail climbs a steep 0.5 mile, looping around the circular summit to the 6011-foot crest of Noble Knob.

Once upon a time, a fire lookout station positioned here enabled the fire watch guard to keep on eye on the forest in all directions, watching for lightning strikes and long fingers of smoke. Today the lookout cabin is gone, but the views remain.

EXTENDING YOUR TRIP

Additional mileage can be enjoyed by turning north (left) toward Twentyeight Mile Lake and following the ridgeline trail for several miles. This offers good views from the meadows along the ridge top.

You can also change up your scenery on the return trip by taking a small spur trail southeast of Mutton Mountain. This trail branches off to the left about a mile before the trailhead, rolling up a small ridge and hooking north for views into the Greenwater Valley before returning to the trailhead. This secondary trail adds about 0.5 mile to the trip.

112 Sheep Lake and Sourdough Gap

RATING/ DIFFICULTY	ROUND-TRIP	ELEV GAIN/ HIGH POINT	SEASON
****/2	7 miles	100 feet/ 6400 feet	July–Oct

Maps: Green Trails Mount Rainier East No. 270 and Bumping Lake No. 271; **Contact:** Okanogan and Wenatchee National Forests,

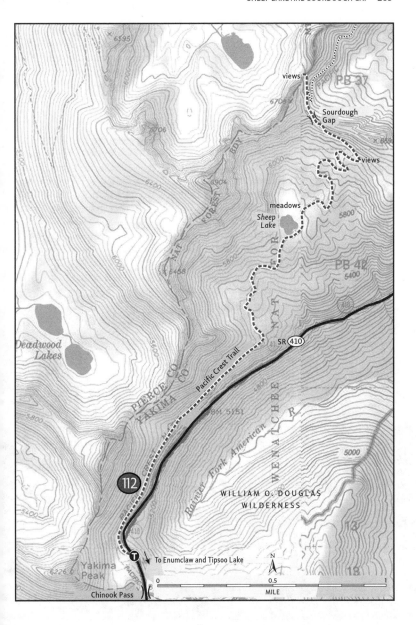

Naches Ranger District, (509) 653-1400, www.fs.fed.us/r6/wenatchee; **Notes:** Northwest Forest Pass required; **GPS:** N 46 55.994, W 121 21.581

🚶 🔪 🐾 *This section of the 2600-mile Pacific Crest Trail (PCT) seems tailor-made for kids and dogs. It's gentle, scenic, and easily accessible, with a great swimming lake, resilient grassy meadows for romping, and easy off-trail scrambles. All this and more awaits hikers willing to share the trail with a lot of fellow nature lovers and the occasional bear— where there are huckleberries, there are sure to be bears, and there are some wonderful huckleberry brambles above this trail. Of course, with plenty of meadows for grazing, rocks to hide among, and trees to perch in, the area is also popular with a host of bird and animal species, including deer, mountain goats, hawks, falcons, marmots, martens, chipmunks, and the ever-faithful friend of hikers, gray jays.*

GETTING THERE

From Enumclaw drive east on State Route 410 (Chinook Pass Highway) to Chinook Pass. Just east of Tipsoo Lake, turn left (north) into a small trailhead parking lot on the north side of the highway. The trailhead is found on the backside of the lot, behind the restrooms. If the parking lot is full, return to the Tipsoo Lake parking lot at the pass and hike the 0.25-mile trail around the lake to the lower lot and the PCT trailhead.

Overlook of the Crystal Lakes basin just beyond Sourdough Gap

ON THE TRAIL

The trail traverses the steep hillside meadows east of Chinook Pass, staying above SR 410 for the first mile. Traffic noise can be heard, and sometimes seen, but the views beyond make up for that. The deep valley of the Rainier Fork American River, with Naches Peak rising on the far side of the valley, is beautiful. Hikers with sharp eyes, or good binoculars, can often pick out hikers rounding the flank of Naches on the PCT, some 3 trail miles to the south.

After the first mile the trail veers north, climbing gently up to a bench below Sourdough Gap. Just past the 2.5 mile mark you'll drop into the Sheep Lake basin. The trail to the gap rounds the east side of the lake and begins a moderately steep climb up the valley wall to the rocky saddle of Sourdough Gap at 3.5 miles. Along the way the trail loops through a few switchbacks and offers wonderful views down to the lake and occasionally all the way back down to the trailhead.

Sourdough Gap is a small saddle in a jagged-edged ridge. You'll find a few spotty views of Mount Rainier during the approach to the gap, but for the really outstanding vistas you'll need to scramble up the steep talus slope on the northwest side of the gap. A faint boot-beaten path leads to the ridge crest—be careful, though, because the far side of the ridge falls away in a 500-foot cliff. From this ridge you'll be able to look southwest onto the Emmons Glacier of Mount Rainier. Directly below your vantage point is the Crystal Lakes basin—be sure to wave to the hikers clustered on the shores of those pretty lakes.

Those who'd rather stick to the established trail will have to forgo views of Rainier, but by continuing on the PCT about 0.25 mile north of Sourdough Gap, you'll find wonderful views east into the meadows of upper Morse Creek, with the blue pool of Placer Lake sitting dead center in the valley. Far beyond is the long spine of American Ridge in the William O. Douglas Wilderness.

EXTENDING YOUR TRIP

From Sourdough Gap adventurous hikers can scramble up a small boot-beaten trail to the ridgeline on the right (north). This provides stunning views down into the Crystal Lakes basin and across the valley to Mount Rainier. You can also add miles to your hike by continuing north on the PCT to Bear Gap and beyond.

113 Naches Peak Loop

RATING/ DIFFICULTY	ROUND-TRIP	ELEV GAIN/ HIGH POINT	SEASON
****/2	3 miles	100 feet/ 6400 feet	July–Oct

Maps: Green Trails Mount Rainier East No. 270 and Bumping Lake No. 271; **Contact:** Okanogan and Wenatchee National Forests, Naches Ranger District, (509) 653-1400, www.fs.fed.us/r6/wenatchee; **Notes:** Northwest Forest Pass required; **GPS:** N 46 52.164, W 121 31.179

This triangular track offers a whole lot of scenery in a short distance. Mount Rainier towers above a rainbow array of wildflower blooms, which fill the air with a fragrant wilderness perfume that drifts on the gentle breezes wafting up from the dry canyons on the east slope of the Cascades. Those same winds coolly caress overheated hikers trekking along the crest. Listen to the marmots whistle at your passing as you pierce sprawling wildflower meadows and enjoy outstanding panoramic views of jagged mountains. Time your visit just right and you can even feast on the sweet nectar of huckleberries.

GETTING THERE

From Enumclaw drive east on State Route 410 (Chinook Pass Highway) to Chinook Pass. Park

on the north side of the highway in the Tipsoo Lake parking area.

ON THE TRAIL

Follow the trail east along the north side of the highway to reach the footbridge that crosses over the road. Join the Pacific Crest Trail (PCT) here.

Meander upward through wildflower meadows for 0.6 mile to the boundary of the William O. Douglas Wilderness. As you stroll up the trail, enjoy masses of western anemone,

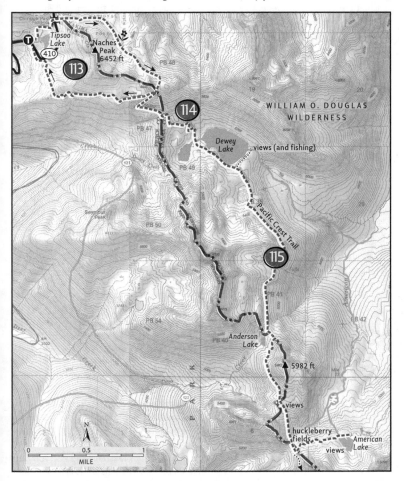

Opposite: Mount Rainier over crimson fall huckleberry colors from Naches Peak

beargrass, lupine, paintbrush, and more. Just 0.25 mile past the wilderness boundary, stop to admire—and maybe wet your toes in—a nameless tarn (elev. 5650 ft) set like a jewel among the green fields of the meadow.

At 1.2 miles stop for a rest or a leisurely lunch at the wide bench overlooking Dewey Lake. The trail splits here, and the loop route goes right. For a longer hike you can continue to your left down the PCT to reach Dewey Lake (Hike 114).

Turn right at the junction and hike west around the southern flank of Naches Peak. You'll soon see Mount Rainier thrusting skyward before you, while more meadows open up at your feet.

At 2.7 miles you'll have looped back around the south and west side of Naches and be back at the highway, opposite Tipsoo Lake. Cross to the north side of the highway and follow the access trails near the lake back to your car.

114 Dewey Lake

RATING/ DIFFICULTY	ROUND-TRIP	ELEV GAIN/ HIGH POINT	SEASON
****/3	6 miles	600 feet/ 5700 feet	July–Oct

Maps: Green Trails Mount Rainier East No. 270 and Bumping Lake No. 271; **Contact:** Okanogan and Wenatchee National Forests, Naches Ranger District, (509) 653-1400, *www.fs.fed.us/r6/wenatchee*; **Notes:** Northwest Forest Pass required; **GPS:** N 46 52.164, W 121 31.179

Alpine lakes stir emotions in people, drawing them into their crystalline beauty and stunning wild settings. Most alpine lakes,

though, are small affairs. Ponds, really, that can be walked around during an after-dinner stroll. Dewey, on the other hand, stands as one of the monarchs of alpine lakes. This long, broad lake boasts scores of shoreline pockets that offer up the elusive solitude often hard to find in a mountain lake basin. Stunning scenery also awaits, with tall Naches Peak towering overhead and a rich forest cradling the opposite lakeshore. If that isn't enough, Dewey hosts an impressive population of trout for the anglers among us. Indeed, the lake is stocked periodically by plane—fish are emptied from tanks in free-fall dives during low overflights of the lake.

GETTING THERE

From Enumclaw drive east on State Route 410 (Chinook Pass Highway) to Chinook Pass. Park on the north side of the highway in the Tipsoo Lake parking area. Cross to the south side of the highway to find the start of the trail.

ON THE TRAIL

Climb the grassy hillside on the south side of the highway and follow the trail as it ascends gradually to the southeast for 0.5 mile. This small connector trail slices through a few small stands of trees but generally rolls through broad meadows of alpine wildflowers. To the west, Mount Rainier fills the horizon.

The trail levels out after 0.5 mile and then reaches a trail junction at 1.5 miles, where you meet the true Pacific Crest Trail (PCT). To the left, a 1.5-mile hike north to SR 410 meets the highway just 0.5 mile east of Tipsoo Lake (see Hike 113).

Turn right instead onto the PCT. It makes a moderately steep descent, dropping some 600 feet in 1.3 miles through a series of gentle switchbacks. You'll pass through old, sun-dappled pine and fir forest to reach a small

Ready to drop down to Dewey Lake

forest clearing on the northwest shore of Dewey Lake.

Continue another mile along the PCT as it follows the western shore of the lake. For the quietest, most solitary picnic sites, find a location on the southwestern shore to enjoy your lunch. For some of the best fishing, scramble around toward the outlet stream on the southeastern edge of the lake. For longer hikes, continue on as described in Hike 115 (American Lake).

115 American Lake

RATING/ DIFFICULTY	ROUND-TRIP	ELEV GAIN/ HIGH POINT	SEASON
****/3	14 miles	1000 feet/ 5700 feet	July–Oct

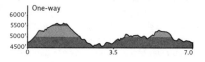

Maps: Green Trails Mount Rainier East No. 270 and Bumping Lake No. 271; **Contact:** Okanogan and Wenatchee National Forests, Naches Ranger District, (509) 653-1400, *www.fs.fed.us/r6/wenatchee*; **Notes:** Northwest Forest Pass required; **GPS:** N 46 52.164, W 121 31.179

William O. Douglas stands as Washington's greatest son. Douglas's lasting claim to greatness is his tenure as a U.S. Supreme Court justice, but he was first and foremost a man of the wilderness. He was a tireless advocate for wildlands, a prolific author of exquisite wilderness adventure narratives and natural history essays, and a lifelong hiker—despite a childhood malady that nearly rendered him an invalid. Douglas refused to submit to illness and took to hiking the hills of the eastern Cascades. By early adulthood he was exploring all the wild country between what are now State

Pacific Crest Trail hikers and their pooch heading to American Lake

Route 410 and US 12—lands that today are protected as the William O. Douglas Wilderness. Hiking American Ridge to American Lake you may find yourself feasting in the same huckleberry fields Douglas himself once enjoyed.

GETTING THERE

From Enumclaw drive east on State Route 410 (Chinook Pass Highway) to Chinook Pass. Park on the north side of the highway in the Tipsoo Lake parking area. Cross to the south side of the highway to find the start of the trail.

ON THE TRAIL

This hike starts as does Hike 114 to Dewey Lake. Follow a connector trail on the south side of the highway for 1.5 miles to its junction with the Pacific Crest Trail (PCT). Stunning alpine meadows and scenic panoramas unfold along this section of trail, setting high expectations for the rest of the hike.

The Naches Peak Loop (Hike 113) goes left at the junction. Turn right (south) instead, and descend 600 feet in the next 1.3 miles, passing through old, sun-dappled pine and fir forest to reach a small forest clearing on the northwest shore of Dewey Lake (Hike 114). From the southeast end of the lake the trail rolls gently south, cutting through huge expanses of huckleberry meadows—excellent places to savor the essence of pine forest. Just be aware that hungry bears also like to gobble the juicy fruit.

You'll reach Anderson Lake at 5 miles. The trail then climbs gently for the next mile, rolling along the western flank of a small unnamed peak (elev. 5982 ft) before reaching the junction with the American Ridge Trail at 6 miles.

Continue east along the ridge for about 1 mile to American Lake, where you'll enjoy more huckleberry fields and scenery that includes a rocky pinnacle to the south and the deep valley of the American River to the north.

116 Mesatchee Creek

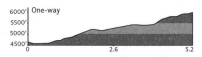

RATING/ DIFFICULTY	ROUND-TRIP	ELEV GAIN/ HIGH POINT	SEASON
**/3	10.4 miles	1300 feet/ 5900 feet	July–Oct

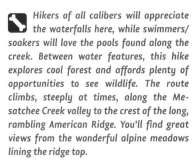

Map: Green Trails Bumping Lake No. 271;
Contact: Okanogan and Wenatchee National
Forests, Naches Ranger District, (509) 653-
1400, *www.fs.fed.us/r6/wenatchee*; **Notes:**
Northwest Forest Pass required; **GPS:** N 46
54.384, W 121 25.251

Bull elk roaming up above Mesatchee Creek

Hikers of all calibers will appreciate
the waterfalls here, while swimmers/
soakers will love the pools found along the
creek. Between water features, this hike
explores cool forest and affords plenty of
opportunities to see wildlife. The route
climbs, steeply at times, along the Mesatchee Creek valley to the crest of the long,
rambling American Ridge. You'll find great
views from the wonderful alpine meadows
lining the ridge top.

GETTING THERE

From Chinook Pass drive east on State Route
410 (Chinook Pass Highway) for 6.5 miles.
Turn right onto a small road (Forest Road
460) leading south about 0.5 mile nearly to

the mouth of the Mesatchee Creek valley. Park at the road end.

ON THE TRAIL

The trail starts up alongside the clear waters of the American River, following an old roadbed for the first mile. A footlog over the river at 1.2 miles marks the start of the workout, as the trail now turns away from the American River and angles up into the Mesatchee Creek valley.

At a trail junction in 0.25 mile, stay left—the right fork leads up the Rainier Fork American River to Dewey Lake (which Hike 114 approaches from a trailhead farther west along

SR 410). The left-hand path stays in the Mesatchee Valley but leaves the creek behind as it gets nasty-steep on a mile-long series of switchbacks heading up the valley wall. Before the creek passes from sight, though, you'll loop close to it on one turn and see a pretty horsetail waterfall cascading over a steep rocky rim.

Once well above the creek level, the trail moderates a bit and enters a long traverse of the slope, angling upstream before crossing the creek just short of the 4-mile mark. You'll find plenty of creekside rest areas if you need to take a break. But don't linger long—you'll

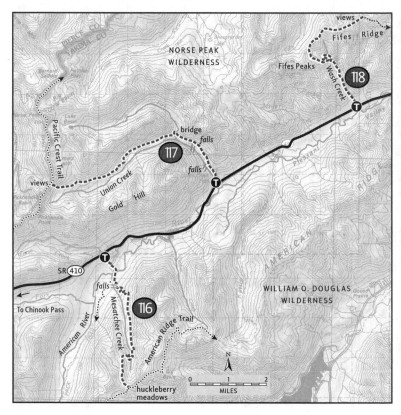

Moon setting over cliffs

want to push on, as there are prettier places to see and enjoy.

The trail moves farther up the creek valley and circles through the upper slopes of the meadow-filled basin at the head of the creek. At 5.2 miles the trail ends at a junction with American Ridge Trail amid a tangle of huckleberries and alpine firs. Enjoy the fruits of the bushes and the fruits of your labor as you bask in the sunshine and take in the views along the ridge and over the deep valley you just climbed.

EXTENDING YOUR TRIP

You can explore east or west along American Ridge's up and down route, finding more local meadows to relax in. The right-hand route eventually links up with Hike 115 to American Lake.

117 Union Creek

RATING/ DIFFICULTY	ROUND-TRIP	ELEV GAIN/ HIGH POINT	SEASON
***/4	14 miles	2500 feet/ 5900 feet	July–Oct

One-way

```
6000'
5000'
4000'
3000'
      0                3.5                7.0
```

Map: Green Trails Bumping Lake No. 271; **Contact:** Okanogan and Wenatchee National Forests, Naches Ranger District, (509) 653-1400, *www.fs.fed.us/r6/wenatchee*; **Notes:** Northwest Forest Pass required; **GPS:** N 46 55.994, W 121 21.581

Pine and fir forest fill the valley of Union Creek, providing a cool retreat from the heat of summer. Explore open meadows and shadow-laden forests, watching for the deer and elk that browse through the valley and the birds that swarm the clusters of berry bushes and bug-rich creekbed. Dippers (a.k.a. water ouzels) plunge into the water to snatch up aquatic insects. Hammer-headed woodpeckers and flickers pound out a bass line behind the melody of twittering nuthatches and trilling juncos. Not everyone will hear these feathered musicians—they have to take a break between sets—but everyone can enjoy the fragrant pine forest and, from the end of the trail, the spectacular views over the valley and beyond.

GETTING THERE

From Chinook Pass drive east on State Route 410 (Chinook Pass Highway) for 9 miles, and turn left into the Union Creek trailhead parking area at the base of Union Creek.

ON THE TRAIL

Start up the trail on the soft path leading north out of the parking lot and in just 0.5 mile enjoy the spectacle of a pounding waterfall on Union Creek. Snap a picture or two to capture the pretty scene, then keep hiking. The trail crosses the creek and angles steeply up the nose of the ridge on the east flank of Union Creek valley. The trail zigs and zags up tight switchbacks before rolling into a long, climbing traverse well above the creek.

At just over 1 mile from the trailhead the path crosses the North Fork Union Creek above another waterfall, then descends to the main trunk of Union Creek to hug the water's edge before climbing onto the wall above the creek once more.

At 4 miles out the trail returns to the creek for a long visit. The trail turns steep once more as it leaves the creek at 4.5 miles for a torturous 2.5-mile climb to the Pacific Crest Trail (PCT) below Blue Bell Pass. From this hard-earned vantage point, enjoy great views of the Norse Peak Wilderness and its rocky summits: Gold Hill, Norse Peak, Pickhandle Point, and the Crystal Mountain peaks.

EXTENDING YOUR TRIP

You can wander north and south along the PCT to explore the ridgetop meadows and alpine summits.

Opposite: Union Creek Falls

Fifes Ridge

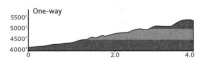

118 Fifes Ridge

RATING/ DIFFICULTY	ROUND-TRIP	ELEV GAIN/ HIGH POINT	SEASON
***/4	8 miles	1200 feet/ 5400 feet	July–Oct

Map: Green Trails Bumping Lake No. 271;
Contact: Okanogan and Wenatchee National
Forests, Naches Ranger District, (509) 653-
1400, www.fs.fed.us/r6/wenatchee; **Notes:**
Northwest Forest Pass required; **GPS:** N 46
57.106, W 121 4.767

The tightly clumped spires of Fifes
Ridge present a formidable sight
from any vantage point, but as you near
the rocky ridge it appears ever more menacing and imposing. Perhaps that's partly

because the trail you have to hike to get
close to the jagged ridge can be menacing
and imposing in its own right. Fortunately,
the views are worth it—and not just the
views at the end of the route. As you climb,
the long, broad basin of American River
and the sweeping line of American Ridge
stretch out before you every time you gain
a vantage point, while Fifes Peaks punctu-
ate the skyline above you.

GETTING THERE

From Chinook Pass drive east on State Route
410 (Chinook Pass Highway) for 13.5 miles,
passing Pleasant Valley Campground. Turn
left onto a poorly marked dirt road just past
milepost 82 and drive up a short distance to
the lower parking area.

ON THE TRAIL

Start hiking up the dirt road, reaching an
upper parking area (accessible only to high-
clearance vehicles) in 0.25 mile. The trail

starts here, crossing into the Norse Peak Wilderness just past the end of the road. The route follows Wash Creek upstream, meandering through a forest filled with vanilla leaf and Indian pipe. Wash Creek has lived up to its name, having washed out a section of the old trail, pushing the newer path up onto the low bench above the creekbed.

At about 1 mile the trail turns steep as it follows the now steeply pitched creekbed upvalley. You'll be sweating buckets even in the frequently dry environment of this heavily forested valley. The trail crosses the creek frequently, allowing you plenty of opportunities to cool yourself in the cold water.

Nearly 3 miles from the trailhead, the path climbs onto a low section of Fifes Ridge and turns east to ascend the ragged rocks of the upper section of the ridgeline. Just past the 3-mile mark you'll cross a rocky summit, affording you wonderful views west to the true summit of Fifes Peaks—vertical walls of rock shoot skyward to form the craggy mountain top. You can also look east along the ridge to view the rampartlike spires and towers of Fifes Ridge. Scan the treetops on the slopes below and you might spot the nests of local raptors.

You can stop at this viewpoint and enjoy the panorama over a leisurely lunch, or push on along the ridgetop trail, finding small meadows higher on the ridge.

Map: Green Trails Old Scab Mountain No. 272; **Contact:** Okanogan and Wenatchee National Forests, Naches Ranger District, (509) 653-1400, www.fs.fed.us/r6/wenatchee; **Notes:** Bat closure Nov 1–Apr 1, Northwest Land Management concessionaire, $5 per vehicle parking fee; **GPS:** N 46 57.106, W 121 4.767

Boulder Cave formed over millions of years from ongoing volcanic action and erosion. Periodic lava flows deposited rock over soft, loose rock and soil. The lava cooled, forming hard layers of basalt and trapping the softer layers of loose sediment between. Wind and water then scoured the softer layers out. Today the cave is home to a dwindling population of Pacific western big-eared bats (a.k.a. Townsend bats), a listed sensitive species in both Washington and Oregon. Only fifty remain of thousands that inhabited the cave in the 1920s and '30s, hence the cave's winter closure to ensure a safe hibernation period. Do bring a reliable light source for exploring the cave.

GETTING THERE

From Chinook Pass drive east on State Route 410 about 26 miles, approaching the town of Cliffdell. Turn right onto a road signed "Boul-

Boulder Cave entrance

119 Boulder Cave

RATING/ DIFFICULTY	ROUND-TRIP	ELEV GAIN/ HIGH POINT	SEASON
****/1	2 miles	300 feet/ 2700 feet	Apr–Oct

der Cave National Recreational Trail." Cross the Naches River on a bridge and almost immediately turn right, following the signs 1.1 miles to the trailhead.

ON THE TRAIL

The Boulder Cave Trail was built by the Civilian Conservation Corps (CCC) in 1935 and was improved in 1987 by the Youth Conservation Corps (YCC), with the voluntary help of a local stone mason. The gravel trail follows the rim of a small gorge that is part of a deep ravine. The path climbs gradually away from the parking area, piercing a pine and fir forest that also supports some big, old maples and alders.

As the wide trail nears the cave mouth, it winds down to the slit in the rock that serves as the cave entrance. Hikers **MUST** have a reliable light source to explore the cave—a bright headlamp is recommended, though a powerful hand-held flashlight would be adequate. A backup light should also be carried just in case your primary light goes dead. You'll also want a jacket to slip on, even in the heat of August. The cave is damp and cool, with temperatures typically hovering in the 50s.

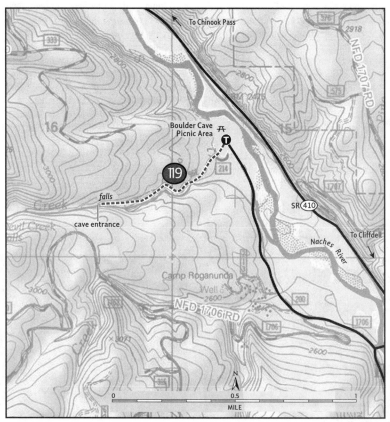

Kevin Altree exiting Boulder Cave

Explore the shallow cave (about 400 feet deep) at your leisure before heading back out the way you came.

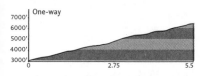

120 Goat Peak

RATING/ DIFFICULTY	ROUND-TRIP	ELEV GAIN/ HIGH POINT	SEASON
****/5	11 miles	3400 feet/ 6473 feet	July–Oct

One-way

7000'
6000'
5000'
4000'
3000'
0   2.75   5.5

Maps: Green Trails Bumping Lake No. 271 and Old Scab Mountain No. 272; **Contact:** Okan-ogan and Wenatchee National Forests, Naches Ranger District, (509) 653-1400, *www.fs.fed .us/r6/wenatchee*; **Notes:** Northwest Forest Pass required; **GPS:** N 46 55.074, W 121 13.868

You want views? We got views. All that's needed is a steep trail and a former fire-lookout site, which is exactly what Goat Peak offers. The peak is the highest point on the long spine of American Ridge, with views galore. Look north to the sheer cliffs of Fifes Peaks. Look south to the blue waters of Bumping Lake, the stark summit of Mount Aix, and beyond to the snow-rimmed peak of Mount Adams. To the west, Mount Rainier stands proud as the monarch of the Cascades. The Goat Peak Trail also

American Ridge near Goat Peak

boasts rich scenery close at hand, with a
bounty of wildflowers and wildlife. But the
trail is dry and sun-baked, so pack plenty
of water to survive the rugged climb to the
old lookout site.

GETTING THERE

From Chinook Pass drive east on State
Route 410 (Chinook Pass Highway) for 19
miles to Bumping River Road (Forest Road
18). Turn right and drive 5.8 miles to the

Goat Peak trailhead near the Cougar Flat Campground.

ON THE TRAIL

The trail climbs steeply from the start, ascending tight switchbacks on the ridge above Goat Creek. The path runs up through forest and then across open, wildflower-dotted hillsides for nearly 4 miles. Along the way, views grow increasingly impressive even as your legs get progressively more tired.

At 4 miles the trail intercepts the long east-west American Ridge Trail. Turn right (east) and follow the ridgetop trail for 1 mile, climbing slightly. It's during this miracle mile that the real payoffs start flowing in. As you stroll along American Ridge you'll enjoy fantastic views north, east, and south. Fifes Ridge cuts the northern skyline. Mount Aix rises firm to the south. To the east, the mighty Cascades taper off to the tawny desert country of the Yakima Plateau.

The American Ridge Trail continues to roll east, but at 5 miles from the trailhead you'll find a small spur trail leading up the final pitch to the summit of Goat Peak. Make this last, steep climb up the final 0.5 mile to reach the awesome views from the 6473-foot summit.

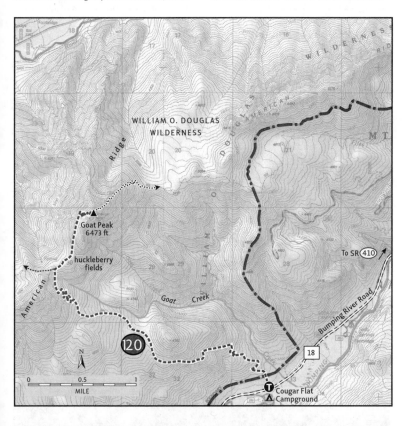

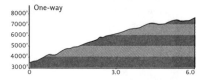

121 Nelson Ridge and Mount Aix

RATING/ DIFFICULTY	ROUND-TRIP	ELEV GAIN/ HIGH POINT	SEASON
****/5	12 miles	4200 feet/ 7766 feet	June–Oct

Maps: Green Trails Bumping Lake No. 271 and White Pass No. 303; **Contact:** Okanogan and Wenatchee National Forests, Naches Ranger District, (509) 653-1400, *www.fs.fed.us/r6 /wenatchee*; **Notes:** Northwest Forest Pass required; **GPS:** N 46 48.848, W 121 18.369

The key to this hike is timing. You want to hit the trail after the route is completely snow-free, but before the heat of summer bakes the trail (and any trail travelers) to a crisp. Or you can try it in autumn, though you'll run the risk of being caught out in an eastern Cascades thunderstorm. Realistically, if you hike in June or September you'll be well served most years. Trail conditions aside, this route requires some serious stamina. It gains 4200 vertical feet in about 5 miles.

Nelson Ridge looking north from the summit of Mount Aix

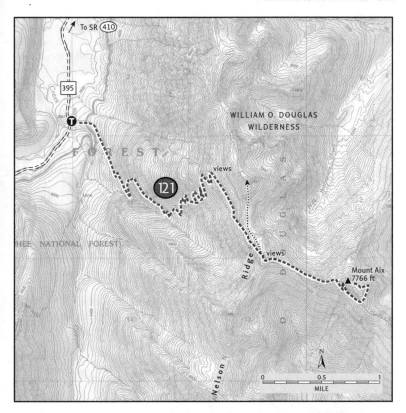

The rewards are great—outstanding views, clean air, and relatively few people to share the trail with—but they come at a substantial price in lung and leg pain. Be prepared to work for every view you get.

GETTING THERE

From Chinook Pass drive east on State Route 410 (Chinook Pass Highway) for 19 miles to Bumping River Road (Forest Road 18). Turn right (south) and drive 12 miles to the end of the pavement, where the road becomes FR 1800 (at the entrance of Bumping Lake Campground). Proceed to a junction and stay straight on what now is Deep Creek Road (FR 395). Drive about 1.5 miles to the Mount Aix trailhead on the left (east) side of the road just before the Copper Creek bridge.

ON THE TRAIL

From the trailhead you'll start upward immediately. The trail climbs through a pine forest, so at least initially you're out of the sun during the workout. This lasts for just over 2 miles, then the closed forest canopy starts to give way to more open alpine forest with a lot of meadows and clearings between timber stands.

The trail also gets steeper, running up through switchbacks until, at 3.7 miles, it levels for a few paces atop a bench (elev. 6400 ft).

Take a breather to enjoy the stunning views, especially to the south (Mount Adams and the jagged teeth of the Goat Rocks) and the west (Mount Rainier).

Just beyond this, at around 5 miles, you'll conquer the ridge, rolling out onto its crest to join the Nelson Ridge Trail. But though you've reached the ridge spine, the spine is steeply slanted and the trail now climbs once more through alpine meadows and scraggly tree stands.

You'll soon find yourself scrambling the final mile to the top of Mount Aix. The last rocky run will tax your strength and endurance, but finally you'll be at the 7766-foot summit with its outstanding 360-degree views. Take a good long rest before starting the knee-grinding descent back down the ruthless trail.

122 Twin Sisters Lakes

RATING/ DIFFICULTY	ROUND-TRIP	ELEV GAIN/ HIGH POINT	SEASON
***/2	5 miles	800 feet/ 5100 feet	June–Oct

One-way

Maps: Green Trails Bumping Lake No. 271 and White Pass No. 303; **Contact:** Okanogan and Wenatchee National Forests, Naches Ranger District, (509) 653-1400, *www.fs.fed.us/r6 /wenatchee*; **Notes:** Northwest Forest Pass required; **GPS:** N 46 45.123, W 121 21.693

Parents, take note. This simple trail offers not one, but two scenic lakes that are set a short distance from the road. A relatively flat trail, great forest and meadow environments to explore, and a pair of cool-water lakes in

which to swim make this one of the more popular William O. Douglas Wilderness day hikes, especially for parents with children. The first of the twins is only about 2 miles down a moderately climbing trail, so plenty of people make their way there. The second lake is 0.5 mile farther and is worth the extra effort, if only to escape the majority of the crowds.

GETTING THERE

From Chinook Pass drive east on State Route 410 (Chinook Pass Highway) for 19 miles to Bumping River Road (Forest Road 18). Turn right (south) and drive 12 miles to the end of the pavement, where the road becomes FR 1800 (at the entrance of Bumping Lake Campground). Proceed to a junction and stay straight on what now is Deep Creek Road (FR 395). Drive to the end of the road and walk to the Twin Sisters trailhead in Deep Creek Campground.

ON THE TRAIL

The trail climbs modestly from the trailhead, rounding the snout of a low ridge above the broad basin of Twin Lakes in about 1.5 miles. The forest along this early section of trail holds a good population of squirrels—you might catch a glimpse of them leaping and gliding from tree to tree. Also listen for the head-banging hammering of woodpeckers as they search for insects in the many dead snags standing in this old forest.

Visit in mid-September and you might earn a special treat. The resident elk go into their rut (mating season) in early autumn as the weather turns colder. As part of the rut ritual, the elk bulls challenge each other with eerie calls. This bugling resonates off the hills, creating a wonderful wild soundtrack for your hiking experience.

After rounding the ridge snout, the trail descends gradually to the first of the twins at

First encounter of Twin Sisters Lakes

2 miles. The path then follows along the shoreline for a few hundred yards before slanting to the left to cross a broad meadowland and, in 0.5 mile, reaching the second, smaller twin.

Continue on around to the southeast side of the lake, branching off to the right into meadows. The main trail continues past the lake basin as described in Hike 123 (Mosquito Valley).

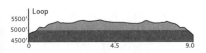

123 Mosquito Valley

RATING/ DIFFICULTY	ROUND-TRIP	ELEV GAIN/ HIGH POINT	SEASON
****/3	9 miles	600 feet/ 5400 feet	June–Oct

Loop elevation profile: 5500', 5000', 4500' from 0 to 9.0, midpoint 4.5

Maps: Green Trails Bumping Lake No. 271 and White Pass No. 303; **Contact:** Okanogan and Wenatchee National Forests, Naches Ranger District, (509) 653-1400, *www.fs.fed.us/r6 /wenatchee*; **Notes:** Northwest Forest Pass required; **GPS:** N 46 45.123, W 121 21.693

The William O. Douglas Wilderness is a water lover's paradise, but is best visited in late summer and fall. The endless ponds, puddles, and lakes also mean endless bugs. This route crosses through Mosquito Valley, after all. Once a few cold nights have thinned the biting population, you'll be able to enjoy unmatched wilderness rambling among sprawling meadows and potholes. You're in the home range of elk here—and black bear territory too. This hike is a good introduction to the

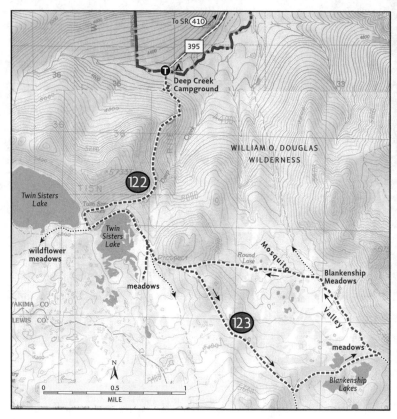

nearly infinite array of loops possible in the William O. Douglas, passing by the dual pools of Twin Lakes, under the shadow of Tumac Mountain's cratered volcanic summit, around Blankenship Lakes, through the sprawling Blankenship Meadows, and, of course, across the heart of Mosquito Valley.

GETTING THERE

From Chinook Pass drive east on State Route 410 (Chinook Pass Highway) for 19 miles to Bumping River Road (Forest Road 18). Turn right (south) and drive 12 miles to the end of the pavement, where the road becomes FR 1800 (at the entrance of Bumping Lake Campground). Proceed to a junction and stay straight on what now is Deep Creek Road (FR 395). Drive to the end of the road and walk to the Twin Sisters trailhead in Deep Creek Campground.

ON THE TRAIL

The trail climbs modestly from the trailhead, following around the snout of a low ridge to reach the first of the Twin Lakes (Hike 122) in about 2 miles. The forest along this early section of trail holds a good population of squirrels—you might catch a glimpse of them

Trail leading into Blankenship Meadows

leaping from tree to tree. Also listen for the head-banging hammering of woodpeckers as they search for insects in the many dead snags.

Move on from the picturesque shores—enjoy a view over the little Twin Sister to Tumac Mountain—and follow the trail as it leads south toward Tumac. About 0.5 mile after reaching the second lake's shore, the trail splits. To the right is a track that leads to the summit of Tumac Mountain. Stay left and skirt southeast around the flank of the cinder cone. In another 0.25 mile reach another junction. This is the start of a loop. Stay right to complete the loop in a counterclockwise direction.

Hike nearly 1 mile south along this trail as it rolls gradually upward through thin forest and scattered clearings before reaching the long, broad meadows of Mosquito Valley. At about 3.5 miles from the trailhead you'll find yet another trail junction—trails crisscross the William O. Douglas Wilderness like strands of a spider web, making for seemingly endless loop-hiking alternatives.

Turn left and amble east through the cluster of Blankenship Lakes. Past the lakes, turn left at yet another junction. This leads along the eastern fringe of Blankenship Meadows, which stretch thousands of acres west and north, broken only by occasional narrow bands of forest. Countless small ponds dot the area, providing drinking water for you (and your dog, if she's along).

In about 1 mile from the previous junction near Blankenship Lakes, reach another junc-

Mosquito Valley leading toward Blankenship Meadows

tion. Turn left once more to hike 1 mile west, closing the loop at the junction just south of Twin Sisters Lakes. Retrace your steps north to those lakes and on out to the trailhead.

124 Cougar Lakes

RATING/ DIFFICULTY	ROUND-TRIP	ELEV GAIN/ HIGH POINT	SEASON
****/3	8 miles	1200 feet/ 5400 feet	July–Oct

Tiger Lily

Map: Green Trails Bumping Lake No. 271; **Contact:** Okanogan and Wenatchee National Forests, Naches Ranger District, (509) 653-1400, *www.fs.fed.us/r6/wenatchee*; **Notes:** Northwest Forest Pass required; **GPS:** N 46 49.836, W 121 22.624

🦴 🐾 *Cougar Lakes boast gently sloped sandy banks, perfect for swimming and sunning after a long dusty hike. Once you've tired of swimming, spend some time foraging for ripe huckleberries— plentiful when in season—or simply scan the talus slopes below House Rock, looking for the ever-present white specks of mountain goats that balance on precarious perches high above green meadows. Don't see any goats? Well, then pull your gaze off the cliffs and scan the meadows below the talus. See any brown blobs moving through the greenery? These are likely big mule deer or possibly even some of the resident elk that make the greater Bumping River basin their home.*

GETTING THERE

From Chinook Pass drive east on State Route 410 (Chinook Pass Highway) for 19 miles to Bumping River Road (Forest Road 18). Turn right (south) and drive 12 miles to the end of the pavement, where the road becomes FR 1800 (at the entrance of Bumping Lake Campground). At 13.5 miles stay left at a road fork, still on FR 1800, and continue to the road end and trailhead about 4 miles farther on the rough, dirt track.

ON THE TRAIL

The trail angles west of the large trailhead parking area (large because it often accommodates numerous horse trailers), leading a

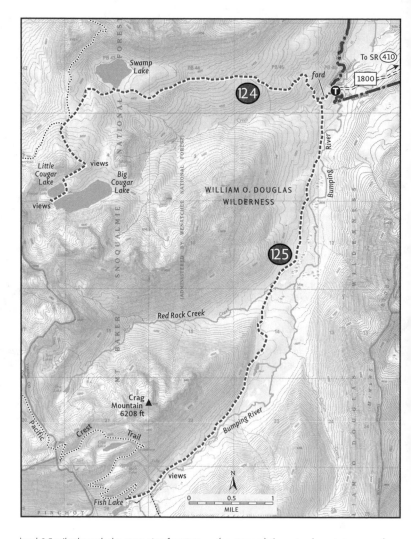

level 0.5 mile through the open pine forest to the banks of Bumping River. Here, you'll have to get wet as the trail cuts through the river at a broad ford. Early in the year, when the snowpack is at full melt stage, the river can be deep and difficult to wade. But by midsummer (most years) the water drops to no more than a knee-deep gentle flow.

Once across the river the trail starts a gentle climb—the route climbs nearly all the way to the trail's end, but never steeply—through the open forest. About 0.5 mile past the ford the trail hits a four-way intersection. Left heads to Fish Lake (Hike 125). Go straight ahead instead, crossing this Bumping River Trail that leads left and right.

The trail then slants up the long, low ridge toward Swamp Lake. The trail here is badly eroded from heavy use by hikers and horses for scores of years. Be careful of the exposed roots and hidden holes. (The Forest Service is working to reroute and rebuild the trail, so conditions are improving.)

At 3.2 miles you'll pass the shallow (but still pretty) Swamp Lake. In less than 0.5 mile past the lake you'll break out of the forest into a broad meadow, only to dip back into the trees for a short forested section, and then erupt back into a meadow at a junction with the American Ridge Trail.

LOW-IMPACT RECREATION

In days gone by, wilderness travelers did as pleased when hiking through the backcountry. If a trail got muddy or wet, a new one was created parallel to the first. If folks wanted a warm drink with lunch, they'd start a campfire. And campers would cut young, fragrant pine boughs to create soft bedding.

As more and more people took to the hills, those actions began to leave large, noticeable scars on the land. Today, with millions of hikers flocking to the backcountry, these kinds of intrusive practices would leave the wilderness blighted for decades to come. To ensure that we don't destroy the essence of the wild country we all enjoy visiting, hikers today are encouraged to employ the Leave No Trace (LNT) principles.

In short, these principles and practices are built around the idea that human visitors to the backcountry should "leave only footprints, take only pictures." In fact, done right, even the footprints will be minimized.

Hikers who encounter mudholes in the middle of trails should suck it up and stride through the puddle rather than stomp down the vegetation around the edge of the mud. Each passing hiker skirts wider and wider around the ever-growing mudhole until the trail is wide enough to drive a truck on, and the vegetation is stomped into oblivion. If you've planned ahead, you're likely wearing hiking boots appropriate for your trail experience, and in Washington that generally means they are waterproof. So stepping in mud does you no harm and helps prevent trail erosion.

Likewise, hikers should resist creating new trails. This doesn't mean you should never step off-trail. By all means, hikers should explore off-trail if comfortable doing so. But when you step off the established trail, you should do it in a place that won't leave a permanent scar; and once off-trail, you need to move well away from the trail. There's no reason to explore off-trail if you're only going to be 20 feet away from that established path. Likewise, cutting across a switchback turn yields you nothing (maybe shaving a couple seconds off your travel time), but it does lasting damage to the trail and the environment around the trail. Cutting switchbacks leads to loss of vegetation and establishment of "cut trails" that channel rainwater and snowmelt. This leads to erosion of the hillside and trail tread.

A willingness on the part of all hikers to practice a little patience and to put up with a little discomfort (such as getting a touch muddy) will help keep our trails open and enjoyable for everyone.

Hiker fording the Bumping River

Turn left on this long path and follow it a mere 0.25 mile before leaving it at another trail junction, this time turning left to climb the Cougar Lakes Trail as it leads up a low ridge before dropping steeply into the Cougar Lakes basin.

You'll first come to Little Cougar Lake. Continue around the east end of Little Cougar and cross the small bridge between the two lakes. The meadows near the inlet stream of Big Cougar show off views of the lakes and the towering hulk of House Rock to the west.

125 Fish Lake

RATING/ DIFFICULTY	ROUND-TRIP	ELEV GAIN/ HIGH POINT	SEASON
***/3	14 miles	1200 feet/ 5400 feet	July–Oct

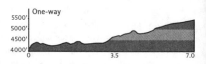

Map: Green Trails Bumping Lake No. 271; **Contact:** Okanogan and Wenatchee National Forests, Naches Ranger District, (509) 653-1400, *www.fs.fed.us/r6/wenatchee*; **Notes:** Northwest Forest Pass required; **GPS:** N 46 49.836, W 121 22.624

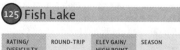 Head up this trail anytime in September and listen closely. If the weather has started to turn cold, with autumn obviously in the air, you might hear the most haunting sound of the American wilderness: bugling elk. Autumn isn't the only time to visit, of course. Though you may not hear

the elk in the summer, you might very well see them in the forest and meadows along Bumping River. This hike is a less-intense outing than some of the higher alpine trails, following an easy grade along the river drainage and gradually gaining elevation into the valley's upper reaches south of Crag Mountain.

GETTING THERE

From Chinook Pass drive east on State Route 410 (Chinook Pass Highway) for 19 miles to Bumping River Road (Forest Road 18). Turn right (south) and drive 12 miles to the end of the pavement, where the road becomes FR 1800 (at the entrance of Bumping Lake Campground). At 13.5 miles stay left at a road fork, still on FR 1800, and continue to the road end and trailhead about 4 miles farther on the rough, dirt track.

ON THE TRAIL

Start out with a 0.5-mile hike along a level track to the edge of Bumping River. Then—after stripping off your boots and socks—ford the river. Early in the year, when the snowpack is at full melt stage, the river can be deep and difficult to wade. But by midsummer (most years) the water drops to no more than a knee-deep gentle flow.

The trail then climbs gently for 0.5 mile to a trail junction. Straight ahead is the Cougar Lakes Trail (Hike 124). Turn left instead and follow the Bumping River Trail upvalley to its headwaters in Fish Lake. The trail parallels the river for the next 8 miles, passing through the occasional forest glade and open meadow but generally sticking to open, airy pine forests, usually well above the river level. About 3 miles from

Old PCT trail marker being eaten by a tree near Fish Lake

the trailhead, you'll cross Red Rock Creek, a good place for a rest stop.

The trail ends at a junction with the Pacific Crest Trail (PCT), about 6.25 miles from the trailhead. Turn right onto the PCT, and in 0.25 mile reach Fish Lake, a broad, swampy body of water at the end of the Bumping River valley. If you haven't seen elk yet, this is a likely place to spot them. The big ungulates love the rich grasses that grow around the lake basin.

Appendix: Conservation and Trail Organizations

Cascade Land Conservancy
615 2nd Avenue, Suite 625
Seattle, WA 98104
(206) 292-5907
info@cascadeland.org
www.cascadeland.org

Conservation Northwest
1208 Bay Street #201
Bellingham, WA 98225
(360) 671-9950
www.conservationnw.org

Issaquah Alps Trail Club
PO Box 351
Issaquah, WA 98027
www.issaquahalps.org

Mountains to Sound Greenway
911 Western Avenue, Suite 523
Seattle, WA 98104
(206) 382-5565
info@mtsgreenway.org
www.mtsgreenway.org

Sierra Club, Cascade Chapter
180 Nickerson Street, Suite 202
Seattle, WA 98109
(206) 378-0114
cascade.chapter@sierraclub.org
www.cascade.sierraclub.org

Volunteers for Outdoor Washington
8511 15th Avenue NE, Room 206
Seattle, WA 98115-3101
(206) 517-3019
info@trailvolunteers.org
www.trailvolunteers.org

Washington Trails Association
2019 3rd Avenue, Suite 100
Seattle, WA 98121
(206) 625-1367
info@wta.org
www.wta.org

Index

About the Author

Dan Nelson's personal and professional life has long focused on the great outdoors of the Pacific Northwest. After a short stint as a newspaper reporter, Dan joined the staff of the Washington Trails Association (WTA) where he worked and played for eleven years as the editor of *Washington Trails* magazine. Currently, Dan serves as the public information officer for the Olympic Region Clean Air Agency—an agency charged with ensuring the air remains clean, clear, and healthy on the beautiful Olympic Peninsula. In addition to loving to walk the wild country, Dan is an avid fly fisher, canoeist, snowshoer, telemark skier, and paraglider pilot. If he's not out enjoying the backcountry, he's indoors writing about it.

In addition to his past work at the WTA, Dan continues as a regular contributor to the *Seattle Times*, *Backpacker* magazine, and *Hooked on the Outdoors* magazine. He specializes in Northwest destinations and outdoor-equipment reviews. He is also author or editor of several outdoor guidebooks published by The Mountaineers Books. He lives in Puyallup with his partner Donna and their yellow lab, Parka (co-researcher for *Best Hikes with Dogs in Western Washington*).

About the Photographer

Alan L. Bauer is a professional freelance photographer specializing in the natural history of the Pacific Northwest and coverage of local history. He is a lifelong resident of the Pacific Northwest, having grown up on a large family farm in Oregon's Willamette Valley and now calling Washington State his home for the past twenty years. Much of his love for the outdoors can be traced back to his life being outside on the farm working and playing—an experience he wouldn't trade for anything!

His work has been published in *Backpacker*, *Odyssey*, *Northwest Runner*, *Oregon Coast*, and *Northwest Travel* magazines as well as numerous publications and books across fourteen countries. He regularly provides images for projects including CD covers, textbooks, websites, presentations, research, and corporate materials. Prior to his involvement with this new book series he was co-author of *Best Desert Hikes: Washington* and *Best Dog Hikes: Inland Northwest* with The Mountaineers Books.

He resides happily in the Cascade foothills east of Seattle with his caring family and border collie. For further information and to see samples of his work, please visit *www.alanbauer.com*.

1% For Trails and Washington Trails Association

Your favorite Washington hikes, such as those in this book, are made possible by the efforts of thousands of volunteers keeping our trails in great shape, and by hikers like you advocating for the protection of trails and wildlands. As budget cuts reduce funding for trail maintenance, Washington Trails Association's volunteer trail-maintenance program fills this void and is ever more important for the future of Washington's hiking. Our mountains and forests can provide us with a lifetime of adventure and exploration—but we need trails to get us there. One percent of the sales of this guidebook goes to support WTA's efforts.

Spend a day on the trail with Washington Trails Association, and give back to the trails you love. WTA hosts over 750 work parties throughout Washington's Cascades and Olympics each year. Volunteers remove downed logs after spring snowmelt, cut away brush, retread worn stretches of trail, and build bridges and turnpikes. Find the volunteer schedule, check current conditions of the trails in this guidebook, and become a member of WTA at www.wta.org or (206) 625-1367.